LUKE THE THEOLOGIAN

Aspects of His Teaching

Joseph A. Fitzmyer, S.J.

PAULIST PRESS   New York/Mahwah

IMPRIMI POTEST
Jacobus A. Devereux, S.J.
Praepositus Provinciae Marylandiae

NIHIL OBSTAT
Rev. Isidore Dixon, S.T.D.
Censor Librorum

IMPRIMATUR
Rev. William J. Kane, Ph.D.
Vicar General for the Archdiocese of Washington

The Nihil Obstat and Imprimatur are official declarations that a book or pamphlet is free of doctrinal or moral error. No implication is contained therein that those who have granted the Nihil Obstat and Imprimatur agree with the contents, opinions or statements expressed.

Book design: Ellen Whitney

Library of Congress Cataloging-in-Publication Data

Fitzmyer, Joseph A.
    Luke the theologian : aspects of his teaching / by Joseph A.
    Fitzmyer.
        p. cm.
    Includes bibliographies and indexes.
    ISBN 0-8091-3058-0 : $7.95 (est.)
    1. Bible. N.T. Luke—Theology. 2. Bible. N.T. Acts—Theology.
    3. Luke, Saint. I. Title.
    BS2589.F58 1989
    226'.406—dc19   89-3042
                                                                    CIP

Published by Paulist Press
997 Macarthur Boulevard
Mahwah, NJ 07430

Printed and bound in the
United States of America

Table of Contents

Preface

This book presents, in a slightly revised form, the Martin D'Arcy Lectures that I was privileged to deliver at Campion Hall in the University of Oxford during the Hilary Term of 1987.

The D'Arcy Lectures commemorate Martin Cyril D'Arcy, S.J. (1888–1976), a literateur, philosopher, and theologian who made a great impact on the growth of English Catholicism during the mid-quarters of the twentieth century. His writings include *Catholicism* (1927), *St. Thomas Aquinas* (1930), *The Nature of Belief* (1931), *The Mind and Heart of Love* (1945), *The Meeting of Love and Knowledge* (1957), and other works of lesser moment. After philosophical studies in Rome and London, D'Arcy came to Oxford in 1927, to Campion Hall, the Permanent Private Hall in the University of Oxford, where members of the Society of Jesus resided and studied. There he began to lecture in philosophy as a member of the Faculty of Literae Humaniores. D'Arcy became Master of Campion Hall in 1933 and engaged the renowned architect, Sir Edwin Lutyens, O.M., to draw up the plans for the new Hall to be built in Brewer Street, close to Christ Church. *The Clarendon Guide to Oxford* describes Campion Hall as "a strikingly original addition to the Oxford scene, the chapel and library being particularly good." D'Arcy remained the Master until 1945, and his own contribution to the Hall lay in the notable collection of works of sacred art—the famous *objets D'Arcy*—that he built up during his time as Master. Thus, Campion Hall itself, its collection of art works, and the recently inaugurated Martin D'Arcy Lectures sponsored each year form a fitting memorial to this great English Jesuit.

Since I have recently finished an extensive commentary on the Lucan Gospel (*The Gospel according to Luke* [AB28, 28A; Garden City, NY: Doubleday, 1981, 1985] pp. xxvi + 1642), one might wonder about the relation of this book to that commentary. In the eight lectures that I was asked to give on Lucan themes and that have become the chapters of this book I have taken up topics that I have only lightly treated in the commentary. But in every case I have gone beyond what is found in the commentary, either in the manner of exposition and discussion or in a fresh approach to new aspects of what is in the commentary. Moreover, what is found in the commentary is often disjointed because of the format of comments and notes used in it. Now a more synthetic and comprehensive approach to the topics discussed has been attempted. For instance, in the discussion of Mary in Lucan Salvation History, elements of the discussion can be found in the commentary in scattered places; but there is no really synthetic treatment of the matter. Again, in the reconsideration of the Lucan authorship of the Third Gospel and Acts I devote more time and space to certain problems that the discussion in the commentary has raised. In this last instance, I am indebted to Prof. John P. Meier, of the Catholic University of America, and Prof. J. Christiaan Beker, of Princeton Theological Seminary, for a stimulating panel discussion of my views at a New York seminar on the New Testament. Much of what appears in the first chapter has grown out of that discussion. I should like, therefore, to express here my gratitude to them for such an interest and stimulation. I have also tried to take into consideration materials that have been written on the aspects of Lucan Teaching treated here since the appearance of my commentary.

My thanks have to be extended in a particular way to the former Master of Campion Hall, the Reverend Paul

Edwards, S.J., who originally contacted me and requested that I give the D'Arcy Lectures, and to the present Master, the Reverend Peter Hackett, S.J., who sponsored them and took such generous care of me during my stay in Campion Hall.

Joseph A. Fitzmyer, S.J.
Georgetown Jesuit Community

Abbreviations

AASF	Annales academiae rerum scientiarum fennicae
AB	Anchor Bible
AnBib	Analecta biblica
ANET	J. B. Pritchard, *Ancient Near Eastern Texts* (Princeton, NJ: Princeton University, 1950)
ANQ	*Andover Newton Quarterly*
ATR	*Anglican Theological Review*
BAGD	W. Bauer, W. F. Arndt, F. W. Gingrich, and F. W. Danker, *Greek-English Lexicon of the New Testament* (2d ed.; Chicago: University of Chicago, 1979)
BBET	Beiträge zur biblischen Exegese und Theologie
BDF	F. Blass, A. Debrunner, and R. W. Funk, *A Greek Grammar of the New Testament and Other Christian Literature* (Chicago: University of Chicago, 1961)
BDR	F. Blass, A. Debrunner, and F. Rehkopf, *Grammatik des neutestamentlichen Griechisch* (Göttingen: Vandenhoeck & Ruprecht, 1976)
BHT	Beiträge zur historischen Theologie
Bib	*Biblica*
BibLeb	*Bibel und Leben*
BJRL	*Bulletin of the John Rylands Library*
BLit	*Bibel und Liturgie*
BNTC	Black's New Testament Commentaries
BR	*Biblical Research*
BSac	*Bibliotheca sacra*
BTB	*Biblical Theology Bulletin*

BZ	*Biblische Zeitschrift*
BZNW	Beihefte zur *ZNW*
CBQ	*Catholic Biblical Quarterly*
CBQMS	Catholic Biblical Quarterly Monograph Series
CCLat	Corpus Christianorum, Latin series
CJRT	*Canadian Journal of Religious Thought*
ConB	Coniectanea biblica
CurTM	*Currents in Theology and Mission*
EKK	Evangelisch-katholischer Kommentar
ETL	*Ephemerides theologicae lovanienses*
EvQ	*Evangelical Quarterly*
EvT	*Evangelische Theologie*
EWNT	H. Balz and G. Schneider (eds.), *Exegetisches Wörterbuch zum Neuen Testament* (3 vols.; Stuttgart: Kohlhammer, 1980–83)
ExpTim	*Expository Times*
HALAT	W. Baumgartner *et al.* (eds.), *Hebräisches und aramäisches Lexikon zum Alten Testament* (4 vols.; Leiden: Brill, 1967–)
HeyJ	*Heythrop Journal*
HTR	*Harvard Theological Review*
ICC	International Critical Commentary
Int	*Interpretation*
JAOS	*Journal of the American Oriental Society*
JBC	R. E. Brown *et al.* (eds.), *The Jerome Biblical Commentary* (Englewood Cliffs, NJ: Prentice-Hall, 1968)
JBL	*Journal of Biblical Literature*
JSNT	*Journal for the Study of the New Testament*
JSNTSup	Supplement to *JSNT*
JSOT	*Journal for the Study of the Old Testament*

JTS	*Journal of Theological Studies*
LCL	Loeb Classical Library
LD	Lectio divina
LTK	K. Rahner, *Lexikon für Theologie und Kirche* (11 vols.; 2d ed. Freiburg im B.: Herder, 1957–67)
LumVie	*Lumière et vie*
MeyerK	H. A. W. Meyer, *Kritisch-exegetischer Kommentar über das Neue Testament* (16 vols.; Göttingen: Vandenhoeck & Ruprecht, 1832– [with many editions and reprints])
NIGTC	New International Greek Testament Commentary
NovT	*Novum Testamentum*
NRT	*Nouvelle Revue Théologique*
NTD	Das Neue Testament deutsch
NTS	*New Testament Studies*
PEQ	*Palestine Exploration Quarterly*
PerspRelStud	*Perspectives in Religious Studies*
PSTJ	*Perkins School of Theology Journal*
RArch	*Revue archéologique*
RB	*Revue biblique*
RechBib	Recherches bibliques
ResQuart	*Restoration Quarterly*
RevQ	*Revue de Qumran*
RevScRel	*Revue des sciences religieuses*
RSR	*Recherches de science religieuse*
RSV	*Revised Standard Version* (of the Bible)
SBJ	*Sainte Bible de Jérusalem* (Paris: Cerf, 1950)
SBLMS	Society of Biblical Literature Monograph Series

SBT	Studies in Biblical Theology
ScEccl	*Sciences ecclésiastiques*
SE VI	*Studia evangelica VI* (= TU 112 [1973])
SJT	*Scottish Journal of Theology*
SNTSMS	Studiorum Novi Testamenti Societas Monograph Series
SNTU	Studien zum Neuen Testament und seiner Umwelt
Str-B	[H. Strack and] P. Billerbeck, *Kommentar zum Neuen Testament aus Talmud und Midrasch* (6 vols.; Munich: Beck, 1922–61)
TBT	*The Bible Today*
TDNT	G. Kittel (ed.), *Theological Dictionary of the New Testament* (10 vols.; Grand Rapids, MI: Eerdmans, 1964–76)
TF	Theologische Forschung
TGl	*Theologie und Glaube*
TS	*Theological Studies*
TTZ	*Trierer theologische Zeitschrift*
TU	Texte und Untersuchungen
TZ	*Theologische Zeitschrift*
VC	*Vigiliae christianae*
WMANT	Wissenschaftliche Monographien zum Alten und Neuen Testament
WUNT	Wissenschaftliche Untersuchungen zum Neuen Testament
ZKT	*Zeitschrift für katholische Theologie*
ZNW	*Zeitschrift für die neutestamentliche Wissenschaft*
ZTK	*Zeitschrift für Theologie und Kirche*

Select Commentaries and Monographs

*(Referred to in the book by either
shortened titles or acronyms)*

Brown, R. E., *The Birth of the Messiah: A Commentary on the Infancy Narratives in Matthew and Luke* (Garden City, NY: Doubleday, 1977). [*Birth*]

————*et al.* (eds.), *Mary in the New Testament: A Collaborative Assessment by Protestant and Roman Catholic Scholars* (Philadelphia: Fortress; New York/Ramsey, NJ: Paulist, 1978). [*MNT*]

Bultmann, R., *History of the Synoptic Tradition* (Oxford: Blackwell, 1968). [*HST*]

Conzelmann, H., *The Theology of St Luke* (New York: Harper & Bros., 1960). [*Theology*]

Creed, J. M., *The Gospel according to St. Luke: The Greek Text, with Introduction, Notes, and Indices* (London: Macmillan, 1930). [*The Gospel*]

Ellis, E. E., *The Gospel of Luke* (Century Bible; 2d ed.; London: Oliphants, 1974). [*Gospel of Luke*]

Fitzmyer, J. A., *Essays on the Semitic Background of the New Testament* (London: Chapman, 1971; repr., Missoula, MT: Scholars, 1974). [*ESBNT*]

————, *The Gospel according to Luke: Introduction, Translation, and Notes* (AB 28,28A; Garden City, NY: Doubleday, 1981, 1985). [*Luke*]

————, *To Advance the Gospel: New Testament Studies* (New York: Crossroad, 1981). [*TAG*]

Hennecke, E. and W. Schneemelcher, *New Testament Apocrypha* (ed. R. McL. Wilson; 2 vols.; London: Lutterworth, 1963–65). [*HSNTA*]

Jeremias, J., *Die Sprache des Lukasevangeliums* (MeyerK; Göttingen: Vandenhoeck & Ruprecht, 1980). [*Die Sprache*]

Jervell, J., *Luke and the People of God: A New Look at Luke-Acts* (Minneapolis: Augsburg, 1972). [*Luke and the People of God*]

Keck, L. E. and J. L. Martyn (eds.), *Studies in Luke-Acts: Essays Presented in Honor of Paul Schubert* (Nashville: Abingdon, 1966). [*SLA*]

Klassen, W. and G. F. Snyder (eds.), *Current Issues in New Testament Interpretation: Essays in Honor of Otto A. Piper* (London: SCM, 1962). [*CINTI*]

Foakes Jackson, F. J. and K. Lake (eds.) *Beginnings of Christianity* (5 vols.; London: Macmillan, 1920–33). [*Beginnings*]

Laurentin, R., *Les évangiles de l'enfance du Christ: Vérité de Noël au-delà des mythes* (Paris: Desclée, 1982). [*Evangiles*] (Now in English translation: *The Truth of Christmas beyond the Myths* [Still River, MA: St. Bede's, 1985.)

McHugh, J., *The Mother of Jesus in the New Testament* (London: Darton, Longman & Todd, 1975). [*The Mother*]

Marshall, I. H., *The Gospel of Luke: A Commentary on the Greek Text* (NIGTC; Exeter: Paternoster; Grand Rapids, MI: Eerdmans, 1978). [*Gospel of Luke*]

Metzger, B. M., *A Textual Commentary on the Greek New Testament* (New York: United Bible Societies, 1971). [*TCGNT*]

Plummer, A., *A Critical and Exegetical Commentary on the Gospel according to S. Luke* (5th ed.; Edinburgh: Clark, 1922; repr. 1964). [*Gospel according to S. Luke*]

Rengstorf, K. H., *Das Evangelium nach Lukas* (NTD 3; 14th ed.; Göttingen: Vandenhoeck & Ruprecht, 1969). [*Das Evangelium nach Lukas*]

Wilson, S. G., *Luke and the Law* (SNTSMS 50; Cambridge: University Press, 1975). [*Luke and the Law*]

1

The Authorship of Luke–Acts Reconsidered

More than twenty years ago W. C. van Unnik, the Dutch New Testament scholar, published an article in which he referred to the author of the Third Gospel and Acts as "the Rev. Mr. Luke—we keep this traditional name for the author . . . without any prejudice." That article, "Luke–Acts, a Storm Center in Contemporary Scholarship," published in 1966,[1] was an invaluable survey of Lucan studies up to that time. In it van Unnik noted how this New Testament author, who was responsible for composing roughly a quarter of the Greek New Testament text, had become "one of the heroes or, perhaps in some cases, more or less the villain of the play on the New Testament stage." Van Unnik's mild skepticism about the identity of the author of the Third Gospel and Acts was not new; for decades before him scholars had entertained doubts about the ancient ecclesiastical tradition, which was often summarily dismissed without much reflection. As a result, that New Testament author had become the whipping-boy on the stage of New Testament study. Today, for many and diverse reasons, interpreters have often sought to modify, or even abandon, some of the positions once adopted about Luke–Acts in the post-World War II period. In such a reassessment, however, the ques-

1

tion of the identity of the author has not played a large part. If I raise it now, it is simply because a renewed critical view of the evidence about "the Rev. Mr. Luke" seems to be in order. The issue is complicated and involves at times more than the Lucan text itself, being tied up with how valuable any of the ancient ecclesiastical tradition about New Testament authors really is and how the author of the Third Gospel and Acts is related to the Apostle Paul.

In the introduction to my commentary on the Lucan Gospel I proposed a nuanced defense of the composition of Luke–Acts by the traditional Luke, called by Paul a "fellow-worker" (Phlm 24) and identified in the Deutero-Pauline letter to the Colossians as "the beloved physician" (4:14). In the pseudepigraphical 2 Timothy he is named as "Paul's sole companion" (4:11). My proposal, based on a renewed reading of the New Testament data and the ancient church evidence, concluded with the "identification of the author of the Third Gospel and Acts as Luke, a Syrian of Antioch, a physician, and a sometime collaborator of Paul."[2]

This identification was based on the title *euangelion kata Loukan* found in the oldest Greek manuscript of the Third Gospel, Papyrus Bodmer XIV or P[75], a codex dating from A.D. 200 (± 25 years), and on a critical reading of the late second-century ascription of the Third Gospel to Luke in the Muratorian Canon, in Irenaeus (*Adv. haer.* 3.1.1; 3.14,1–3), in the Greek form of an ancient extratextual prologue to the Gospel (often called—questionably—the Anti-Marcionite Prologue), and in Tertullian (*Adv. Marcionem* 4.2,2). In this ecclesiastical tradition I tried to sort out what might have been deduced from the New Testament itself about this author: e.g., that he was a physician, a companion or collaborator of Paul, a disciple who had not witnessed Jesus' ministry, and who began his account with a story about John the Baptist—and who had composed the Acts of the Apostles, writing both books in good Greek style. Such details form part of the tradition in one writer or another and could have been deduced from the New Testament itself by an astute church writer. But other details in that tradition are not so obviously deduced from New Testament evidence, e.g., the ascription itself of the Third Gospel and Acts to Luke, or the description of him as a Syrian of Antioch (or of Rome or Bithynia); or the details that he died in Boeotia or Thebes, unmarried, childless, and at the age of 84. The second-century tradition, especially as it was later repeated and embellished in the forms handed on by Origen, Eusebius, and Jerome, gathered legendary accretions. Dismissing such accretions, I limited the non-deduced details to the ascription of the Third Gospel and Acts to Luke and to his origin in Antioch of Syria (i.e., Antioch on the Orontes or Antioch near Daphne). Antioch is not only the most frequently mentioned place of origin for Luke in this tradition, but it also has no apologetic or theological concern; the plausibility of the author's Antiochene origin has been argued by A. Strobel and R. Glover[3] on the basis of data given in Acts about the early Christian community found there (11:19–20; 13:1–4; 14:26–28; 15:1–3,13–40; 18:22–23).

I further insisted that one had to read the material in Irenaeus about Luke more critically than had usually been done in the past. Irenaeus partly based his identification of Luke as the author on the so-called We-Sections of Acts (16:10–17; 20:5–15; 21:1–18; 27:1–28:16): "Luke . . . companion of Paul (*akolouthos, sectator*) set forth in a book the gospel as preached by him" (i.e., by Paul; *Adv. haer.* 3.1,1). But he further claimed on the basis of these sections that "this Luke was inseparable from Paul" (*Adv. haer.* 3.14,1). Since I reckoned with the probability that the best explanation of the

We-Sections was still that they stemmed from "a diary of the author, later used in the composition of Acts,"[4] I was, in effect, accepting the internal evidence used for Irenaeus' conclusion—to the extent at least that the author had been a companion or collaborator of Paul. But I took the We-Sections at face value and concluded against Irenaeus that these passages did not reveal that the author of Acts had been an "inseparable" companion, as Irenaeus had maintained. The evidence of the We-Sections shows that he was at most a sometime companion of Paul. Thus this position was based in part on Paul's own statement in Phlm 24, where "Luke" is mentioned among his *synergoi,* and in part on the restricted evidence of the We-Sections themselves that suggest that the author of Acts was a companion of Paul for a time.

The We-Sections begin in the middle of Paul's second missionary journey, as we usually label it today, viz., at Acts 16:10, where Paul in Troas has a night-vision of a Macedonian beseeching him to come over and help him and others. The author of Acts writes, "We sought to go to Macedonia." That initial passage ends at 16:17, in the midst of the account of Paul's reaction to the Philippian girl "who had a python-spirit," which he eventually drives out (16:18). The We-Section is at an end, and the narrative continues in the third person.

The second We-Section is found at Acts 20:5–15, which recounts the departure of Paul and the author from Philippi by ship for Troas (where Paul delivers his long-winded speech), and they eventually travel to Assos, Chios, Samos, Miletus, etc. Now the question is, Where was the author of Acts between the episode in 16:10–17 (the first We-Section, which ends in Philippi) and that in 20:5–15 (the second We-Section, which begins in Philippi)? From these passages one could deduce that the author was Paul's *akolouthos* or *sectator,* as did Irenaeus. But the implication contained in them may be more eloquent than is generally recognized, since the second passage is related to Paul's return to Jerusalem at the end of his so-called third missionary journey. Now if one may conclude from the absence of We-Sections between the middle of the second missionary journey and the end of the third journey that the author of Acts was not present with Paul, but had been left as *synergos* in Philippi or Macedonia during that time, the implication would be that the author was not with Paul during very important phases of the latter's career. On Paul's way back to Jerusalem at the end of his third missionary journey the author of Acts becomes again not only *synergos,* but even *akolouthos.* I follow the generally accepted dating of Pauline chronology.[5] Paul's first visit to Philippi would have occurred sometime in late A.D. 50, as he arrived in Corinth for the first time in early A.D. 51. His return to Jerusalem at the end of the third journey would have been in the late spring of A.D. 58. Yet the period A.D. 50–58 is precisely the time when Paul had his battles with the Judaizers and the charismatic factions of Corinth and when he wrote most of his important letters.

Now if the author of Acts were separated from Paul during this period of A.D. 50–58 and were not Paul's close collaborator during this time, this would explain two things. First, the brief association of the author of Acts with Paul would reveal why he might want to make Paul the hero of the second part of Acts, the one who would carry "the word of the Lord" to "the end of the earth" (Acts 1:8). Second, it would also explain why the author of Acts seems to be unaware of Paul's important writings, unaware of much of his theology, and why he depicts Paul as he does, as one who carried to the end of the earth a view of Christianity that does not coincide in all respects with the ideas of Paul himself. In 1950 P.

Vielhauer composed his highly regarded article, "Zum 'Paulinismus' der Apostelgeschichte,"[6] in which he showed how different the Paul of Acts appears from the Paul of the undisputed letters. Vielhauer listed a difference of ideas in four crucial areas: natural theology, the Mosaic law, christology, and eschatology. Even though Vielhauer's article itself needs critical scrutiny in some details, the thrust of it has been generally accepted, and we have come to recognize that the depiction of Paul in Acts differs somewhat from the picture of the Apostle and his theology that are enshrined in his own letters. Moreover, the difference in the portrayal of Paul in Acts is to be explained not only by the author's literary purpose, but also by the author's lack of acquaintance with the Paul of history and with his letters at a crucial period. Voices are raised from time to time to maintain Luke's acquaintance with the letters of Paul,[7] but they do not carry conviction, since Acts is singularly deficient in expressing major tenets of Pauline teaching. How else can one explain why the author of Acts depicts Paul preaching justification by faith only once (in the synagogue of Antioch in Pisidia, 13:38–39): "Therefore, let it be known to you, brethren, that through this man (Jesus) forgiveness of sins is proclaimed to you, and by him everyone who believes is acquitted of everything, of which you could not be acquitted by the law of Moses." Here the verb *dikaioun*, "acquit," is used, indeed, and in a context that mentions faith (*pas ho pisteuōn*), but it lacks the precision of Pauline formulation.[8] Justification has rather been subsumed under the author's own doctrine of *aphesis hamartiōn*, "forgiveness of sins," and subordinated to it. "Forgiveness of sins" is not one of the ways in which Paul expresses an effect of the Christ-event in his undisputed letters.[9] *Aphesis tōn hamartiōn* is found in Col 1:14, and *aphesis tōn paraptōmatōn* in Eph 1:7, but the phrases in question, related to the Lucan phrase (Luke 1:77; 3:3; 24:47; Acts 2:38; 5:31; 10:43; 26:18), are part of the reason why one regards Colossians and Ephesians as Deutero-Pauline.[10] Yet this rare instance of Paul preaching justification in Acts and the treatment that it receives under the author's pen are to be attributed to the author not having been with Paul at the time when he struggled through the controversy with the Judaizers and had to formulate his doctrine of justification by grace through faith.[11]

So much, then, for a summary of the position proposed in my commentary on the Lucan Gospel about its author. The acceptance of the We-Sections as part of a diary that the author of Acts incorporated at places into his account of Paul's ministry and the restriction of its data to their face value allows one to conclude that the author of the Third Gospel and Acts was indeed Luke, a Syrian of Antioch on the Orontes, a physician (as he is called in Col 4:11), and a sometime collaborator of Paul the Apostle.

Discussion with others and further reflection have been the background for the reconsideration of this proposal. I do not mean "reconsideration" in the sense of retraction. On the contrary, I plan now to review certain aspects of the proposal in the light of such discussion and reflection. I shall review the matter under three headings: (1) problems in the second-century tradition; (2) Philippians and Luke's presence in Philippi and Macedonia; and (3) the literary character of the We-Sections.

I. *Problems in the Second-Century Tradition*

By "problems" is meant aspects of the second-century tradition that I perhaps did not consider sufficiently. The

first of these is the date of the Muratorian Canon. It is
known that A. C. Sundberg, Jr. has argued strongly that this
canonical list of New Testament books dates not from the
end of the second century, as had normally been held, but
rather from the fourth century.[12] Indeed, the popular and
widely used *Interpreter's Dictionary of the Bible* in its supplementary volume[13] espouses the fourth-century dating. If that
dating were acceptable, it would mean the elimination of
what has been regarded as the earliest prop for the second-
century tradition about Luke as the author of the Third
Gospel and Acts.

However, the article on the Muratorian Canon in that
supplement has been authored by Sundberg himself and is
scarcely an independent testimony. Moreover, apart from R.
F. Collins,[14] I have been able to find no other scholars who
have accepted Sundberg's thesis. W. G. Kümmel has called
Sundberg's dating of the Muratorian Canon "arbitrary,"[15]
and H. Y. Gamble, E. Ferguson, and F. F. Bruce have come
out strongly against his position.[16] I personally have often
been uneasy with Sundberg's arguments and now welcome
this recent reaction to them. Yet even if the second-century
dating of the Muratorian Canon were widely questioned, the
second-century tradition about the Lucan authorship of the
Third Gospel and Acts, pared down to what I salvage from it,
does not depend on this canonical list alone, since apart from
it there is the testimony of Irenaeus and Tertullian and there is
now the evidence of the title, *euangelion kata Loukan,* in
Papyrus Bodmer XIV,[17] published only in 1961. No one has
claimed, so far as I know, that that title on a late second-
century codex of Egyptian provenience is demonstrably dependent on either Irenaeus or Tertullian. It is an important
independent witness to what was the tradition at the end of
the second century in the Egyptian church.

Second, I am also aware that the ancient extratextual prologue to the Third Gospel is likewise dated to the fourth—or even fifth—century, e.g., by J. Regul.[18] But whereas that late date may be admissible for the final redaction of that prologue, which is clearly composite, I still prefer to regard its first paragraph in the Greek form as coming from the second century.

Third, another aspect of the ancient ecclesiastical tradition that should be considered is the possibility that the ancient witnesses to Lucan authorship "show that speculation on the origin of the New Testament books was already abundant in the second century."[19] Speculation based on New Testament data could, indeed, have given rise to such traditions about authorship. Irenaeus so argued from the We-Sections of Acts to show that Luke was Paul's "inseparable" companion. Though I question whether the data enable one to conclude to the "inseparability" of that relationship, Irenaeus' use of those sections reveals such speculation. If one were to examine Acts alone, the treatment of Peter and Paul in it as the two main heroes might suggest companions of either of them as candidates for the authorship of that writing. In the case of Peter, Silvanus and Mark are mentioned as collaborators of Peter in 1 Pet 5:12–13. But in the case of Paul, the candidates are more numerous: e.g., Timothy, Lucius, Jason, Sosipater (Rom 16:21); Sosthenes (1 Cor 1:1); Epaphroditus (Phil 2:25)—not to pass over the others named in the passages where Luke himself is mentioned: Epaphras, Mark, Aristarchus, Demas (called "fellow prisoners" or "fellow workers" in Phlm 23–24); Aristarchus, Mark (cousin of Barnabas), Jesus called Justus (all Jewish Christians); Epaphras and Demas (Gentile Christians, as Luke is undoubtedly so regarded in Col 4:12–14). In 2 Tim 4:11 Luke is said to be the only one with "Paul," whereas Demas, Crescens, Titus,

Tychicus have gone off or have been sent elsewhere. Even though we may maintain today the Deutero-Pauline or pseudepigraphical character of Colossians or 2 Timothy, patristic writers of the second century would not have shared that view. As far as they were concerned, the data in the Pauline corpus would have to be taken as a block. Yet even so, can such a list of collaborators of Paul enable one to home in on Luke as the author of the Third Gospel and Acts?

Some of the names could be eliminated by astute speculation: e.g., Aristarchus (Phlm 24; Col 4:10) is probably the same person as the one mentioned in Acts 27:2, who is said to be "with us" (hence "with" the author of Acts, not identical with him). The fact that Aristarchus, Mark, and Jesus called Justus are said to be "the only ones of the circumcision" (i.e., Christians of Jewish background) in Col 4:10–11, whereas Epaphras, "who is one of yourselves" (i.e., a Christian of Gentile background—in which category Luke and Demas are also mentioned) would not rule out any of the first three as the possible author of Acts. It is scarcely a foregone conclusion that a Jewish Christian could not have written the good Greek of the Third Gospel and Acts. Granted that the thought patterns, style, and language of these New Testament writings call for a Christian author of Gentile background (as we judge today), it is far from certain that ancient writers would have concluded so precisely. Moreover, there is the opinion of Eusebius (*Pan.* 51.11), repeated by some modern commentators, that Luke was actually Jewish, one of the seventy disciples, and the companion of Cleopas on the road to Emmaus.[20] True, Mark, Titus, and Timothy might also have been eliminated from consideration, given the fact that early tradition already associated them with other New Testament writings. In this sort of speculation one wonders why "Paul" asks Timothy to come to him and "bring along the cloak which he ("Paul") had left at Troas with Carpus, also the books and especially the parchments" (2 Tim 4:13). Would not such a context suggest that Carpus of Troas would be the likely candidate for the author of the Third Gospel and Acts? I find it very difficult to think that, because "Paul" says that Luke is the only one with him (2 Tim 4:11), Luke thus becomes the *only* candidate that a second-century speculation would focus on, as one considered the We-Sections as autobiographical, regarded Colossians and 2 Timothy as genuine Pauline writings, and failed to distinguish various imprisonments of Paul. In all of this there is more than a mere hint of arguing *a posse ad esse*. As I read Irenaeus, I detect this second-century Church Father looking for arguments from the New Testament to bolster an existing tradition. Irenaeus had no superior knowledge; I refer merely to a tradition independent of his speculation and his analysis of New Testament writings. In all of this one has to ask how a Church Father would have come to ascribe the Third Gospel and Acts to such an obscure Christian as Luke, a person who was not one of the Twelve, if there were not some basis for the traditional ascription. It seems rather that writers such as Irenaeus, Tertullian, and others were tributary to a tradition that they sought to bolster—one that is now attested independently in the Egyptian papyrus Bodmer XIV.

II. Philippians and Luke's Presence in Philippi

If my conclusion from the We-Sections is that Luke stayed in Philippi or Macedonia from the middle of Paul's second missionary journey to the end of the third journey (roughly A.D. 50–58) and that he was not around when Paul was formulating his major theological teachings and so did not really come to comprehend them, would it not also mean that Luke would have been in Philippi or its vicinity about the time that Paul sent his letter to the Philippians? The answer to this question is complicated because of the nature of the letter to the Philippians and the date of its composition.

In modern discussion of Philippians one often encounters the suggestion that the letter is a conflation of three short letters that Paul sent at different times to the Christians at Philippi. This analysis of Philippians is based in part on the ancient tradition attested by Polycarp that Paul, in communicating with the Philippian Christians, *egrapsen epistolas,* "wrote letters" (*Phil.* 3.2).[21] In part, it is also based on the abrupt transitions in the existing letter: the beginning after a farewell at 3:2; the tone of 3:2–4:3, so different from the rest; the character of 4:10–20, where gratitude is expressed after a "farewell" (4:4–9). Various proposals are made for the division of the existing conflated letter into three sources; they do not concern us now, but the proposals raise the question when these letters would have been sent and whether Luke would have known any of them, were he in or near Philippi.

The question is further complicated by the attempt made to identify the provenience of Philippians either as a unit or as shorter letters. In the existing letter Paul writes as a prisoner (1:7,13,14,17). Philippians is one of the Captivity Letters. Traditionally, it has been associated with Colossians, Ephesians, and Philemon and ascribed to Paul's Roman house-arrest (Acts 28:16b,30a). This place for the composition of Philippians was used by Marcion and has been advocated in modern times by such interpreters as F. W. Beare, C. O. Buchanan, C. G. Caird, L. Cerfaux, C. H. Dodd, D. Guthrie, E. F. Harrison, and J. Schmid. Obviously, if Paul wrote Philippians from the Roman house-arrest (roughly A.D. 61–63), then Luke, who would not have been in or near Philippi after A.D. 58 according to my proposal, would never have had the opportunity to read Philippians.

Other proposals, however, have been made for the place of composition of Philippians (as one or three letters). There is the theory that it was composed during Paul's imprisonment in Caesarea Maritima (A.D. 58–60), as H. E. G. Paulus once proposed; he has been followed by M. Dibelius, E. Lohmeyer, O. Pfleiderer, B. Reicke, and F. Spitta. Again, that would have followed upon the stay of Luke in or near Philippi, since that imprisonment would have followed upon the return of Paul to Jerusalem at the end of the third missionary journey. It should be noted in passing that, though the We-Sections precede and follow the story of Paul's arrest after his arrival in Jerusalem (21:1–18 and 27:1–28:16), neither of these passages has anything to do with Paul's imprisonment in Jerusalem or Caesarea Maritima (Acts 21:33–26:32). The author of Acts never implies that he was with Paul during the time of the Jerusalem or Caesarean imprisonment.

A number of interpreters of Philippians, however, in more recent years have found the dates implied in the Roman and Caesarean imprisonments to be too late for the problem addressed in Phil 3:2–4:3, a passage that seems to cry out for a relationship of it with the period of Paul's battle with the Judaizers and with such writings as Galatians, 1–2 Corinthians, and Romans. Consequently, they have proposed an Ephesian imprisonment of Paul as the place where Philippians would rather have been composed. Paul may refer vaguely to such an imprisonment in his mention of fighting wild beasts in Ephesus (1 Cor 15:32; cf. 4:9) or the

affliction that he experienced in Asia (2 Cor 1:8). First proposed as the provenience of Philippians by H. Lisco in 1900,
this Ephesian imprisonment has found many advocates since
then: P. Benoit, A. Deissmann, G. S. Duncan, P. Feine, M.
Goguel, and W. Michaelis. If this place of origin were correct for Philippians, then it would have been written sometime during Paul's third missionary journey, when he was
mainly based in Ephesus (roughly A.D. 54–57). If his imprisonment had anything to do with the riot of the silversmiths
(Acts 19:23–41), it would be closer to A.D. 57 than to the
beginning of Paul's stay there. In any case, if Paul wrote
Philippians (as a unit or as three shorter letters) from such an
Ephesian imprisonment, it/they would have come to Philippi
while the author of Acts was still in or near that town,
according to my proposal. How then explain the author's
apparent unacquaintance even with this undisputed Pauline
letter?

In Philippians Paul refers to the contentious women,
Euodia and Syntyche, who had labored with him "in the
gospel" (4:2–3) along "with Clement and the remaining
fellow-workers" (*kai tōn loipōn synergōn*). Though Paul em-
ploys the plural of the noun *synergos,* which he uses of Luke
in Phlm 24, there is not the slightest hint that he would have
considered Luke to be among such *synergoi* at Philippi.

Certainly, the sole reference to Paul's preaching of justification by faith in Acts 13:38–39, to which I have already
referred, is not obviously dependent on Phil 3:9. There Paul
speaks about having a "righteousness" that is not his own,
not "based on the law," but one which is "through faith in
Christ, the righteousness from God that depends on faith."
The use that Luke makes of his sole reference to justification
and faith needs some other explanation for its origin.

Would the author of the Third Gospel and Acts, who

lived for at least twenty years beyond the death of Paul, have so severed connections with an area such as Philippi in which he would have labored for about eight years, if my hypothesis has any validity? Here the silence of Acts is involved; we note it, but we cannot explain it except to say that Acts is really not autobiographical—apart from the few We-Sections, wherein the emphasis is not on the author but on Paul. Again, even though the ancient title of the Lucan second volume, *Praxeis Apostolōn,* is scarcely original, it still remains true that the major "apostles" whose deeds are recounted in this work are Peter and Paul, whereas all others are insignificant actors, among whom would be the author of Acts himself. If the author of Acts had kept up contacts with the community at Philippi, how could he have failed to learn about the letter(s) to the Philippians? To answer such a question would involve trying to explain why the author of Acts never depicts Paul writing any letters at all or solving problems by epistolographic means in localities in which he was not present. This question is related to the purpose the author had in writing Acts and to his casting Paul in the role of the one who carries the word of the Lord *viva voce* "to the end of the earth" (1:8). Acts, indeed, reveals the author's awareness of Paul's night-vision at Troas, which is an important stage in the development of that role; it is for him important as the beginning of the Macedonian mission that was thus sparked.

Even if one were to admit that the author of Acts finally accompanied Paul to Rome and was somewhere in the imperial capital during the two years of Paul's house-arrest, of which Acts 28:30 speaks, can one deduce from that presence in Rome that the author of Acts must have read Paul's letter to the Romans (sent there in A.D. 58 from Corinth or its port Cenchreae, before Paul left to pass through Philippi on the way back to Jerusalem)?

In this entire debate about the author of Acts and the letter to the Philippians the argument runs once again *a posse ad esse;* the author of Acts was in or near Philippi from A.D. 50–58 and he could have read the letter to the Philippians. Yes, he could have, but did he?

A sort of corollary to this argument might concern the question whether Paul himself kept copies of the major letters that he composed. The author of Acts, who was near Paul during certain occasions toward the end of his life, might then have had access to such copies. Whether or not Paul had a copy of his major letters (e.g., that to the Romans) is anyone's guess. I have not yet been able to discover what the ancient custom was in this regard, or how many copies would have been made of such letters. Apart from such a theoretic possibility, Acts seems to have been composed quite independently of copies of Paul's letters. This is explained by the distance that I strive to put between the time that Luke served as Paul's sometime companion (A.D. 50, 58–61) and the period when he finally composed the Third Gospel and Acts, *ca.* A.D. 80–85.

III.   The Literary Character of the We-Sections

In general, three explanations have been proposed for the character of the We-Sections of Acts: (1) they are autobiographical, reflecting common experiences of the author and Paul recorded in what we would call a diary; (2) they are drawn from an itinerary-record, from which the author of Acts culls and which he rewrites in his own style and inserts into his narrative, preserving the "we" of the original writer's record; and (3) they are creations of the author of Acts who adopts a literary form in using "we" for certain passages related to sea voyages, thus imitating a "conventional generic style within Hellenistic literature."[22] In my commentary on the Lucan Gospel, I adopted the first explanation, which had often been used before,[23] because it seemed to me the best explanation of these passages in Acts.

The second explanation seems somewhat arbitrary. Whose itinerary-record would it have been, if it stems from someone other than the author of Acts? The explanation copes with the uniformity of style found in the We-Sections and the rest of Acts; but this is precisely the reason why I prefer to think that the We-Sections stem from the author's own diary-like record. Moreover, the second explanation raises again the general question of the sources of Acts and, particularly in this case, it is open to all the difficulties about such sources once raised by J. Dupont.[24] If one is going to explain the use of "we" in these sections by an appeal to an earlier existing text, then the better explanation is that they stem from a record kept by the author of Acts himself.

I did not give sufficient attention in my commentary to the third explanation, especially to the proposal made by V. K. Robbins.[25] I have been, however, skeptical about this literary explanation of the We-Sections that assimilates them to a conventional literary style in contemporary Greco-Roman literature. It is not that I would want to deny the existence of such a "conventional generic style," but I find some of the evidence for its use forced and the application of it to the passages of Acts even more so. My skepticism rests on several factors.

First, if it is a studied literary device used by the author of Acts, then why does it appear only where it does—from Troas to Philippi, from Philippi to Jerusalem, and from Caesarea to Rome? Sailing is mentioned in Acts 13:4, from

Seleucia, the port of Antioch on the Orontes, to Salamis in Cyprus; in 13:13, from Paphos on Cyprus to Perga in Pamphylia; in 14:26, from Attalia near Perga back to Antioch. Sailing is, moreover, implied in Acts 17:14, where the brethren in Beroea "sent Paul off to make his way to the sea." It is further mentioned in Acts 18:18, where Paul at the end of his second missionary journey departs from Corinth for Syria, and in 18:21, where he sails from Ephesus to Caesarea Maritima. The author of Acts records that Paul departed from Ephesus for Macedonia and Greece (20:1–2), but he supplies no details about the journey, during which Paul would have had to cross at least the Hellespont by ship. In none of these passages, either implicitly or explicitly referring to sea voyages, is the first plural narrative form employed.[26]

Second, further difficulty is sensed in the first We-Section (16:10–17), where the "we" may be appropriate in vv. 10–12, which refer to the journey from Troas to Philippi by sea via Samothrace and Neapolis. But why is the "we" continued in the story of Paul's going to a place of prayer at some riverside site, in the story of his sojourn at Lydia's house, and in only the first part of the story about Paul's exorcism of the girl with the python-spirit (16:13–17)? Moreover, v. 10 itself is a declaration of intention, and the We-Section itself should more properly begin with v. 11, if the "we" is to be explained by a sea voyage connection. Hence one may ask how appropriate the explanation is for the *entire* passage in which this "we" occurs. Similarly, one would have to ask the same question about Acts 20:7–8, which provides the setting for Paul's long winded speech in Troas and the Eutychus incident. Eventually, vv. 13–16 continue in the first plural, but v. 16, which tells about Paul sailing "past Ephesus," recounts it in the third singular; this is also found in vv. 9–12. Again, why does the "we" continue during the account of the overland journey from Ptolemais to Caesarea Maritima (Acts 21:7–8a), during the story about Philip the evangelist and his daughters and Agabus (21:8b–14), and during the narrative of the further overland journey from Caesarea to Jerusalem (21:15–18)?

Third, I have difficulty with some of the examples used by Robbins and claimed by him to be part of contemporary "Hellenistic literature." He maintains in general that "sea voyages are often couched in the first person narrative,"[27] yet he begins citing examples of such narration from ancient Egyptian tales, e.g., *The Story of Si-nuhe,* dating from roughly 1800 B.C., and *The Journey of Wen-Amun to Phoenicia,* dating from roughly 1100 B.C. Aside from the fact that these tales are scarcely part of "Hellenistic literature," they are narratives using the first person singular, not the plural. Moreover, Robbins does not tell us that in the *Story of Si-nuhe* almost the entire tale is recounted in the first singular; it is not restricted to sea voyages or lake crossings. Si-nuhe's dealings with Ammi-enshi, the ruler of Upper Retenu (somewhere near Byblos), where he spent a year and a half, and then his "many years" of married life and military service are all recounted in the first singular. J. A. Wilson, who translates the tale in *ANET,* writes about it as "pompous and overstyled in wording and phrasing."[28] In other words, one wonders about the use of this tale as an extrabiblical example of sea voyage narrative style using "we." The same has to be said about the Wen-Amun report. The first person singular is used not only for the journey from Tanis across the great Syrian Sea to Dor (on the north coast of Palestine) and then to Byblos, but also for all the account of Wen-Amun's dealings with the Prince of Byblos.[29]

Robbins further cites the Akkadian *Epic of Gilgamesh,*

yet the narrative in the first singular is not confined to the
journey to Mount Nisir, but includes the building of the ship,
the pouring of a libation on a mountaintop, and the granting
to Atrahasis to see a dream. Moreover, the third plural is
also used with reference to a boat voyage: "Gilgamesh and
Urshanabi boarded the boat; [they launch]ed the boat on the
waves [and] they sailed away."[30]

Similarly, examples drawn from Homer's *Odyssey* prove
little, since they are not examples of the first person plural
introduced into a narrative when a sea voyage is involved.
Rather, Odysseus is engaged in telling a *story* to King
Alcinous and the Phaeacians at a banquet about his personal
experiences, which happen to include a sea voyage. In modern usage it would all be set in quotation marks, and this is
quite different from use of "we" in Acts. Robbins makes
much of the Homeric shift from the first singular to the first
plural, "a formulaic means for launching the ship, sailing for a
number of days, and beaching the ship at the end of a voyage."[31] But he does not tell us that the first plural is also used
in the account of the capture of wives and the looting of the
city of Cicones (*Od.* 9.41), or about how the evil doom of
Zeus "attended us ill-fated men" (*Od.* 9.52–53). There is,
moreover, a constant shift back and forth between the first
singular and the first plural even in the story being recounted
in direct discourse about Odysseus' sea voyage. Robbins has
simply concentrated on the first plural and has not sufficiently
attended to the use of the first singular. The same has to be
said about the passage cited by him from Virgil's *Aeneid* 3.1–
9. It is part of the story being recounted by Aeneas at Dido's
banquet, and his story moves back and forth from the first
singular to the first plural; and the latter is not restricted to sea
voyage accounts.

The examples that Robbins has cited from more contemporary Hellenistic literature are, in general, more pertinent. But how much can one really draw from Varro's *Menippean Satires* (nos. 276, 473), when they are only one- or two-line epigrams? Those quoted deal, indeed, with boating, but there are other epigrams using the first plural that deal with dining (nos. 102, 103). Similarly, one may query the relevance of the example cited from the seventh discourse of Dio Chrysostom. According to Robbins, there is recounted "a sea voyage, which ends in a shipwreck and a journey . . . ," in which "first person narration" is used. But the whole discourse begins, "I shall now relate a personal experience of mine, not merely something I have heard from others" (7.1). The author then recounts a trip in a small boat, a storm encountered, and the beaching of the boat—all in either the first singular or the third plural. Then, in the passage cited by Robbins (7.10) the author says, "As we proceeded on our way. . . ." The narration has nothing to do with a sea voyage; it is an overland journey, recounted in the first plural. Is any of this relevant to the narrative style of Acts in which the We-Sections occur?

Similarly, one may ask how relevant the passage from Petronius, *Satyricon* 114 really is. Again, even in the Josephus passage (*Life* 3 § 14–16) the narrative does shift at one point from the first singular to the first plural, but later on (which Robbins does not make clear) Josephus reverts and says, "I and some others, about eighty in all . . ." (*egō te kai tines heteroi peri ogdoēkonta sympantes*). Then the rest continues, as one would expect in an autobiographical writing, in the first singular.

As for other examples that Robbins cites, I have little difficulty; they show that one can speak of a sea voyage genre (or possibly even of a shipwreck genre) in first-century Greco-Roman literature. I have no difficulty with the suggestion that Acts 27 may have been composed in dependence on such a genre.[32]

The use of the first plural on board ship may be more naturally explained as an expression of the sociological character of such an experience. Robbins himself acknowledges this.[33] But the question rises whether that sociological experience is ever so recounted by those who have not been part of it—or, at least, who want to give the impression that they have been part of it, sea voyage, shipwreck, or what have you. That there may have been such a sea voyage genre I am ready to admit; that it was used in fiction is also admissible. But that it accounts for the We-Sections in Acts is another matter, even if one wants to admit that the imitative historiography in which the author writes might tolerate it.

For reasons such as these I have been skeptical about Robbins' explanation of the We-Sections and have preferred the first explanation, viz., that they are drawn from a diary-like record that the author of Acts once kept and give evidence that he was for a time a companion of Paul—not an inseparable companion, as Irenaeus would have us believe, but a sometime companion of the Apostle.[34]

Notes

[1] *SLA,* 15–32.

[2] *Luke,* 53.

[3] See A. Strobel, "Lukas der Antiochener (Bemerkungen zu Act 11,28D)," *ZNW* 49 (1958) 131–34; R. Glover, " 'Luke the Antiochene' and Acts," *NTS* 11 (1964–65) 97–106.

[4] *Luke,* 36–37; see further part III below.

[5] See my recent book, *Paul and His Theology: A Brief Sketch* (Englewood Cliffs, NJ: Prentice-Hall, 1989) 3–19.

[6] *EvT* 10 (1950–51) 1–15. The English version, "On the 'Paulinism' of Acts" has appeared in various places: *PSTJ* 17 (1963) 5–17; reprinted, *SLA,* 33–50; abridged in W. A. Meeks (ed.), *The Writings of St. Paul* (Norton Critical Edition; New York: Norton, 1972) 166–75.

[7] See M. S. Enslin, " 'Luke' and 'Paul,' " *JAOS* 58 (1938) 81–91. J. Knox, "Acts and the Pauline Letter Corpus," *SLA,* 279–87. E. E. Ellis, *Gospel of Luke,* 50–51. M. D. Goulder, "Did Luke Know Any of the Pauline Letters?" *PerspRelStud* 13 (1986) 97–112 (he probably knew 1 Thessalonians and 1 Corinthians). Contrast S. Brown, *Apostasy and Perseverance in the Theology of Luke* (AnBib 36; Rome: Biblical Institute, 1969) 2–3 (Luke lacks knowledge of all New Testament writings save Mark and "Q").

[8] See further S. G. Wilson, *Luke and the Law,* 59.

[9] See *Paul and His Theology* (n. 5 above) 67.

[10] The idea of "forgiveness, remission" of sins may not be wholly absent from undisputed Pauline writings, since it may be expressed by *paresis* (Rom 3:25), a word whose meaning is much disputed. See *EWNT* 3. 92; cf. U. Wilckens, *Der Brief an die Römer* (3 vols.; EKK 6/1–3; Einsiedeln: Benziger; Neukirchen-Vluyn: Neukirchener-V., 1978–82) 1. 196.

[11] It may be noted in passing how this important doctrine of Pauline theology is rephrased in terms of "salvation" in Deutero-Pauline Eph 2:8–10. As Ephesians reveals, "justification" was reformulated as "salvation" with the passage of time, once the judaizing controversy had disappeared; so too Acts depicts Paul preaching justification, subsumed under a different theologoumenon, probably because the author of Acts never fully realized how important the doctrine of justification was in Pauline thinking.

[12] "Canon Muratori: A Fourth-Century List," *HTR* 66 (1973) 1–41; "Towards a Revised History of the New Testament Canon," *SE VI,* 452–61.

[13] See "Muratorian Fragment," *The Interpreter's Dictionary of the Bible: Supplementary Volume* (ed. K. Crim; Nashville: Abingdon, 1976) 609–10.

[14] See *Introduction to the New Testament* (Garden City, NY: Doubleday, 1983) 35.

[15] *Introduction to the New Testament* (rev. ed.; Nashville: Abingdon, 1975) 492 n. 69.

[16] See H. Y. Gamble, *The New Testament Canon: Its Making and Meaning* (Philadelphia: Fortress, 1985) 32 n. 25; E. Ferguson, "Canon Muratori: Date and Provenance," *Studia patristica* 18 (3 parts; ed. E. A. Livingstone; Oxford: Pergamum, 1982) 2. 677–83; F. F. Bruce, "Some Thoughts on the Beginning of the New Testament Canon," *BJRL* 65 (1982) 37–60, esp. 55–57, 59. Cf. D. Farkasfalvy, "The Early Development of the New Testament Canon," *The Formation of the New Testament Canon* (ed. W. R. Farmer and D. Farkasfalvy; Theological Inquiries; New York: Paulist, 1983) 161 n. 1; J. Beumer, "Das Fragmentum Muratori und seine Rätsel," *TP* 48 (1973) 534–50.

[17] See R. Kasser (ed.), *Papyrus Bodmer XIV–XV:*

Evangiles de Luc et Jean (2 vols.; Cologny-Geneva: Bibliothèque Bodmer, 1961).

[18] *Die antimarcionitischen Evangelienprologe* (Vetus Latina, Aus der Geschichte der lateinischen Bibel 6; Freiburg im B.: Herder, 1969). Cf. R. G. Heard, "The Old Gospel Prologues," *JTS* ns 6 (1955) 1–16, esp. 16.

[19] See H. J. Cadbury, *Beginnings,* 2. 259.

[20] See W. F. Albright, "Luke's Ethnic Background," in J. Munck, *The Acts of the Apostles* (AB 31; Garden City, NY: Doubleday, 1967) 164–67.

[21] See K. Lake, *The Apostolic Fathers* (LCL; 2 vols.; Cambridge, MA: Harvard University, 1965) 1. 286.

[22] See V. K. Robbins, "The We-Passages in Acts and Ancient Sea Voyages," *BR* 20 (1975) 5–18, esp. 6. See further F. Bovon, "Luc: Portrait et projet," *LumVie* 153–54 (1981) 9–18, esp. 17 ("le 'nous' . . . est certes un subterfuge littéraire").

[23] E.g., see J. Munck, *Acts* (n. 20 above) xliii.

[24] See *The Sources of Acts: The Present Position* (London: Darton, Longman and Todd, 1964).

[25] See n. 22 above; cf. "By Land and Sea: The We-Passages and Ancient Sea Voyages," *Perspectives on Luke–Acts* (ed. C. H. Talbert; Danville, VA: Association of Baptist Professors of Religion, 1978) 215–42.

[26] See W. S. Kurz, Review of my commentary, *CBQ* 44 (1982) 673.

[27] "The We-Passages" (n. 22 above), 5.

[28] See J. B. Pritchard, *ANET,* 18–22, esp. 18.

[29] Ibid., 25–29.

[30] See XI.256–57 (ibid., 96).

[31] "The We-Passages" (n. 22 above).

[32] See S. M. Praeder, "Acts 27:1–28:16: Sea Voyages

in Ancient Literature and the Theology of Luke–Acts," *CBQ* 46 (1984) 683–706.

[33] "The We-Passages" (n. 22 above), 6.

[34] See further J. Dupont, *Les Actes des Apôtres* (Paris: Cerf, 1954) 145; also p. 112. A. George, "Luc," *Catholicisme* 7 (1975) 1226–31.

2

Problems in the Lucan
Infancy Narrative

More than any other part of the Lucan writings
the infancy narrative in chaps. 1–2 of the Gospel continues
to be its most sensitive area. For some reason, not wholly
clear, it is the area wherein interpreters are prone to introduce considerations from other standpoints, as if the herme-
neutics involved in these chapters must be different from
those used in a critical interpretation of the rest of the Lucan
writings. Problems in the first two chapters of the Lucan
Gospel remain, and they have to be faced as honestly as
those in other parts of it.

My reconsideration of the Lucan infancy narrative is not
intended as a retraction of what I have said about it in my
commentary on this Gospel. Certain aspects of the narrative, however, call for further discussion, aspects that I
treated only in disjoined comments on phrases in the infancy
narrative and aspects that have emerged in more recent
discussions. Some of the latter have already been treated in
the survey of studies of the Matthean and Lucan infancy
narratives recently published by R. E. Brown.[1] In it he has
reviewed in excellent fashion many of the writings devoted
to these narratives in the decade since 1976, i.e., from the
time of the publication of his own monumental study of
them, *The Birth of the Messiah.*[2]

Before I take up the topics that I propose to discuss in this chapter, a word should be said about the name for Luke 1–2 and the function that these chapters have in the Gospel as a whole. "Infancy narrative" is the name frequently used for this part of the Gospel, but sometimes commentators prefer to speak of it as the "birth narrative." Such a title, however, seems less adequate since the Lucan narrative includes an episode of Jesus' childhood, at the age of twelve (2:41–52), the details of which have nothing to do with birth. Apart from the fact that it is unique even in these early Lucan chapters, being form-critically a pronouncement story that differs so much from the rest of the episodes in chaps. 1–2, it creates a problem even for the title that I have preferred, the "infancy narrative," because it is no more closely related to Jesus' infancy. If "infancy narrative" better covers the majority of the episodes dealing with the conception, birth, etc. of John the Baptist and Jesus, it still does not do justice to the childhood episode of 2:41–52. At times the name "infancy gospel" has been preferred, but that seems even less suitable, because Luke has not only avoided the term *euangelion,* at least in his first volume,[3] but the association of it with the later noncanonical infancy Gospels might give it an undue connotation.

Related to the problem of the name for these first two chapters of the Lucan Gospel is the question whether 1:5–2:52 really forms a unit in the Gospel distinct from chapters 3–4. Some writers have maintained that 1:5 (or even 1:1) to 4:22a forms the opening part of this Gospel.[4] However, it is not merely that the Lucan Gospel agrees with the Matthean in having an infancy narrative prefixed to the beginning of the account of the ministry of John the Baptist and eventually of Jesus. To use such a reason would be to admit a guiding factor that is extrinsic to the Lucan writing itself. But the Lucan narrative in chaps. 1–2 is markedly different from chaps. 3–4, not only in its style and language, which many interpreters find heavily semitizing, but also by the relation of 3:1–2 to the prologue of 1:1–4, a relation that cannot be glossed over. Luke 3:1–2 stands today as part of the larger unit 3:1–6, which introduces the ministry of John the Baptist as the introduction to the ministry narrative of the Third Gospel. Yet vv. 1–2 are constructed as a long periodic sentence, perhaps not as polished as that of the prologue (1:1–4), but definitely resembling it. Its sixfold synchronism sets the stage for the call of John in the desert to go forth and preach "a baptism of repentance for the forgiveness of sins." The matter that it thus introduces reveals that this part of the Lucan Gospel begins where Mark 1:3–4 begins; it also corresponds to the first episode in the Matthean Gospel after the infancy narrative. Indeed, 3:1–2 may have been the opening sentence of the original composition of Luke, to which he subsequently prefixed the prologue and the infancy narrative (at the time that he decided to divide his work into two volumes).[5] For when Luke in the present prologue of Acts refers to this *prōtos logos,* his "first volume," and briefly summarizes its contents, he speaks "of all the things that Jesus began to do and to teach," but not a hint is given of the infancy narrative. The prologue of Acts thus seems to allude to the original function of 3:1–2 in the Gospel. For these reasons it seems preferable to regard the infancy narrative of chaps. 1–2 as the initial unit of the Gospel as we now have it. Even though the Lucan infancy narrative functions in relation to the rest of the Gospel, as does the Matthean infancy narrative in relation to the rest of the First Gospel, it is not so regarded merely for this extrinsic reason. In both cases, the infancy narrative acts as a kind of overture to the Gospel as a whole to which it is prefixed, often sounding for the first time chords that will be later orchestrated in the work as a whole. These preliminary remarks serve to introduce the Lucan infancy narrative.

Two aspects of the narrative will be the subject of the rest of my discussion in this chapter: (1) the historicity of the Lucan infancy narrative: Why is it problematical? and (2) the character and purpose of Luke 1:26–38: Is it a mariological commission or a christological identification?

I. The Historicity of the Lucan Infancy Narrative: Why Is It Problematical?

It is widely admitted today that the canonical infancy narratives are a late development in the gospel tradition. This tradition has itself grown out of the primitive *kērygma* or "proclamation" of the good news of Jesus Christ. First to develop from that proclamation was the part of the tradition normally regarded as the passion narrative, common to all four Gospels, to the Synoptic as well as the Johannine, despite the diversity of details in these specific forms of such a narrative. In time the gospel tradition prefixed to the passion narrative the narrative of his ministry, the account of what Jesus did and taught (in an effort to explain why the passion narrative recounts what it does). Eventually, that tradition took on two further developments, the so-called resurrection narratives (the accounts of the appearances of the risen Christ to his followers and of the commission that he gave to them) and the infancy narratives (or other Gospel beginning).

If there is any validity to this summary of the development of the gospel tradition, it accounts for the lack of an infancy narrative in the earliest Gospel, that according to

Mark. In the case of the Johannine Gospel, which is admittedly late at least in its final redaction, it too knows nothing of a development of the tradition with an infancy narrative. It begins rather with the quasi-poetic prologue about the Logos, with its prose inserts about John the Baptist sent by God to bear witness to the Logos. It is not without significance that, when one drops the infancy narrative from the Matthean and Lucan Gospels, one notes that they begin their third chapters where Mark begins, with the ministry of John the Baptist and his relation to a coming Mightier One. Similarly, when one distinguishes the quasi-poetic Johannine prologue about the Logos from its prose inserts and its immediate sequel (John's testimony), one notes again that in each case all four Gospels have John the Baptist and his ministry as the initial marker of the ministry narrative in the developing gospel tradition. Hence, what precedes that ministry, be it infancy narrative or prologue about the Logos, represents an ulterior development in that tradition.

As for the Matthean and Lucan infancy narratives these developments reflect the stage when early Christians were beginning to show an interest in Jesus' origins. This has been called the biographical concern, a concern that is almost wholly absent from the Marcan Gospel:[6] Who was he? Where did he come from? Who were his parents, his family, etc.? However, that the infancy narrative was a later development in the gospel tradition does not *per se* say or imply that it is any less historical than other parts of that tradition. The extent to which one accords it historical value must be judged on other grounds than its late development in the gospel tradition.

There is another facet to this consideration, viz., the continued development of the gospel tradition beyond the canonical bounds. Such development was not arrested with the emergence of the last parts of the canonical tradition, the resurrection narratives and the infancy narratives. The development pressed on in the apocryphal Gospels, among which there are not only the *Gospel of Peter* and the *Gospel of Thomas,* but also specific infancy Gospels, such as the *Protevangelium of James,* the *Infancy Gospel of Thomas,* etc.[7] The legend-full character of the latter Gospels reveals a significant aspect of the developing gospel tradition. For this reason one has to be cautious in general about the historical value of even the late-developing infancy narratives within the canon.

Indeed, attempts have been made in recent times to find in the extracanonical gospel tradition elements of an authentic Jesus-tradition equal to or even alleged to be superior to what is found in the canonical tradition. In this regard one may recall the recent discussions of H. Koester and J. D. Crossan.[8] That some genuine Jesus-tradition may be preserved in such apocryphal writings is *per se* plausible; some of the parallels in the apocryphal Gospels to ministry episodes in the canonical Gospels have been shown to be more primitive in their forms, and thus closer to the genuine forms.[9] But the validity of such claims,[10] if pressed to include the infancy narratives, has still to be shown. In this instance, in my view at least, the development in the extracanonical infancy writings is manifestly dependent on the canonical narratives in both their inspiration and their legendary thrust, and therefore it is of secondary value.

In trying to assess the historical value of the Lucan infancy narrative, one cannot help but begin by comparing it with its counterpart in the Matthean Gospel. In such a comparison, one clearly realizes soon enough that neither Matthew nor Luke has derived such material from earlier Marcan or "Q" traditions. Both stem from an independent strain and are usually ascribed to sources private to the two later Synoptic evangelists. Moreover, there is no persuasive evidence that Matthew and Luke, who have otherwise made use of both Mark and "Q," have been tributary to each other. This is maintained not only for the Gospels as a whole, but in particular for their infancy narratives. In using the so-called Modified Two-Source Theory as the solution to the Synoptic problem, I would ascribe the matter used in the infancy narratives to the evangelist's private source, often designated "M" or "L." In making use of this theory, I am lining myself up with the majority of Gospel interpreters today.[11] I find no convincing value in other attempts to solve the Synoptic problem, be it the Augustinian, the Griesbachian, that of Vaganay, Léon-Dufour, or others.[12] Specifically, in the Augustinian or Griesbachian solutions, it is inexplicable why Mark, if he were presenting in his Gospel an abridgement, digest, or conflation of the Matthean and/or Lucan Gospels, would drop *all* the details of the infancy narratives, especially those about the conception of Jesus by Mary through the power of the holy Spirit. Mary goes not without mention, to be sure, in the Marcan Gospel (6:3); nor does the holy Spirit, who often appears. But what would have possessed this evangelist to omit such important data? It is far more intelligible to maintain that the tradition about the virginal conception of Jesus through the power of the holy Spirit was not yet part of the common developing gospel tradition by the time that Mark wrote.[13] Recently, C. S. Mann, who has just published a commentary on the Marcan Gospel in the Anchor Bible series, espouses the Griesbachian solution and maintains that "Mark is dependent on both Matthew and Luke," but he has to admit that a serious question remains unanswered in that hypothesis, "notably, why did Luke not make substantial use of the nativity narra-

tives in Matthew?"[14] That question, serious though it is for
the Griesbach hypothesis, is, however, less telling than the
Marcan omission of all details of the Matthean and Lucan
infancy narratives. There are, however, more problems with
the Griesbach hypothesis than I can discuss here; they do not
concern us now.[15] I have introduced it here only to exclude
it, because it has indirectly a connection with the Lucan
infancy narrative and the problem of its historical value.

Attempts have also been made at times to explain the
Matthean and Lucan infancy narratives as dependent on
each other. For instance, R. H. Gundry in his commentary
on the First Gospel thinks that this evangelist has worked
with the Lucan infancy narrative before him.[16] Matthew is
said to follow "the pattern of the annunciation to Zechariah"
or "the designation of Joseph as Mary's husband again
comes from the annunciation to Mary (see Luke 1:27)." Or
again, Matthew "changes the sacrificial slaying of 'a pair of
turtledoves or two young pigeons,' which took place at the
presentation of the baby Jesus in the Temple (Luke 2:24; cf.
Lev 12:6–8) into Herod's slaughtering of the babies in Bethlehem."[17] The far-fetched character of such a suggestion that
the Herodian slaughter of the innocents in Matthew 2 is a
development of the Lucan story about the sacrifice of turtledoves and pigeons is obvious; it needs no further comment.
Moreover, the dependence of Matthew on the Lucan infancy
narrative remains an assumption that is asserted, but unsub-
stantiated. The same would have to be said for the dependence of Luke on Matthew, a solution espoused in some
quarters today.

The thrust of the Lucan infancy narrative, however, is so
different from that of the Matthean Gospel that one has to
insist on the free composition of each infancy narrative as a
whole. Each evangelist has, indeed, made use of preexisting

Christian tradition and details, but he has also cast them in a new literary framework for specific theological and religious purposes. This composition is postulated by the very structure of the two narratives. Matthew's narrative has an undeniable literary structure in that, after the introductory genealogy that relates Jesus to Abraham and David, it is articulated about five Old Testament quotations, with which the episodes end or in which they come to a climax. Each quotation is distinctively marked by the introductory fulfillment formula, making it a *Reflexionszitat*. However, Luke's narrative, though also marked by a literary structure, is dominated by a parallelism of announcements of the conception of John the Baptist and Jesus and of their birth, circumcision, and manifestation to Palestinian neighbors of the region. It is a parallelism worked out with an antithetic comparison—what has been called one-up-manship, in which Jesus always comes off as the superior figure among these newborn, heaven-sent agents of salvation for humanity.

Such a comparison of the structure of the Matthean and Lucan infancy narratives is well known and has long since been recognized, but the consequences of this difference of structure, details, and composition in the two narratives are not always drawn so clearly as they might be, especially in terms of the problems affecting the historical value of the accounts. These consequences have to do with certain points of similarity and discrepancy that are found in these independent compositions.

On the one hand, there are twelve items that the two narratives share in common despite their independent literary structure and composition. In both infancy narratives:

1. Mary is explicitly referred to as a "virgin" (*parthenos*, Matt 1:23—Luke 1:27).

2. Jesus' parents, Mary and Joseph, are depicted as

engaged, then married, but without marital intercourse (Matt 1:18,25—Luke 1:27,34).

3. The Davidic descent of Jesus is mentioned (Matt 1:16,20—Luke 1:27,32).

4. An angel announces the conception and future birth of Jesus (Matt 1:20–23—Luke 1:30–35).

5. The conception of Jesus takes place apart from Joseph (Matt 1:20,23,25—Luke 1:34).

6. The role of the holy Spirit in the conception of Jesus is explicitly mentioned (Matt 1:18,20—Luke 1:35).

7. The heavenly imposition of the name of Jesus is noted (Matt 1:21—Luke 1:31).

8. Jesus is regarded as "savior" (Matt 1:21—Luke 2:11).

9. Jesus' birth occurs after the parents have come together (Matt 1:24–25—Luke 2:5–6).

10. Jesus' birth takes place in the days of Herod the Great (Matt 2:1—Luke 1:5).

11. Jesus' birth takes place in Bethlehem of Judea (Matt 2:1—Luke 2:4–6).

12. The child Jesus is reared in Nazareth (Matt 2:23–Luke 2:39).

The least one can say about these common details is that they have come to the evangelists from a preexisting Christian tradition, through "M" and "L" respectively, otherwise it is not possible to explain their independent common use. Moreover, because they are used independently by Matthew and Luke, one Gospel serves as a check on the use in the other. Hence, the minimal historical background of the Lucan infancy narrative would be identified with these twelve items. Indeed, certain of the items even find support elsewhere in the New Testament, and this would bolster up their historical character: e.g., the Davidic descent of Jesus (Rom 1:3) or his birth from a Jewish mother (Gal 4:4).

On the other hand, there is also a discrepancy in details in the two infancy narratives. Though such a discrepancy may not *eo ipso* call in question the historical character of items to which it is related, it may reveal the free literary composition of the evangelist. The greatest discrepancy is found in the content of the various episodes that make up chap. 2 in each narrative. In the Lucan account there is nothing about Herod's reaction to the news of the birth of the child Jesus, of the flight to Egypt, of the massacre of the Bethlehem innocents, or of the reason for the family's withdrawal to Nazareth. Similarly, in the Matthean account there is not a word about John the Baptist, the circumcision of Jesus, the presentation of him in the Temple, or the loss and finding of him as a twelve-year-old.

A further, perhaps more crucial, discrepancy of detail affects one of the commonly shared items, viz., the angelic announcement of the conception and birth of Jesus (#4 above). In Matthew the announcement comes to Joseph "in a dream" (*kat' onar*, 1:20), whereas in Luke it comes to Mary, the virgin and highly favored One (1:30–33). This difference of detail gives rise to obvious questions, which no harmonization of the texts can solve. Is it likely that the angelic announcement would have been made to both Joseph and Mary? *Per se* this is not impossible; but such a reflection is not very satisfying or convincing, because in each case the announcement is set in a context that preoccupies the evangelist: Matthew uses the announcement to reassure Joseph who is minded to divorce Mary "found to be with child," whereas Luke uses it to allay Mary's fear and awareness of no sexual relations with "a man." No little part of the problem in this instance is precisely Matthew's wording, "before they came to live together, she was found to be with child *of the holy Spirit*" (1:18). That she was "found to be with child" is intelligible enough, but that it was found to be "of the holy Spirit" is perplexing. Everyone who reads this Matthean verse realizes that it is the evangelist's clear affirmation of the virginal conception of Jesus. But his language has got ahead of his narrative. As D. O. Via has put it, ". . . this is a victory of Matthew's theological eagerness over his craft as a story teller. . . . Matthew introduces the audience into the marvelous world at the discourse level before he introduces Joseph into it at the story level."[18] In any case, one is tempted to ask, "Well, who really received the angelic announcement, Mary or Joseph?" Put this way, the answer can only be agnostic. If harmonization of the two annunciation accounts does not solve the problem, one must realize that the question about such a historical detail rises from neither account alone, but from our (modern) comparison of the two accounts. If I am right that the Matthean and Lucan infancy narratives were independent compositions that made use of preexisting Christian traditions of factual character, then they were not composed to be so compared. Each of the accounts conveys its formal message about the virginal conception of Jesus by Mary and about the role of the Spirit in that conception. The revelatory character of the communication made is guaranteed in both narratives, and each narrative proclaims that conception as an item of Christian faith. That is the essential religious import of the accounts, despite the discrepancy in detail. Even if they do not satisfy the inquisitive mind of the modern reader in all respects, the basic affirmation they make still has historical value.[19]

There are, however, other details in the Lucan infancy narrative that cause discrepancy when a comparison with the Matthean narrative is made. Thus, according to Matt 2:11 Mary and Joseph live in a "house" in Bethlehem, whereas in Luke they cannot find room in the Bethlehem "lodge" (*kata-lyma*), and Mary has to lay her newborn child in a manger of an animal-shelter (2:7). Again, the commonly-shared item is the birth of Jesus in Bethlehem of Judea (#11 above), but the details do not agree, despite well-known efforts to harmonize them. The Matthean account, if read for what it alone narrates, gives the impression that Joseph and Mary are residents in the town of Bethlehem; it has not a hint that they have had to come from Nazareth in Galilee to register in accord with Caesar Augustus' decree or the census of Quirinius. The only chronological peg in the Matthean narrative is "in the days of Herod" (2:1), which is shared by Luke 1:5, but otherwise there is no room in its narrative thrust for any further extrabiblical chronological pegging.

When one examines the Lucan infancy narrative in and for itself, and not in comparison with the Matthean narrative, there are a few further problems that bear on its historical character. The most notorious of these is the problem of Luke's mention of the birth of Jesus "in the days of Herod" (1:5) and about the time of the decree of Caesar Augustus and the census of Quirinius (2:1–2). This is not the place for a repetition of a detailed discussion of this problem.[20] Suffice it to say that the most plausible solution is not to press for the historicity of details in this matter; one should rather resort to a vagueness of recollection for the two important events in the history of Palestinian Jews that are here run together in the Lucan narrative. In my opinion, the best explanation has been proposed by an expert Roman historian, R. Syme, who wrote:

Two striking events in Palestinian history would leave
their mark in the minds of men. First, the end of Herod
in 4 B. C., second the annexation of Judaea in A.D. 6.
Either might serve for approximate dating in a society
not given to exact documentation. Each event, so it
happened, led to disturbances. More serious were those
in 4 B. C., according to Josephus. Varus the legate of
Syria had to intervene with the whole of his army. But
the crisis of A. D. 6 was more sharply remembered
because Roman rule and taxation were imposed. Thus,
in Acts 5,37, the speech of the Pharisee Gamaliel: 'In
the days of the census.'[21]

Another problem is met in the mention of "their purification" in Luke 2:22: "when the days of their purification had
passed." To whom does "their" refer?[22] Mary and Joseph?
Or Mary and Jesus? There was, however, no requirement in
the Old Testament for the purification of the husband after
the birth of a child, and since Joseph was not involved to
begin with, the "their" can scarcely include him. But after
childbirth the mother had to be purified (Lev 12:2–8); and
the firstborn son had to be "redeemed" (Exod 13:1–2; Num
3:47–48). In using "their," Luke manifests his lack of detailed or accurate knowledge of Palestinian Jewish customs;
he has telescoped the reference to the two obligations (purification and redemption of the firstborn son) and grouped
them under "their purification," which makes little sense.

Moreover, within the Lucan narrative itself certain details in chap. 2 are introduced with no reference to the
virginal conception of Jesus in chap. 1. For instance, Mary
and Joseph are referred to as Jesus' "parents" (*goneis,*
2:27,41,43) or as his "father and mother" (2:33) or (on
Mary's lips) as "your father and I" (2:48). Totally missing in

these verses is any qualifying adjective with "father" such as "putative" or "foster." This situation stands in contrast to the clarification offered at the beginning of the genealogy in 3:23, "as was supposed" (*hōs enomizeto*), i.e., in the minds of the people he was "the son of Joseph." One can, of course, exaggerate the import of such phrases in chap. 2. They merely bear witness to the inconsistency with which Luke has composed his work—an inconsistency noted elsewhere. But they also reflect undoubtedly an early Christian way of talking about Joseph and Mary that was already part of the tradition that Luke inherited and used in chap. 2. In any case, the discrepancy of detail in these cases underlines the problematic character of the historicity of the infancy narrative as such.

When one reflects on these aspects of the Lucan infancy narrative—its parallel structure, its use of items of preevangelical tradition in common with Matthew, its discrepancy in details when compared with the Matthean narrative, and its own distinct problems, one can see why one must be cautious in asserting the overall historicity of this Lucan account. Before I terminate my remarks on this character of the infancy narrative, two last problems have to be considered, viz., the sources that Luke might have used and their bearing on the kind of historiography in which he is engaged.

In his prologue Luke maintains that he has done his homework: he has consulted "original eyewitnesses and ministers of the word" (1:2). Clearly, this refers at least to apostles and disciples who were witnesses of Jesus' ministry from his baptism on, as the Lucan sense of "from the beginning" (1:3) has to be understood in accordance with his use of the phrase elsewhere (cf. Luke 3:23; 23:5; Acts 1:1,22; 10:37).[23] Now, however, the question is, Can it in any sense be pressed back to "the beginning" of Jesus' earthly life? In such a case, who would be the eyewitnesses (and ministers of the word)? The elderly Zechariah and Elizabeth? The census-registrants? The Bethlehem shepherds? Joseph? Mary? In such a line-up of possibilities only the last two could be seriously considered. Yet Joseph further appears in the Lucan Gospel only at the beginning of the genealogy (3:23) and in the question asked about Jesus' parentage (4:22). In effect, he is an actor in the Lucan Gospel only in part of the infancy narrative (1:27; 2:4–7,16–51); and the usual explanation for his disappearance from the rest of the Gospel narrative is that he was no longer alive, when Jesus began his ministry (as is assumed in the interpretation of other Gospels).

As for Mary, it must be remembered that the last appearance that she makes in the whole New Testament is at Acts 1:14, where she sits with the disciples and other women awaiting the gift of the Spirit. In other words, her last attested appearance is pre-Pentecostal, and there is no reason to think that Luke himself was among the disciples mentioned in that passage of Acts. Those who try to maintain that Luke got information about the infancy and childhood of Jesus from Mary herself often appeal to certain verses in the infancy narrative. Thus, after the shepherds depart, Mary is said to have "treasured all these things and pondered over them" (2:19); again, after the finding of the child Jesus in the Temple, "his mother cherished all these things within her" (2:15). E. Osty once queried apropos of 2:19, "Is this a delicate way of letting it be known that Luke has garnered the confidence of Mary?"[24] Such a suggestion is sometimes proposed more elaborately: The beloved disciple who stood at the cross (John 19:26) is taken to be John the son of Zebedee, with whom Mary would have lived after the crucifixion (19:27)—indeed, to a ripe old age. To this John, Mary would have confided all the details about Jesus' infancy and childhood. From such a person Luke would eventually have garnered his information. Indeed, J. McHugh asserts that "the affinity between Luke's Gospel and the Fourth Gospel is nowhere more marked than in the Infancy Narrative, and the Fourth Gospel cannot be wholly detached from John the son of Zebedee."[25] Similarly, R. Laurentin writes:

> Mary is in the end the only possible source of an episode like the annunciation, and the obvious source (*source toute indiquée*) of a number of others; the visitation, and even the circumcision of John the Baptist (according to our analysis of 1:56), Christmas, the presentation and the finding of Jesus (Luke 2). Otherwise, the gospel of the infancy would be fiction and in contradiction with Luke himself (Prologue 1:1–4).[26]

But all of this amounts to nothing more than speculation; one is merely analyzing the narrative and looking for *possible* candidates from whom Luke could have derived his information about details in the infancy narrative—details that often differ from those in the Matthean infancy narrative. There is, in fact, not a shred of evidence to support such speculation. Moreover, none of the standard studies of the relation of John's Gospel to the Synpotics, or to the Lucan Gospel in particular, ever considers the infancy narrative.[27] Moreover, the suggestion rides roughshod over the major problem about John the Baptist in the Lucan and Johannine Gospels. The Lucan infancy narrative implies that John the Baptist and Jesus were kinsmen and that they must have known each other. But the Johannine Gospel portrays the Baptist as saying explicitly twice, "I myself did not know him. . . . I myself did not know him, but he who sent me to baptize with water told me, 'The one on whom you see the Spirit descend and remain is the one who baptizes with the holy Spirit' " (1:31,33). This creates the problem about the relation of John the Baptist and Jesus, and in my opinion makes it very difficult to establish that the Lucan infancy narrative has been influenced by the Johannine Gospel or its tradition.

That family secrets were eventually divulged to the church at large is likewise problematical, especially when one considers that the Lucan mention of Mary "treasuring" and "cherishing" things, over which she pondered, has to be understood in the light of another Lucan passage. These are comments of the evangelist himself, and they have to be interpreted against Simeon's words to Mary in 2:34bc–35ab: "This child is marked for the fall and the rise of many in Israel, to be a symbol that will be rejected—indeed, a sword shall pierce you too—so that the thoughts of many minds will be laid bare." This is part of the way that Luke depicts Mary—about which more in chapter III. To what extent, then, is it legitimate to interpret Mary's treasuring and cherishing of such details as *memories* about Jesus' infancy and childhood that would be exploited by the evangelist? That is to read too much into such verses. In the long run, though we have already conceded that Luke has worked with preexisting Christian tradition about the conception and birth of Jesus, we simply do not know how such "L" material has come to him. To maintain that Mary herself is the source is to affirm more than what one has evidence for.

The studied parallelism of the stories about John the Baptist and Jesus in the infancy narrative[28] and its mimetic character likewise affect the historical character of the account. For at least 1:5–25,57–66b I reckon with a Baptist source that Luke may have inherited. The question of such a source is not original with me, having been postulated earlier by such interpreters as M. Dibelius, R. Bultmann, A. R. C. Leaney, and G. Schneider.[29] I restrict this source to the episodes about the announcement of John's conception, his birth, circumcision, and manifestation.[30] Using such preexistent material, Luke has created his story of the announcement of the conception of Jesus, his birth, circumcision, and manifestation in imitation of the Baptist source. But the mimetic character of the Lucan infancy narrative is not limited to such imitation and the resultant parallelism, since no one who reads Luke 1–2 fails to miss its further imitation of the Samuel story in 1 Samuel 1–3; the influence of this Old Testament material on the Lucan composition has often been noted. This mimetic character is, in part at least, why the Lucan infancy narrative differs so much from the Matthean.

Years ago E. Burrows coined the term "imitative historiography,"[31] which I borrow from him because it expresses well the kind of historical writing that Luke is engaged in—at least in the infancy narrative. In other words, the historical data that the evangelist has inherited have been assimilated to other literary accounts either biblical or nonbiblical. Thus, Luke's story of Jesus' origins not only parallels what he has inherited from the Baptist source about John's origins but is also heavily colored by continual reminiscences of the story of the birth and childhood of Samuel in the Old Testament. One has only to look at the marginal notes in a critical Greek New Testament to find some of the allusions to that story, and Burrows himself has set forth a list of twenty-five of them.[32]

If these aspects of the Lucan infancy narrative merit serious consideration, then one realizes why its historical character is regarded at times as problematical. My concern is not to demolish the historical import or these Lucan chapters. On the contrary, the historical material that is presented in them is laced with the aspects set forth above, and they reveal that a preoccupation with historicity is not of prime concern in such a narrative. Even though the Roman Catholic understanding of Scripture would consider Luke 1–2 as graced with inspiration, that inspiration always remains analogous,[33] adapted to the literary form used by the evangelist. Hence, though an inspired infancy narrative, it is an inspired piece of imitative historiography, not without its problems.

II. The Character and Purpose of Luke 1:26–38:
Is It a Mariological Commission or a
Christological Identification?

The scene of Gabriel's announcement to Mary the virgin that she is to conceive and bear Jesus (1:26–38) is familiar, and its parallelism with that of the announcement to Zechariah about the conception and birth of John has already been discussed. In my commentary on the Lucan Gospel,[34] I followed the analysis of the scene used in the study produced by the ecumenical task-force, *Mary in the New Testament,* of which I was one of the co-editors.[35] That analysis compared the annunciation scene with Old Testament announcements of the birth of various important figures in Israelite history, e.g., the announcement of the birth of Isaac to Abraham (Genesis 17) and of Samson's birth to his parents (Judges 13). This too was part of the mimetic character of the scene, mentioned in general in part I above. In that analysis a pattern of five elements was distinguished:

    1. The appearance of an angel (Gen 17:1; Judg 13:3,9,11).

2. A reaction of fear or awe (Gen 17:3; Judg 13:6,22).

3. The announcement about the birth of a child (Gen 17:5; Judg 13:3). This announcement has various sub-elements:

    a. Name or title of the person addressed (Gen 17:5);

    b. Mention of conception, present or future (Gen 17:16,19; Judg 13:3);

    c. Naming of the child to be born (Gen 17:19);

    d. Future accomplishments of the child (Gen 17:19; Judg 13:5).

4. An objection from the person addressed (Gen 17:17; Judg 13:17).

5. A reassuring sign given by the angel (Judg 13:9,18–21).

Even though the announcement does not concern birth in the annunciation-scenes recounted about Moses (Exodus 3) and Gideon (Judges 6), many of the same elements are also found in these episodes: Exod 3:2,6,4 and 10,11,12; Judg 6:11–12,22–23,12 and 14,15,19–22.

The pattern seems to be found in the Lucan scenes of the annunciation to Zechariah (1:5–15) and the shepherds (2:9–12); but I shall concentrate on the annunciation to Mary, since recent discussion has centered on it. In 1:26–38 the five elements and their subelements seem to be present: in vv. 26–27, Gabriel's appearance; in vv. 29–30, Mary's reaction; in vv. 28–35, the double announcement made to Mary, who is addressed by name and title (vv. 28,30), told that she will conceive and bear a son (v. 31); the child is named (v. 31), and his future accomplishments stated (vv. 32,33,35); in v. 34 Mary's objection is uttered; and in vv. 36–37, the reassuring sign is given (Elizabeth's conception in her old age).

Because, however, the annunciation pattern does not always concern birth in the Old Testament and because one or other element or subelement has been found wanting at times (e.g., the reaction of fear), it has seemed to some commentators that the pattern present in Luke 1:5–25; 1:26–38; and 2:1–9 is rather that of an Old Testament commissioning story or of an Old Testament story of prophetic election.[36] In such a commissioning form one finds a similar pattern of various elements:

1. An introduction stating the circumstances.

2. The confrontation of the commissioner and the commissioned one.

3. A reaction of fear or unworthiness.

4. The commission (inauguration of a prophet or judge).

5. A protest (objection to the words of the commissioner).

6. A reassurance given to the commissioned one.

7. A conclusion.

This pattern has been well studied by B. J. Hubbard, who has likewise gathered extrabiblical examples from ancient Near Eastern literature. He has also applied it specifically to the three Lucan scenes.[37] One cannot help but note a certain similarity in the patterns drawn from the Old Testament accounts, whether they be of announcement of birth or of commission for a role in salvation history.

When Luke 1:26–38 is considered from these different standpoints, a difference of emphasis is conveyed. Whereas in the first case (the Old Testament pattern of birth-announcement) the emphasis falls on the child to be born, in the second case (the Old Testament pattern of commission) the emphasis falls rather on the person addressed. If Luke 1:26–38 be a scene understood as a literary form of commissioning, it would mean that in its primary thrust

Mary is being commissioned by God to play a distinctive role in his plan of salvation. Her vocation or election would be analogous to that of Gideon in Judg 6:11–14 or to some prophet of old. No one will contest such an analysis of this Lucan scene; it is valid in that Mary is commissioned to be the mother of the Davidic heir and of the Son of God. By her humble acquiescence to the commission as the hand-maid of the Lord (1:38), she becomes in the Lucan Gospel an instrument as chosen as any Old Testament prophet or agent; but that does not say it all, as will be seen in chapter III.

However, this analysis of 1:26–38 shifts the emphasis in the episode unduly; it centers it on a secondary aspect. It does not really cope with the details that have to do with the virginal conception of Jesus, his heritage on the Davidic throne, or the christological titles that are given to him in the episode. Moreover, the parallelism with the annunciation to Zechariah makes it clear that, if 1:5–15 be also understood as a commissioning form, then Zechariah, a rather minor figure in the whole story, becomes instead the vessel of election. True, Zechariah is only a foil for Mary in the stepped parallelism of the Lucan annunciation stories. But even so, the comparison reveals that the emphasis is mis-placed when these episodes are understood as commission-ing stories. For in both instances the emphasis is rather on the sons to be born, by extraordinary conception, indeed, and on the roles that each is to play in God's salvific plan for humanity. As R. E. Brown has recently noted, "That most of the verses in Luke 1:26–38 concern Jesus (what he will do; who he is) and that the scene is prefaced to a Gospel about Jesus should make it evident that the primary purpose of this scene is not mariological."[38]

E. W. Conrad has recently proposed an amendment of

the elements in the Old Testament birth-announcement form and has added other Old Testament examples to the discussion.[39] Though he has modified the pattern somewhat, he has made it clear that Luke 1:26–38 is to be understood primarily as a birth-announcement form. The elements of a vocation or commissioning narrative that may be present in it are wholly secondary. The upshot of this discussion, then, is that this Lucan pericope presents not primarily a mariological commission, but a christological identification.

There may be, of course, other problems in the Lucan infancy narrative, but I have preferred to concentrate on these two because of recent developments.

Notes

[1] "Gospel Infancy Narrative Research from 1976 to 1986: Part I (Matthew) and Part II (Luke)," *CBQ* 48 (1986) 468–83, 660–80. See further S. Muñoz Iglesias, *Los evangelios de la infancia II: Los anuncios angélicos previos en el evangelio lucano de la infancia* (BAC 479; Madrid: Editorial Católica, 1986). M.-V. Leroy, "Evangiles de l'enfance," *RevThom* 85 (1985) 131–39. L. Legrand, *L'Annonce à Marie (Lc 1.26–28)* (LD 106; Paris: Cerf, 1981).

[2] *A Commentary on the Infancy Narratives in Matthew and Luke* (Garden City, NY: Doubleday, 1977). Brown's discussion of the infancy narratives has been subjected to considerable criticism by R. Laurentin, *Les évangiles de l'enfance du Christ: Vérité de Noël au-delà des mythes* (Paris: Desclée, 1982). Brown has answered Laurentin in an article, "More Polemical than Instructive: R. Laurentin on the Infancy Narratives," *Marianum* 47 (1985) 188–207; this article has also been used by Brown in parts of his recent book *Biblical Exegesis and Church Doctrine* (New York: Paulist, 1985) 74–85, 156–61. Cf. R. Laurentin, "Vérité des évangiles de l'enfance," *NRT* 105 (1983) 691–710.

[3] See *Luke,* 148.

[4] See W. G. Kümmel, *Introduction to the New Testament* (rev. ed.; Nashville: Abingdon, 1975) 125. J. Schmid, *Evangelium nach Lukas* (RNT 3; Regensburg: Pustet, 1960) 33. R. Morgenthaler, *Die lukanische Geschichtsschreibung als Zeugnis* (2 vols.; Zürich: Zwingli, 1949) 155, 165. W. Wilkens, "Die theologische Struktur der Komposition des Lukasevangeliums," *TZ* 34 (1978) 1–13. L. T. Brodie, "A New Temple and a New Law: The Unity and Chronicles-based Nature of Luke 1:1–4:22a," *JSNT* 5 (1979) 21–45. C. H. Talbert, *Reading Luke: A Literary and Theological Com-*

mentary on the Third Gospel (New York: Crossroad, 1982) 13–48 (Luke 1:5–4:15, Prophecies of Future Greatness, constitutes the first section after its prologue).

⁵ This was undoubtedly also the time that he added to his narrative the genealogy of 3:23–38.

⁶ The biographical concern may represent a development of the Marcan reference to Jesus' "family" (the *RSV* translation of Greek *hoi par' autou,* Mark 3:21) or his "mother and brothers" (3:31; cf. 6:3).

⁷ There are also other fragmentary and gnostic examples of such Gospels. See *HSNTA* 1. 363–417.

⁸ See H. Koester, "Apocryphal and Canonical Gospels," *HTR* 73 (1980) 105–30. Cf. J. D. Crossan, *Four Other Gospels: Shadows on the Contours of Canon* (Minneapolis: Winston, 1985).

⁹ See *Luke,* 1279–81.

¹⁰ See now the recent discussion of R. E. Brown, "The *Gospel of Peter* and Canonical Gospel Priority," *NTS* 33 (1987) 321–43.

¹¹ Even though he does not espouse it himself, J. Drury (*Tradition and Design in Luke's Gospel: A Study in Early Christian Historiography* [London: Darton, Longman & Todd, 1976] 40) admits that this is the opinion of the majority.

¹² See W. R. Farmer, *The Synoptic Problem: A Critical Analysis* (New York: Macmillan, 1964; slightly rev. ed., Dillsboro, NC: Western North Carolina, 1976). L. Vaganay, *Le problème synoptique: Une hypothèse de travail* (Bibliothèque de théologie 3/1; Tournai: Desclée, 1954). X. Léon-Dufour, "Redaktionsgeschichte of Matthew and Literary Criticism," *Jesus and Man's Hope* (Perspective Books 1; 2 vols.; Pittsburgh: Pittsburgh Theological Seminary, 1970) 1. 9–35. Cf. *Luke,* 63–106.

[13] See further my article, "The Virginal Conception of Jesus in the New Testament," *TAG,* 41–78, esp. 48–49.

[14] *Mark: A New Translation with Introduction and Commentary* (AB 27; Garden City, NY: Doubleday, 1986) 56.

[15] See *Luke,* 65, 69, 73–75; cf. "The Priority of Mark and the 'Q' Source in Luke, *Jesus and Man's Hope*" (n. 12 above) 1. 131–70; reprinted, *TAG,* 3–40.

[16] *Matthew: A Commentary on His Literary and Theological Art* (Grand Rapids, MI: Eerdmans, 1982) 20–21. The dependence of Matthew on Luke is otherwise hardly espoused today; see W. G. Kümmel, *Introduction* (n. 4 above), 64; A. R. C. Leaney, *A Commentary on the Gospel according to St. Luke* (BNTC; 2d ed. London: Black, 1966) 13–16.

The dependence of Luke on Matthew is assumed by A. N. Sherwin-White, *Roman Society and Roman Law in the New Testament* (Sarum Lectures 1960–1961; Oxford: Clarendon, 1963) 122–25, 167. Similarly J. Drury, *Tradition* (n. 11 above), 40. Many others have espoused this dependence (K. Rengstorf, A. Schlatter, C. Butler, A. Farrer, N. Turner, W. R. Farmer, etc.). For the main arguments to the contrary, see W. G. Kümmel, *Introduction* (n. 4 above), 64.

[17] *Matthew,* 34–35.

[18] See D. O. Via, "Narrative World and Ethical Response: The Marvelous and Righteousness in Matthew 1–2," *Semeia* 12 (1978) 123–49, esp. 133. Cf. C. T. Davis, "Tradition and Redaction in Matthew 1:18–2:23," *JBL* 90 (1971) 404–21, esp. 413.

[19] One has to insist on this nuance, even though one may agree, as did the task-force of Protestants and Roman Catholics, "that the historicity of the virginal conception could not be settled by historical criticism" (*MNT,* 35–37,

esp. n. 26). For Roman Catholics, however, it is an item of traditional Catholic faith, infallibly taught by the ordinary magisterium.

[20] See *Luke*, 392–405; cf. R. E. Brown, *Birth*, 547–56.

[21] "The Titulus Tiburtinus," *Akten des vi. internationalen Kongresses für griechische und lateinische Epigraphik, München 1972* (Vestigia, Beiträge zur alten Geschichte 17; Munich: Beck, 1973) 585–601, esp. 600.

[22] The reading in the best Greek manuscripts is *autōn*, "their." In ms. D. one reads *autou*, "his" (presumably Jesus'). In the Latin Vulgate one finds *eius*, which probably reflects the reading of ms. D, but the gender is now common, and it could mean "her" (i.e., Mary's). But the reading of neither ms. D nor the Latin Vulgate is to be preferred to that of the majority in the Greek manuscript tradition. For this reason one should beware of the use of Codex Bezae in the interpretation of this passage given by R. Laurentin, *Evangiles*, 92.

[23] See *Luke*, 298.

[24] *L'Evangile selon Saint Luc* (SBJ; Paris: Cerf, 1948; 3d ed., 1961) 39.

[25] *The Mother*, 147. McHugh lists on pp. 8–10 themes that he claims are common to Luke and John, especially in the infancy narrative and prologue, but the relationship is often overdrawn.

[26] *Evangiles*, 543. Yet even Laurentin, at the end of his special note on the question, has to admit, "In short, the multiple convergences seem to us to make it sure that Mary is the source, but they do not allow us to say how."

[27] See J. A. Bailey, *The Traditions Common to the Gospels of Luke and John* (NovTSup 7; Leiden: Brill, 1963). R. E. Brown, *The Gospel According to John* (AB 29,29A; Garden City, NY: Doubleday, 1966–70) xlvi–xlvii.

R. Schnackenburg, *Gospel According to John* (3 vols.; New York: Herder and Herder, 1968–82) 1.30–32. Indeed, as R. E. Brown points out (*Birth,* 238) John's Gospel shows no awareness of the birth and childhood stories of Jesus, save possibly that he was from Bethlehem, *if* John 7:41–42 be interpreted ironically.

²⁸ See *Luke,* 313–14.

²⁹ See M. Dibelius, "Jungfrausohn und Krippenkind," *Botschaft und Geschichte* (2 vols.; Tübingen: Mohr [Siebeck], 1953) 1.1–78. R. Bultmann, *HST,* 294–95 [Germ. orig., 316–28]. A. R. C. Leaney, *A Commentary* (n. 16 above), 32. G. Schneider, *Das Evangelium nach Lukas* (2 vols.; 2d ed.; Gütersloh: Mohn; Würzburg: Echter-V., 1984) 76–79.

³⁰ I do not ascribe to it the hymns of the Lucan infancy narrative.

³¹ See *The Gospel of the Infancy and Other Biblical Essays* (Bellarmine Series 6; London: Burns Oates and Washbourne, 1940) 1–58.

³² Ibid., 6–27.

³³ See A. Bea, *De Sacrae Scripturae Inspiratione* (2d ed.; Rome: Biblical Institute, 1935) 106: "Sua cuique generi literario est veritas" (Each literary form has its own truth).

³⁴ *Luke,* 334–36.

³⁵ *MNT,* 112–13, 125–26. Cf. R. E. Brown, *Birth,* 156–57, 318.

³⁶ See T. Y. Mullins, "New Testament Commission Forms, Especially in Luke–Acts," *JBL* 95 (1976) 603–14. B. J. Hubbard, "Commissioning Stories in Luke–Acts: A Story of Their Antecedents, Form and Content," *Semeia* 8 (1977) 103–26, esp. 115–16. K. Stock, "Die Berufung Marias (Lk 1,26–38)," *Bib* 61 (1980) 457–91. F. O'Fearghail, "The Literary Forms of Lk 1,5–25 and 1,26–38," *Marianum* 43 (1981)

321–44. I. de la Potterie, "L'annuncio a Maria," *La Madre del Signore* (ed. C. Vagaggini; Bologna: EDB, 1982) 55–73. P. Bellet, "Estructura i forma: Annunciació de naixement i forma d'elecció profética (Lc 1,26–38)," *Revista catalana de teología* 7 (1982) 91–130. H. Verweyen, "Mariologie als Befreiung: Lk 1,26–45.56 im Kontext," *ZKT* 105 (1983) 168–83.

37 "Commissioning Stories" (n. 36 above).

38 "Gospel Infancy Narrative Research" (n. 1 above), 663.

39 See "The Annunciation of Birth and the Birth of the Messiah," *CBQ* 47 (1985) 656–63. Conrad refers further to birth-announcements introduced by "behold," the giving of a name, and the determination of the child's role. Note also the association of "fear not" with the promise of a child in Gen 15:1; 26:24; 43:1–7; 44:1–5; Jer 30:10–11; 46:27–28.

3

Mary in Lucan Salvation History

In the New Testament Mary is mentioned by
name only in the Synoptic Gospels and Acts. In the Johannine
Gospel she appears in two episodes, but only under the designation of either "the mother of Jesus" (2:1,3) or "his mother"
(2:5,12; 19:25, 26). If it had been left to this Gospel, we would
never have learned her name. Among the Synoptic evangelists Mark mentions her by name only once (6:3) and refers to
her in yet another episode (3:31–35), and Matthew uses her
name five times in three episodes (1:16,18,20; 2:11; 13:53)
and refers to her once again (12:46–50); but Luke outdoes
them both. He mentions her by name thirteen times in five
episodes 1:27,30,34,38; 1:39,41,46,56; 2:5,16,19; 2:34; Acts
1:14) and refers to her three times again without mentioning
her name (Luke 2:41–51; 8:19–21; 11:27–28). From such a
survey it becomes clear that the Lucan portrait of Mary has
most influenced the church's mariological tradition.[1]

It remains a puzzle, of course, why Mary is not mentioned in any of the other twenty-two New Testament writings, apart from a possible, highly disputed allusion to her in
Rev 12:1–17.[2] Yet many of these other New Testament
writings are concerned either with early Christian exhorta-
tion or with *ad hoc* problems or with an interpretation of

Christ Jesus and his significance for human history, where
mention of her would be uncalled for. Not even Gal 4:4
("born of a woman, born under the law") escapes such a
category since the first phrase there is meant to affirm the
Son's humanity and the second his native ties to God's
chosen people in his role as the Father's instrument for the
redemption of human beings in view of their adoption as
children of God. Paul's affirmation is markedly soteriological and uninterested in Jesus' pedigree; hence the mention of
"woman" is generic, scarcely specific.[3]

In view of this general picture of Mary in the New
Testament, and even of the benign neglect of her in much of
it, one realizes better the significance of her appearance in
the Lucan writings.[4] It is of a different sort and has played its
own part in later mariological thinking. In his Gospel Luke
has made use of materials inherited from the gospel tradition
which existed before him,[5] but he has introduced Mary into
such materials widely and hence depicted her in more important roles than the other Synoptic evangelists. He even mentions her at the beginning of his second volume (Acts 1:14),
but then only to refer to her never again. In that New
Testament writing she appears like Matthias (1:23–26) to
play a role briefly, being mentioned only once, and is passed
over in silence thereafter.[6] We never learn anything more
about either of them after the first chapter of Acts. Yet
because of the Lucan treatment of Mary and because that
has been read at times in various ways, there is reason to
look at it again and strive to isolate the genuine Lucan
emphases. How, then, has Luke presented Mary in his un-
folding story of salvation history? To answer that question, I
shall consider two topics: (1) Lucan salvation history; and
(2) Mary's role in it.

I. Lucan Salvation History

It is sometimes queried whether one should speak about *Luke's* salvation history. Is not this term a mere modern hermeneutical device, of use perhaps today in interpreting the New Testament, but really foreign to Luke himself, or to any New Testament writer? Clearly the term "salvation history" is modern, and it implies a definite view of human history. It tends to regard that history not as cyclic in the ancient Greco-Roman sense, according to which events involving human beings moved from one age to another only to recur again in renewed forms, cycles, or periods.[7] It rather regards human history as uni-linear in the ancient Jewish sense, according to which events involving human beings moved from a beginning (*genesis,* Hebrew *rēʾšît*) and were aimed at an end (*eschaton,* Hebrew *qēṣ*). God the creator was thought of as its initiator, and he was also its term or goal.[8] Human history, thus conceived, was moreover regarded as salvific, because God was envisaged not as an aloof, transcendent being enjoying isolated celestial bliss, but as the lord of history, directing its course with wisdom and intervening in it with concern for the deliverance or salvation of his people.

Such a view of salvation history is not spelled out in detail by any New Testament writer, but it is clear that at least some New Testament writers were working with such a conception.[9] It is, then, no mere hermeneutical device, born in the minds of twentieth-century interpreters seeking to give a rational explanation of elements in an ancient text. Moreover, though Luke works with such a construct, he cannot be said to be the inventor of salvation history. S. Schulz would have us believe, however, that "the Hellenist Luke is the creator of Salvation History,"[10] but this view is

scarcely correct, as a number of other New Testament interpreters have noted.[11] For apart from the fact that "salvation"
is for Paul one of the effects of the Christ-event (2 Cor 7:10;
Rom 1:16; 5:9–10; 10:10; 13:11),[12] he too has a view of
human history guided by God's salvific activity. He alludes
to such a conception in 1 Cor 7:29–31; 10:11; 2 Cor 6:2; Rom
4:23; 5:14; 10:4; 13:11–14 with reference to ages or periods
of human history: from creation to Moses; from Moses to
the Christ (the risen Lord); from his resurrection to his
parousia. Paul's salvation history may be a view of human
history seen through modified rabbinical spectacles,[13] but it
is no less a view of God's purpose in directing history than is
Luke's. Paul appeals to the "will" (*thelēma*) of God, which
has directed his own movements (Rom 1:10; 15:32), has
summoned him to apostolic service (1 Cor 1:1; 2 Cor 1:1),
and delivered us "from the present evil age" (Gal 1:4).
Intimately involved in that Pauline view of human history is
God's "purpose of election" (Rom 9:11; cf. 8:28). The specific stages of that history may differ in the Pauline writings
from those in the Lucan, but they reveal that Christians
before Luke had already evolved a notion of God's direction
of history.

If Luke, then, has not invented salvation history, it is
precisely a view of history that enables him to relate the
story of the Jesus-movement which he recounts in his Gospel
to its sequel (the story in Acts) and to events in the Old
Testament. It is clear to modern interpreters of the Lucan
writings that the evangelist's purpose in writing his two volumes was to continue the biblical writing of old. He may well
have written the first life of Christ, but he has also seen "the
events that have come to fulfillment among us" (Luke 1:1) as
related to Old Testament history and as realizations of God's
direction of history. Luke boasts of having investigated

"everything" and of having recounted the events "systemati-
cally," i.e., in a given literary order, periodized, and guided
by promise and fulfillment. At times Luke alludes to a basic
"plan" for the salvation of human beings that comes to
realization in the activity of Jesus of Nazareth, in his ministry, passion, death, resurrection, and exaltation. This is
"God's design" (*hē boulē tou theou,* 7:30), thwarted perhaps
by Pharisees and Scribes, but nonetheless come to fulfillment (cf. Acts 2:23; 4:28; 13:36; 20:27). He depicts Jesus
praying on the Mount of Olives, referring explicitly to the
Father's "will" (*thelēma,* 22:42), the same expression for the
divine guidance of events as that used by Paul (cf. also Acts
21:14; 22:14; 1:7). Luke speaks, moreover, of God's prede-
termination of events (Luke 22:22), of his having preor-
dained Jesus to be the judge of the living and the dead (Acts
10:42; cf. 17:26,31). This too is the reason for the Lucan
insistence on the "necessity" with which Jesus did or said
something. The impersonal verb *dei,* "it is necessary," carries this nuance, and it appears twenty-eight times in Luke–
Acts in contrast to isolated, single occurrences of it in Mark
(8:31) and Matthew (16:21). Furthermore, Luke has more
instances of expressions of "fulfillment" than any other evangelist; in these he is consciously linking events in the life and
ministry of Jesus with Old Testament precedents. Such elements in the Lucan writings put a stress on salvation history
in a way that is not so obvious in other New Testament
writers; and so, even though Luke may not be the inventor
of salvation history, he has his own way of referring to it.[14]

Since early in this century interpreters of the Lucan
writings have proposed a threefold division of salvation history as operative in them. H. von Baer (*Der heilige Geist in
den Lukasschriften*[15]) seems to have been the first to have
proposed it (in 1926), and more recently it has been elabo-

rated by H. Conzelmann (*The Theology of St Luke*[16]).
Though Conzelmann's specific proposal has at times come
under critical fire (from W. G. Kümmel, U. Luck, C. H.
Talbert, F. Bovon),[17] I continue to regard it as basically
sound, even if in need of some modifications.

Kümmel and others prefer to think of Lucan salvation
history in two stages: promise and fulfillment. These ideas
are involved in the Lucan view, as we have mentioned, but
they are scarcely distinctive or adequate expressions of his
view; one also finds promise and fulfillment in both the
Matthean and the Johannine Gospels.

However, in the Conzelmann proposal, Luke 16:16
plays an important role: "Up until John it was the law and
the prophets; from that time on the kingdom of God is being
preached. . . ." The interpretation of this verse has been
hotly debated ever since, for it alludes specifically to only
two periods of salvation history, with John the Baptist as the
caesura or turning-point; yet one cannot ignore the further
periodization that is implicit in Lucan thinking when one
considers Acts as the sequel to the Third Gospel. Only Luke
has composed such a sequel, and indeed with an explicit
reference to a new period in the context of the ascension,
when the apostles are depicted asking, "Lord, is it *at this time*
that you are restoring the kingdom to Israel?" (1:6). Luke is
thus presenting another caesura or demarcation of salvation
history, differentiating "this time" from what preceded. This
caesura or break is also indicated by the double account of
the ascension of Jesus (Luke 24:50–52 and Acts 1:3–11). For
such reasons I prefer to follow Conzelmann's threefold division of Lucan salvation history.

Conzelmann sees the Lucan view of salvation history
structured as follows: (1) *Period of Israel,* from creation to
(the imprisonment of) John the Baptist; (2) *Period of Jesus,*

from his baptism through his public ministry to his ascension; and (3) *Period of the Church under Stress,* from Jesus' ascension to his parousia.[18] (The further subdivision of the Period of Jesus, proposed by Conzelmann, need not detain us now.)[19]

A difficulty with Conzelmann's presentation, one which has tended to discredit his basic proposal, is his neglect of the Lucan infancy narrative. For some strange reason he has regarded Luke 1–2 as not really Lucan, as not pertaining to Lucan theology.[20] In this regard he has been criticized by P. S. Minear, H. H. Oliver, R. Morgenthaler, R. Laurentin, *et al.*[21] We shall have more to say below about the picture of John the Baptist in the Lucan writings.[22] At present we insist that both the infancy narrative with its theology and John the Baptist play more integral roles in the Lucan writings than Conzelmann has been willing to accord them. Conzelmann's neglect of the infancy narrative results in his practically ignoring the role of Mary in Lucan salvation history.

With such comments on the Lucan view of salvation history, we may now turn to the second point.

II. Mary's Role in Lucan Salvation History

We have already noted that Mary is named in five Lucan episodes and that reference is made to her in three others. I shall examine each of these episodes briefly in an effort to bring out how Luke has depicted her in his view of salvation history.

At the outset, however, it is important to note that Luke fits the data that he has inherited from the tradition about Mary into his own *literary* account of the Jesus story and of the movement that began with him. This means that what we read about Mary in the Lucan Gospel and Acts is part of what has been called Stage III of the gospel tradition. To explain this, let me digress for a moment on the stages of the gospel tradition.

Ever since the form-critical study of the Gospels began in the early part of this century, we have learned to distinguish three stages in the gospel tradition—stages that are of prime importance for the interpretation of the canonical Gospels. Stage I, representing roughly A.D. 1–33, has to do with what the Jesus of history did and said. What remains of that stage has been embellished in the preaching and teaching of early Christian disciples. Stage II, representing roughly A.D. 33–65, has to do with what those disciples preached and taught about Jesus, now regarded as the risen Christ. In this stage, he who was the kingdom preacher of Stage I has become the preached one, and his message is carried forth by others. Stage III, representing roughly A.D. 65–95, has to do with the tradition that the evangelists culled from Stage II, synthesized, and explicated or explained in their written Gospels, refining and adapting their material for the sake of various Christian communities. Stage III is rooted in Stages I and II, but it represents neither a stenographic nor a cinematographic report of what the Jesus of history did and said. A fortiori, it presents us with no such report of what the Mary of history did or said. We must remember this especially in our quest for how Mary is depicted in the Lucan view of salvation history. Luke writes from Stage III, and it would be only a form of fundamentalism to try to equate Stage III with Stage I.[23]

In trying, then, to present the Lucan portrait of Mary, we deal first of all with her appearance in the Lucan infancy narrative, where she is presented as a figure in the Period of Israel. As we have seen above,[24] the differences in the Lucan and Matthean infancy narratives, composed independently of each other, make it impossible to harmonize the details and the scenes in them. Yet the two accounts serve as checks on those details that they do share in common. I have singled out twelve such items, the commonly inherited pre-gospel tradition in these narratives.[25] This has been utilized by each evangelist in his own creative way.

In the first episode in which Mary appears in the Lucan Gospel (1:26–38) we see her confronted by the angel of the Lord, Gabriel, who announces to her that she is to become the mother of a son, whom she is to call Jesus and who will not only sit on David's throne, but will also be recognized as the Holy One, the Son of God. That scene is patterned on scenes of the announcement of the birth of Old Testament agents in the history of God's people.[26] It is also patterned after that of John the Baptist, whose conception and birth were made known to his father, Zechariah. Here Lucan parallelism is clearly at work. There is also the similarity of the story of the announcement made to Mary with that of 1 Samuel 1–3. As we have already seen, "imitative historiography" has been used. In this episode, as God favored Hannah of old and now the barren Elizabeth in her old age, so he also favors the virgin Mary, chosen to be the mother of a child to be born as the agent of God's new mode of salvation for humanity. Now heaven's message and grace are made known to Mary; she is the favored one in the Period of Israel, as Luke sees it. God's undeserved grace is at work in her; she has been chosen to conceive and bear him who is the Son of God, the Son of the Most High.

The primary emphasis in this first scene in which Mary appears is on its christological identification.[27] Its intent is to identify the child who is to be born of Mary, the virgin, by the power of the Most High: "You will name him Jesus"

(1:31) and "he will be called the Son of God" (1:35). He will be "great" (1:32), i.e., he will bear the title *megas* that the Greek Old Testament bestows on Yahweh himself (Pss 48:2 = 145:3; 86:10; 135:5)—and not just "great in the sight of the Lord," as was said of John the Baptist (1:15). He will inherit "the throne of his father David" (1:32); he will be "the Son of the Most High" (1:32) and will be "king over the house of David forever" (1:33). So this child to be born to Mary is identified in a double description, which echoes in its own way 2 Sam 7:9–16, the dynastic oracle of Nathan, the prophet of old. He is to be a Davidic Messiah, but even more, the Son of God. To this destiny Luke links the pre-gospel tradition about his virginal conception and that about the heavenly imposition of his name (Jesus). Thus, the primary Lucan emphasis in this first scene in which Mary appears falls on its christological affirmation.

A secondary affirmation, however, is mariological, in that it sets forth the *virginal* conception of Jesus by Mary. This conception is never described in a biological sense, for the figurative nuance of the verbs used in v. 35 is clear: *eperchesthai,* "come upon" (said of the holy Spirit) and *episkiazein,* "cast a shadow over" (said of the power of the Most High). Neither of them implies *per se* any sort of intercourse, not even of the sort of *hieros gamos.* What is to be wrought in Mary is the work of the holy Spirit, God's creative power present to her. The affirmation of Mary's virginity *ante partum* is evident, even if one cannot establish any connection between this scene and Isa 7:14, understood as in the LXX, as one can clearly do in the Matthean annunciation scene. That connection is a Matthean nuance, the note of fulfillment—of which Luke knows nothing. Yet the affirmation of Mary's conception of this child is not simply the removal of barrenness, as in the case of her kinswoman,

Elizabeth (or in the case of Hannah in 1 Samuel 1); it is rather a conception that is without the experience of male intercourse (*apeiros andrōn*).[28] It is meant to stress the extraordinary character of the child to be born, one greater than John, because this child is destined for an extraordinary role in God's salvation history. Mary's role thus serves her son's role, and it all makes its beginning in the Period of Israel.

There is still another mariological nuance to be noted, for the scene ends with the Lucan portrayal of Mary as an example of how God can make out of human nothingness an exalted instrument. A mere Jewish virgin, expecting to be married to her fiancé Joseph, finds her role reversed. Whereas she and her husband-to-be are unrecognized individuals in the Period of Israel, she has become *kecharitō-menē*, "the favored one" (1:28), graced by God's election and called to be the mother of the Davidic Messiah and the Son of God.[29] The reversal of roles, announced by the heavenly messenger, elicits from her a cooperative response: She is "the handmaid of the Lord," the servant of Yahweh, his obedient, fully responsive instrument in the birth and destiny of the child who is to bring salvation, forgiveness of sins, and peace to humanity in a new way. Thus God, the lord of history, manifests his choice of an instrument to realize his plan of salvation, and Mary's *fiat* becomes the expression of her willing acceptance in that realization and of her cooperation with divine grace.

We cannot leave this first scene without a few comments on Mary's words to Gabriel in v. 34. When one concentrates on the Lucan emphasis in this presentation of Mary (Stage III of the gospel tradition), one realizes how futile it has been to indulge in the age-old explanations of the inner psyche of the Mary of history: whether this scene represents "an account of some more spiritual and wholly

interior experience, of which no bystander could have been
a witness";[30] or whether Mary was referring to a vow of
perpetual virginity, when she asked, "How can this be,
since I have no relations with a man?"; or perhaps to some
sort of "resolve"; or whether she was protesting because,
supposedly recalling Isa 7:14 (according to the LXX, to
boot!—with *parthenos,* "virgin," as the translation of Hebr.
galmāh), she realized that according to such a tradition the
mother of the Messiah was to be a "virgin," whereas she
was already engaged to be married to Joseph; or whether
she was expressing surprise that she, as Joseph's fiancée but
not yet cohabiting with him, was conceiving then and there;
or even that she was already with child and was protesting
in the past tense, *quoniam virum non cognovi,* as the Old
Latin and some patristic writers have understood the words
of the text.[31] Today we realize that Luke's text should
never have been subjected to such psychological queries,
born of a fundamentalism that confuses Stage III of the
gospel tradition with Stage I. Rather, Mary's question to
Gabriel in v. 34 must be recognized for what it is, a storyteller's device to advance the heavenly communication to
her about the birth of the child to be born. It is an example
of an objection in the pattern of birth-announcements derived from Old Testament accounts.[32] It functions in this
scene in the same way that the objection of Zechariah
functions in the scene of the announcement of the conception and birth of John. In this case, its purpose is to prepare
for the second part of the heaven-sent message about the
extraordinary child to be born and for the angel's reassurance; he would be not just "great" or the heir to "the
throne of his father David," but would be "the Holy One,
the Son of God" (1:35). This is why his birth is
extraordinary—why he is born of a virgin.

In the second Lucan episode in which Mary is named, her visit to her kinswoman Elizabeth (1:39–56), Mary's role in the Period of Israel is further recognized.[33] Filled with the holy Spirit, Elizabeth acknowledges Mary's greeting and formulates her double role: (1) Mary is addressed in the second singular as one personally "blest" (*eulogēmenē*) by Yahweh, above and beyond all women because of the fruit of her womb: "blest" in the child she is to bear and "blest" as the mother of the Lord—the *Kyrios*-title is now transferred to Mary's child. Thus Elizabeth recognizes the first way in which Mary has been "favored" (1:28)—in her motherhood. In this she has become a figure important in the Period of Israel. (2) Mary is also addressed as "blessed" (*makaria*), because she "has believed" (*hē pisteusasa*, "the believing one," v. 45). Now she is addressed in the third singular: she has reacted to the word of God in faith.[34] Thus Luke in his Gospel portrays Mary as the first believer; and over her the first Lucan beatitude is uttered. Because of such faith, "what the Lord has promised will see fulfillment."[35] So Elizabeth is depicted acknowledging Mary's double role in this stage of salvation history: Yahweh's handmaid is to bring into the world of human beings its savior-to-be; but she is also the first to believe in this savior-to-be, the first to take God's new word to herself. Thus both her motherhood and her faith are extolled.[36]

Mary's reaction to Elizabeth's acknowledgement and praise is couched in the Magnificat,[37] in which she declares the greatness of Yahweh. She recognizes that God has chosen one of low degree to be his handmaid and to serve Israel (Abraham and his descendants forever), and for this reason to him all praise is due. Moreover, Mary realizes that because of such heavenly favor "all generations will count me blessed" (*makariousin*).[38] Thus, with the aid of a borrowed pre-Lucan liturgical hymn the evangelist paints with deft strokes the praise that Mary sings on this occasion as her double role in the Period of Israel is again formulated: She is "blest" as the mother of the Lord and "blessed" as the first believer in him; she is "favored" by Yahweh and so is to be counted "blessed" forever. An important link in the first two scenes is not to be missed: each mother has learned from heaven about the child of the other. Mary has learned from Gabriel about Elizabeth's child; Elizabeth learns about Mary's child through her own child, John, who still in the womb leaps in greeting as one filled with the holy Spirit (1:15). Thereupon, Elizabeth, likewise filled with the Spirit, praises Mary; and Mary, declared both "blest" and "blessed," praises God himself. The Magnificat thus celebrates the gifts of God to Mary in the past, present, and future. Elizabeth's child, John, in leaping in the womb, begins his role as the precursor of Jesus in the Lucan Gospel.

The third episode in which Luke mentions Mary by name is that of the birth of Jesus (2:1–10).[39] Mary gives birth to "her firstborn son" (2:7) and thus brings to fulfillment what has been promised to her by heaven itself. Through the angelic choir heaven itself now celebrates the birth of him who is "Savior, Messiah, and Lord" (2:11). The angels' Gloria sums up an effect of his birth on human history: "Peace on earth for people whom God favors" (2:14). Thus Luke formulates one of the ways he uses to describe effects of the Christ-event.[40] This "peace" comes to humanity through the birth of Jesus from his handmaid-mother.

The scene ends with the evangelist's comment, "Mary treasured all these things and pondered over them" (2:19), seeking to hit upon the real meaning of all that she had witnessed, heard about from the shepherds, and experienced. In the Lucan story, Mary has not yet perceived the deep implications of all these things, even though she has learned that her child would be "Messiah" (1:32; cf. 2:11), "Son of God" (1:35), "Lord" (1:43; cf. 2:11), and now even "Savior" (2:11) and the bearer of God's "peace" to humanity (2:14). For the implications of these things await an important Lucan qualification, to be provided in the next episode. Moreover, it is not Mary herself who tells us that she treasured all these matters, but rather the evangelist, the storyteller Luke.

In the fourth scene in which Mary appears, that of the circumcision and manifestation of Jesus (2:21–40), she is at first referred to along with Joseph as "the child's father and mother" (2:33). A double manifestation of Jesus is then made, first to the upright and devout Simeon, then to the elderly prophetess Anna. Joseph and Mary are surprised at what Simeon declares about the child in his canticle, the Nunc Dimittis: Jesus is recognized as the personification of God's "salvation," made ready in the sight of all peoples, "a light to give revelation to Gentiles and glory to his people Israel" (2:30–32). Yet Simeon's further declaration has an ominous tone: he utters an oracle over Mary, "Look, this child is marked for the fall and the rise of many in Israel, to be a symbol that will be rejected—indeed, a sword shall pierce you too—so that the thoughts of many minds will be laid bare" (2:34–35). In these difficult verses the child's destiny is set forth: he will be a source of division in Israel. He will cause many in it to fall (by rejecting him); he will cause many in it to rise (by accepting him). The Lucan Mary will also be caught up in this critical aspect of her child's mission, for a discriminating sword shall also pierce her soul. She will have to learn what division can come into a family by such a son as she has borne. Her relation to him will not be merely motherly, but one that will transcend such familial ties, i.e., it will be that of faithful follower who may be tried. Later on, the Lucan Jesus will himself comment on this role of his mother in his life and ministry—and, in fact, in salvation history. Hence the discriminating sword—a motif adopted by Luke from Ezek 14:17[41]—has to be seen in the role that it plays in the Lucan story itself, and one of its effects will be seen in the following episode in which Mary appears.

But before we examine that episode, it is important to exclude from the understanding of this one two other interpretations of the piercing sword that have often been proposed. The first is that of the symbol of the anguish that Mary would experience at Jesus' passion, as she sees Jesus crucified or his side pierced with a lance—the traditional *Mater Dolorosa* motif. That may be her role in the Johannine Gospel, where she does stand at the foot of the cross (19:25–27). In the Lucan Gospel, however, Mary is never so depicted.[42] Those who stand at the cross in this Gospel (23:49) are "the women who had followed him from Galilee" (see also 23:55) and "his acquaintances" (*hoi gnōstoi,* masculine).[43] Yet there is no indication in this Gospel that Mary is among these people. Hence the sword that will pierce her soul according to Simeon is not symbolic of her anguish at the cross.

The second interpretation is one that dates from patristic times and is still used today, that Mary in Simeon's oracle symbolizes Israel.[44] This interpretation, however, is eisegetical; it has been freely read into the text, since no real basis can be shown that in the Lucan Gospel Mary represents Israel, even though she is a favored or chosen figure in the Period of Israel. Moreover, since Israel itself is clearly meant in the rest of Simeon's oracle and the *sou autēs tēn psychēn,* lit., "your own soul" (in the second singular feminine) stands in obvious contrast to "Israel," mentioned explicitly in v. 34 (as masculine *tō Israēl*), this interpretation is simply unconvincing.

No, the discerning sword in Simeon's oracle is said to pierce Mary's own being, and an example of that will be given in the following Lucan episode, the last one in the infancy narrative (2:41–50), the story of the loss and finding of the twelve-year-old Jesus.

Mary is not explicitly named in it, but she is referred to under such designations as "his parents" (2:41,43,48), "his mother" (2:48a,51), or "your father and I" (2:48b). The last designation becomes the springboard for Jesus' first pronouncement in the Lucan Gospel, "Why are you searching for me? Did you not know that I had to be in my Father's house?" (2:49). The evangelist's comment on that pronouncement is not to be glossed over: "But they did not understand what he was saying to them" (2:50). The contrast in this scene is noteworthy: the anguished Mary and Joseph, terribly worried about their twelve-year-old, and the confident self-assurance of the child. In the parental incomprehension one sees the Lucan sword of discrimination at work. It severs Jesus from his natural, earthly parent and dedicates him to his heavenly Father's service. It is Luke's way of putting the matter, that Mary and Joseph have yet to come to a proper understanding of the relation of this child to them and to his heavenly Father. The Lucan Mary may have "cherished all these things within her," for she has been, indeed, in this story "the mother of the Lord" (1:43); she has been told that her child was to be the Messiah, the Son of God, Lord, Savior, and bearer of God's peace. But now she is depicted in anguish over this child born to her, not yet comprehending what his dedication to his heavenly Father might mean in *her* life. "The incomprehension that she manifests in 2:48,50 reveals that she has much to learn."[45] Once again, one has to resist trying to psychoanalyze the Mary or Jesus of history, as if one were dealing in this scene with Stage I of the gospel tradition. In Stage III the evangelist uses Mary as a means to get across to his readers the difficulty that Jesus' contemporaries, and even his own family, had in trying to comprehend rightly who he really was. Luke, however, does this without depicting Mary and the rest of the family with the stigma that they bear in the Marcan and Johannine traditions. In Mark 3:21 Jesus' "family" is presented as convinced that "he is beside himself," and they come to take him away. In John 7:5 we read that "even Jesus' brothers did not believe in him." This detail from the Marcan and Johannine traditions may or may not have been known to Luke; if it had been, he has chosen rather to present it as the incomprehension of Joseph and Mary.

As Jesus himself, Mary thus becomes an important figure in the Period of Israel, in the first phase of Lucan salvation history. By his circumcision, his being offered in the Temple of Jerusalem, his training as a young Jewish male in the observance of Jerusalem feasts by "his parents," he has been incorporated into the Israel of old. He is thus a figure in the Period of Israel, just as the mother who bore him and trained him. As he was chosen to be his Father's choice instrument of human salvation, so Mary has been shown favor, being chosen to be this Son's mother. Yet she is not only "the mother of the Lord" (1:43), but the one first depicted as a "believer," with all the doubts and anguish that that relationship to him will always entail. With this note the Lucan Period of Israel comes to an end. When John the Baptist appears in the following Lucan episodes, the *archē*, "beginning" of the Period of Jesus is announced.[46] This is the period in which "salvation" is accomplished for humanity and the promise of release announced by Isaiah (61:1–2) begins to be realized (Luke 4:16–21).[47]

When we come to the Lucan episodes in the Period of Jesus itself, Mary is never mentioned in them by name, but she is referred to in two scenes. The first of them is 8:19–21, the scene that follows on the parables of the sowed seed and the lamp. It is the closing scene of a subsection about Jesus' ministry in the Lucan Gospel, a subsection that I have entitled "the preached and accepted Word of God" (8:4–21). In it the Lucan Jesus comments on the various ways in which his preaching of the Word is received; vv. 19–21 form the subsection's climax, fashioned by Luke from material that he has taken over from his Marcan source (3:31–35) and transposed to this point, with his own redactional modifications. In the Marcan parallel the material is related to what preceded in 3:20–21. Jesus' relatives or family have been reacting negatively toward him and have come to get him, because they were thinking, "He is beside himself."[48] This is ascribed by Mark to *hoi par' autou,* "those about him," which the latest edition of the *RSV* translates as "his family." Then in vv. 31–35, when Jesus is told that his mother, brothers, and sisters are standing outside summoning him, he looks around at those sitting in the circle before him and says, "Here are my mother and my brothers; whoever does the will of God is brother and sister and mother to me." Thus the Marcan Jesus substitutes for his natural family his followers, or what has been called his "spiritual" family or his "eschatological" family.[49] Further on in the Marcan Gospel (6:4) Jesus remarks, "A prophet is not without honor save in his own country, among his own kin, and in his own house." In that Gospel one never finds Jesus' mother or kin among his followers, even if Mark does not go so far as the

Johannine tradition to assert that "not even his brothers
believed in him" (7:5). But all such negative reaction to
Jesus on the part of his kin disappears in the Lucan Gospel.
First of all, Luke omits any parallel to Mark 3:20–21. Second, he tones down the remark about the prophet being
honored (Luke 4:24): the prophet finds no acceptance in his
own country; nothing is said about house or family. Third,
Luke presents Jesus' mother and brothers (omitting all mention of the sisters) as the model disciples in the Period of
Jesus: "My mother and my brothers, they are the ones who
listen to the word of God and act on it" (8:21, using the
present participles, *akouontes kai poiountes*). Thus in the
Lucan story Jesus' mother and brothers become the prime
examples of those who listen to the Word of God "with a
noble and generous mind" (8:15), i.e., prime examples of
the seed which takes root in good soil, the ones who produce
a crop through persistence. In this way, Luke has eliminated
all criticism of Jesus' family and casts Mary, his mother, as
the ideal hearer of the Word of God. The anguish and
incomprehension of 2:41–50 have passed, and she is now
cast again in her role as the first believer, as she was in the
Period of Israel. Thus she is once again the obedient, responsive, cooperative handmaid of the Lord. The "Word of
God" will continue to be proclaimed in the Lucan Gospel
and further in Acts, where it will go even to "the end of the
earth" (1:8).[50]

The other Lucan episode in the Period of Jesus in which
Mary is referred to is 11:27–28.[51] There a woman from the
crowd that has been listening to Jesus preaching cries out,
"Blessed is the womb that bore you and the breasts that you
fed on." But Jesus replies, "Blessed rather are those who
listen to the word of God and observe it." Here a Palestinian
Jewish woman, charmed by Jesus' eloquence and message,

exclaims about how wonderful a mother such a preacher-son must have had—a typical mother's reaction. Her exclamation and the beatitude that she uses serve as a foil for Jesus' own corresponding beatitude. The woman's utterance echoes Elizabeth's beatitude in 1:45 and even Mary's own words in 1:48, "From now on all generations will call me blessed." But Jesus' beatitude is corrective: one should not judge God's blessings by charming words or exorcisms, but by obedient observance of his word. Even more is implied, because, as we have seen, Elizabeth's words to Mary made it clear that Mary was not only "blest" as the one chosen to be Jesus' physical mother (1:43), but also "blessed" because of her faith (1:45). Now the second beatitude in this episode, uttered by her own son, is phrased generically and praises all those who hear and observe God's word. This second beatitude does not negate the first, as it has at times been understood, but rather formulates what Jesus considers of greater importance. The particle *menoun* means in this context, not "nay, rather," but "yes, but. . . ."[52] The Lucan Jesus thus admits that his mother is worthy of praise, not just because she has given birth to him, but because she too, especially in the Lucan story, has learned to meet the criterion of discipleship; she is among those who have listened to the Word of God, have believed it, and have acted on it (8:21).

Finally, Mary appears again in the Lucan story at the end of the Period of Jesus and at the very beginning of the Period of the Church under Stress. In Acts 1:14 we read, "All these [the Eleven just named] with one accord devoted themselves to prayer, together with the women and Mary the mother of Jesus, and with his brothers." Thus Luke describes the Jerusalem nucleus community that awaits the inauguration of the Period of the Church, when the "promise of my Father" (24:49; cf. Acts 1:4) is to be poured out on them. As Luke has depicted Mary from the beginning as a believer (1:45), as the model disciple who not only listens to the Word of God but acts on it (8:21; 11:28), so now he portrays her in "the upper room" (Acts 1:13) in the company of the Eleven, the "women" (the devoted followers of Luke 8:2–3; 23:49,55; 24:10), and "his brothers." They are presented in a characteristically Lucan attitude of discipleship, viz., at prayer.[53] Mary is thus part of the concord that reigns among believers in the nascent pre-Pentecostal church of the Lucan second volume. This scene (Acts 1:14) makes it clear that the Lucan Mary, "the handmaid of the Lord," has weathered the crisis of losing her son in death. If the discriminating sword has shown its edge again in her life, it has not severed her ties to her son as a devoted follower and believer. After this pre-Pentecostal scene Mary disappears from the Lucan story, but the evangelist has left us with his own lasting impression of her: a believer at prayer. Thus in the Lucan story Mary does not grow to a ripe old age or dwell in the house of a follower of Jesus.

Before we terminate our remarks on Mary's role in Lucan salvation history, we may reflect on one other passage in the Third Gospel, the genealogy of Jesus in 3:23–38, with its description of Jesus as the "supposed" son of Joseph, for it has an indirect bearing on our topic. Being part of a genealogy, with its implied reference to history, and tracing Jesus' lineage back to Adam and to God himself (which the Matthean genealogy does not do), it not only echoes the affirmation in the infancy narrative about the virginal conception of Jesus, but also reaffirms in its own way what was said about him in the baptismal scene by the heavenly voice, "You are my beloved son; in you *I have taken delight*" (3:22, with an allusion to the Servant Song of Isa 42:1). All of this pertains to the inauguration of the Period of Jesus, as he begins to announce the Word of God in a new way and initiates the salvific ministry for which he was sent by the Father. We may leave to speculation whether the Lucan genealogy originally stood nearer the beginning of the two-volume work than it does at present, since many interpreters hold that the infancy narrative was added after the rest of the Gospel and Acts were actually composed. More intriguing is whether or not the genealogy originally included the clause, "in the minds of the people" (lit., "as was supposed")—said of Joseph's paternity. There is no way to be sure; in any case, it stands today as a corrective to the genealogy in the light of the affirmation of the virginal conception in the infancy narrative itself. At any rate, there is not a shred of evidence that the Lucan genealogy was meant to set forth Mary's pedigree, rather than Joseph's, as has at times been maintained, for Mary is not even indirectly mentioned in it.[54]

Notes

[1] H. Conzelmann (*Theology*, 172 n. 1) strangely enough writes: "Mary disappears to a greater extent in Luke than in Mark and Matthew." One must remember that for Conzelmann the infancy narrative is not part of genuine Lucan theology; see *Luke*, 310. Moreover, in the note just referred to Conzelmann even goes so far as to suspect "that Acts i, 14 is an interpolation."

[2] See further *MNT*, 219–39.

[3] H.-D. Betz (*Galatians* [Hermeneia; Philadelphia: Fortress, 1979] 207) regards the whole statement as reflecting an essentially pre-Pauline christology.

Apropos of Gal 4:4, J. McHugh (*The Mother*, 274–75) tries to argue from the failure of Paul to use *gennasthai*, "the normal New Testament word meaning 'to be born.' " According to him, Paul, in employing rather *ginesthai*, would actually have been thinking of Jesus' "virginal conception." McHugh also refers to Rom 1:3 and Phil 2:7, where *ginesthai* again occurs, and contrasts Job 14:1, where "born of a woman" is rendered in the Septuagint as *brotos gar gennētos gynaikos* (cf. 15:14; Matt 11:11). Yet that reference to Job scarcely clinches the matter, and McHugh has to admit (p. 275) that *genomenos* (Phil 2:7) "does not refer directly to the virginal conception."

For what it is worth, BAGD (158), in listing *ginomai*, gives as its first meaning (I/1), "be born or begotten" and refers to Wis 7:3; Sir 44:9; 1 Esdr 4:16; Tob 8:6. Moreover, as New Testament instances of this meaning, it lists explicitly John 8:58; Rom 1:3; and Gal 4:4. Cf. Josephus, *Ant.* 2.9.3 # 216; Epictetus 2.17.8; Dittenberger, *Sylloge*[3] 1186:6; Athenaeus 13.37. Similarly W. Hackenberg, *"Ginomai," EWNT* 1. 594–96, who notes, however, that the meaning "geschaffen/

geboren werden" is relatively rare, but lists both Rom 1:3 and Gal 4:4 as examples of it.

⁴ The Johannine portrait is also important, filling in aspects of mariology that the Lucan does not present; but even those are limited. See *MNT,* 179–218.

⁵ See *Luke,* 63–106.

⁶ The choice of Matthias is recounted because of the need felt at that point in the Lucan story to reconstitute the Twelve after the death of Judas; see K. H. Rengstorf, "The Election of Matthias," *CINTI,* 178–92. That need is no longer felt when James, the son of Zebedee, is put to death by Herod Agrippa (Acts 12:2), because the Twelve have likewise ceased to be mentioned in Acts (since 6:2–6).

⁷ Recall Virgil, *Eclogues* 4.4–11.

⁸ Recall 1 Cor 8:6.

⁹ See further O. Cullmann, *Salvation in History* (New York: Harper & Row, 1967); cf. J. Frisque, *Oscar Cullmann: Une théologie de l'histoire du salut* (Cahiers de l'actualité religieuse 11; Tournai: Castermann, 1960).

¹⁰ "Gottes Vorsehung bei Lukas," *ZNW* 54 (1963) 104–16, esp. 104.

¹¹ See, e.g., U. Wilckens, "Interpreting Luke–Acts in a Period of Existentialist Theology," *SLA,* 66. W. G. Kümmel, "Current Theological Accusations against Luke," *ANQ* 16 (1975) 131–45, esp. 137; "Heilsgeschichte im Neuen Testament?" *Neues Testament und Kirche: Für Rudolf Schnackenburg* (ed. J. Gnilka; Freiburg: Herder, 1974) 434–57.

¹² For an explanation of the effects of the Christ-event in Pauline theology, see my article, "Reconciliation in Pauline Theology," *No Famine in the Land: Studies in Honor of John L. McKenzie* (ed. J. W. Flanagan and A. W. Robinson; Missoula, MT: Scholars, 1975) 155–77, esp. 155–56; reprinted, *TAG,* 162–85, esp. 163–64.

[13] See further my revised essay, *Paul and His Theology: A Brief Sketch* (Englewood Cliffs, NJ: Prentice-Hall, 1989) 44–46. For a view of Matthean salvation history, see J. P. Meier, *The Vision of Matthew: Christ, Church, and Morality in the First Gospel* (New York/Ramsey, NJ: Paulist, 1979) 26–33.

[14] For details on this topic, see *Luke*, 18–22, 171–92. Cf. J. B. Stanek, "Lukas—Theologie der Heilsgeschichte," *Communio viatorum* 28 (1985) 9–31.

[15] (BWANT 39; Stuttgart: Kohlhammer, 1926).

[16] His study is better entitled in the German original, *Die Mitte der Zeit: Studien zur Theologie des Lukas* (Tübingen: Mohr [Siebeck], 1954).

[17] W. G. Kümmel, "Current Theological Accusations" (n. 11 above), 138. C. H. Talbert, "Promise and Fulfillment in Lucan Theology," *New Perspectives from the Society of Biblical Literature Seminar* (ed. C. H. Talbert; New York: Crossroad, 1984) 91–103. F. Bovon, "Luc: Portrait et projet," *LumVie* 153–54 (1981) 9–18, esp. 13.

[18] *Theology*, 12–17. Cf. W. C. Robinson, Jr., *Der Weg des Herrn: Studien zur Geschichte und Eschatologie im Lukas-Evangelium: Ein Gespräch mit Hans Conzelmann* (Theologische Forschung 36; Hamburg-Bergstedt: Reich, 1964).

[19] See *Luke*, 183–86.

[20] See *Theology*, 18 n. 1, 22 n.2, 24–25, 75 n. 4, 172, 174 n.1, 193 n. 5.

[21] See P. S. Minear, "Luke's Use of the Birth Stories," *SLA*, 111–30. H. H. Oliver, "The Lucan Birth Stories and the Purpose of Luke–Acts," *NTS* 10 (1963–64) 202–26. R. Laurentin, *Evangiles*, 47–52. R. Morgenthaler, *Die lukanische Geschichtsschreibung als Zeugnis: Gestalt und Gehalt der Kunst des Lukas* (2 vols.; Zurich: Zwingli-V., 1949)

1.96–105; "Statistische Beobachtungen am Wortschatz des Neuen Testaments," *TZ* 11 (1955) 97–114.

[22] See pp. 86–116.

[23] See further the 1964 Instruction of the Biblical Commission, "On the Historical Truth of the Gospels," which has explicitly adopted this threefold division of the gospel tradition. An English translation of the Instruction and a commentary upon it can be found in my booklet, *A Christological Catechism: New Testament Answers* (New York/Ramsey, NJ: Paulist, 1982) 97–142, esp. 111–19, 133–37, 141–42.

[24] See pp. 32–39.

[25] See pp. 35–36 above; cf. *Luke,* 307; also 73–75.

[26] For the announcement-pattern, see pp. 46–50 above.

[27] See *Luke,* 340–41. He is called by both a human and a divine name, "Jesus" and "Son of God" (see R. Laurentin, *Evangiles,* 89–91).

[28] On *parthenos,* "virgin," see BAGD, 627; J. A. Fitzmyer, *"Parthenos,"* *EWNT,* 3. 93–95, esp. 94. Cf. J. McHugh, *The Mother,* 281–83.

[29] See now I. de la Potterie, *"Kecharitōmenē* en Lc 1,28: Etude philologique," *Bib* 68 (1987) 357–82, 480–508. He would translate the angelic greeting as "Rejoice to have been transformed by grace."

[30] As J. McHugh (*The Mother,* 128–29) puts it.

[31] For details on these age-old explanations, see *Luke,* 348–50; cf. R. Laurentin, *Evangiles,* 492.

[32] See p. 47 above.

[33] See further J. McHugh, *The Mother,* 68–72; R. Laurentin, *Evangiles,* 197–201.

[34] *Pace* H. Räisänen, the emphasis is not solely on Mary's faith, but on both her motherhood and her faith. Cf.

Die Mutter Jesu im Neuen Testament (AASF B158; Helsinki: Academy of Sciences, 1969) 110.

[35] The clause introduced by *hoti* (v. 45) could also be translated as the object of the participle *pisteusasa*, "Blessed, indeed, is the woman who has believed that what the Lord has promised her will see fulfillment." See *Luke*, 365.

[36] In saying that Mary is depicted in the Lucan Gospel as the first "believer," I do not mean that she is already portrayed as a "Christian." Christian faith implies belief in Jesus as Lord, as the risen Christ—and that is not yet the burden of Luke's depiction of Mary. She is still a figure in the Period of Israel, but one on whom the Spirit of the Lord has already been poured out. She is thus among "the servants and the handmaids" of the Lord (Acts 2:18, quoting Joel 2:29).

[37] On the problems of the Magnificat, see *Luke*, 358–69; cf. R. E. Brown, *Birth*, 346–66; *MNT*, 137–43.

[38] See J. McHugh, *The Mother*, 99–112.

[39] Ibid., 80–98.

[40] See *Luke*, 224–25.

[41] "Or if I bring a sword against that land and say, 'Let a sword pass through the land'; and I cut off from it man and beast." Cf. *Sib. Or.* 3.316. See further *Luke*, 429–30; *MNT*, 155–57.

[42] See *MNT*, 156; cf. H. Räisänen, *Die Mutter* (n. 34 above), 133.

[43] For what is implied here, see pp. 126–127 below.

[44] See J. McHugh, *The Mother*, 110–11. He follows P. Benoit, " 'Et toi-même, un glaive transpercera l'âme' (Luc 2,35)," *CBQ* 25 (1963) 251–61; repr., *Exégèse et théologie III* (Paris: Cerf, 1968) 216–27.

[45] See *Luke*, 438. Contrast R. Laurentin, *Evangiles*, 103–13.

[46] For the significance of *archē* (and cognate expressions) in the appearance of John the Baptist and the beginning of the Period of Jesus in Lucan salvation history, see Luke 1:3; 3:23; 23:5; Acts 1;1,22; 10:37. Cf. *Luke,* 298, 499. See pp. 106–10 below.

[47] See *Luke,* 528–30; cf. H. Conzelmann, *Theology,* 36–38.

[48] See G. D. Kilpatrick, "Jesus, His Family and His Disciples," *JSNT* 15 (1982) 3–19, esp. 9–12. The *RSV* understands *elegon,* "they were saying," generically, "for people were saying," but "people" is not in the Greek text and the "they" has to refer to the *hoi par' autou* themselves.

[49] See *MNT,* 56–58.

[50] For this meaning of Acts 1:8, see *Ps. Sol.* 8:15, where the Roman Pompey is alluded to and said to be brought *ap' eschatou tēs gēs* (a similar allusion to Rome as the "end of the earth"). For another, hardly likely interpretation of the Lucan phrase, see D. R. Schwartz, "The End of the *Gē* (Acts 1:8): Beginning or End of the Christian Vision?" *JBL* 105 (1986) 669–76.

[51] See J. McHugh, *The Mother,* 347.

[52] See *Luke,* 928–29; *MNT,* 171; cf. M. E. Thrall, *Greek Particles in the New Testament* (NTTS 3; Leiden: Brill, 1962) 35. Thrall clearly adopts the latter sense.

[53] See pp. 136–37 below.

[54] See *Luke,* 497–98 for details.

4

The Lucan Picture of John the Baptist as Precursor of the Lord

Each year, as the liturgical cycle begins, Christians celebrate four weeks of Advent. On two of the Sundays of Advent, and at times during the weeks, the Gospels read at the liturgy are passages taken from the New Testament about John the Baptist, traditionally hailed as the precursor of the Lord. In recent times it has been queried whether this role of John is presented in the Lucan writings, and the topic merits some discussion. But the New Testament data about John the Baptist and his relation to Jesus are complicated and need to be sorted out. So it may be of interest to look once again at the ancient texts that tell us about John and his relation to Jesus, and especially at the role that the former plays in the Lucan writings.

On a few things there is a remarkable consensus among the four evangelists about John the Baptist.[1] In each of the four Gospels the evangelists have presented his ministry as the occasion for that of Jesus; each depicts him, with slightly different nuances, to be sure, as a Jewish reform-preacher, living out in the desert of Judea and proclaiming a baptism of repentance for the forgiveness of sins. In each account he is identified as a person fulfilling the words of Isa 40:3, "the voice of someone crying out in the desert, 'Make ready the way of the Lord' " (Mark 1:3; Matt 3:3; Luke 3:4; John 1:23). In each Gospel John announces that his baptism of water is but a foreshadowing of another baptism, sometimes said to be of fire and the Spirit, which would be administered by one who is coming after him, mightier than he. So runs the generic picture of John the Baptist in the canonical Gospels.

Strikingly enough, the Synoptic and Johannine evangelists each begin their ministry narratives with details about John the Baptist. In the earliest Synoptic Gospel, the Marcan, the account opens with John in the desert—after the first verse, which is a sort of title for that Gospel: "The beginning of the gospel of Jesus Christ, the Son of God" (1:1). Then it immediately goes on, "As is written in Isaiah the prophet, 'Behold, I am sending my messenger before your face, who will prepare your way—the voice of someone crying out in the desert' " (1:2). Within the Synoptic tradition, the other two Gospels usually parallel Mark, but each of them has prefixed an infancy narrative, after which chap. 3 begins where Mark 1 begins. John's Gospel provides again a remarkable parallel in that, though it begins with the prologue to the Logos (1:1–18), that quasi-poetic composition is punctuated with prose inserts about John that may have introduced his testimony to Jesus that otherwise follows in v. 19. Thus the early Christian tradition bears a constant, if slightly diversified, testimony to the relationship of the ministry of John to the beginning of that of Jesus.

When one looks at the infancy narratives of the Matthean and Lucan Gospels, one notes that the former is completely unaware of any tradition about John's conception, birth, circumcision, or manifestation to the people, whereas the latter makes use of such a tradition. Indeed, the Lucan infancy narrative explains the relationship of

John the Baptist to Jesus indirectly as one of kinship, by depicting Elizabeth, John's mother, as a "relative" or "kinswoman" of Mary, the mother of Jesus (1:36). As we have seen, such a detail is hard to assess, since it seems to be in conflict with what John himself says in the Johannine Gospel (1:31,33).[2]

These comments serve as a generic introduction to three more specific questions that have to be considered: (1) the historical John the Baptist; (2) John the Baptist in the Marcan and Matthean Gospels; and (3) the Lucan picture of John the Baptist. For the Lucan picture of John is best studied in contrast to what is otherwise known about him.

I.   The Historical John the Baptist

To try to uncover today the John of history is as complicated a problem as that of the Jesus of history. At the outset, we make clear a distinction between the John or Jesus of history and the historical John or historical Jesus. That Jesus and John the Baptist were figures of ancient history is not at issue and is not doubted; but we have to distinguish such a "Jesus of history" or "John of history" from "the historical Jesus" and "the historical John," meaning by the latter what one can discover about them by the critical reading of ancient texts and sources bearing on them and the times in which they lived. The reconstruction of the historical Jesus or John may only correspond in part to the Jesus of history or the John of history.

Part of the problem facing one in the discussion of the historical John the Baptist is the nature of the ancient documents in which he is mentioned. They were not written *per se* as historical accounts or as annals intended to preserve records or items of bygone significance for future generations. The texts from which we learn most about John form part of the gospel tradition of the Christian church, composed to stir up faith in Jesus of Nazareth and in his meaning for human destiny. It is not that such religious writings lack historical worth, but rather that they must be read critically, which involves a comparing of the data they present with other canonical and extracanonical data that are relevant.

Moreover, in asking about the historical John the Baptist, we are trying to probe the tradition to find out something about its Stage I.[3] In probing the tradition in this way, one has to avoid two pitfalls, "the fundamentalism of the fearful" that would equate Stage III with Stage I and "the cynicism of the foolish" that would write off all the historical value in the tradition.[4] This is, moreover, the point of the introductory remarks about John already made: in two traditions in the Gospels, the Synoptic and the Johannine, we have independent testimony that agrees in relating the ministry of John to the beginning of that of Jesus. It is an example of what has been called the principle of multiple attestation in New Testament writings, one of the criteria for historical judgment.

Before we investigate further the gospel tradition, we may consider some of the extracanonical data about John that is available to us. Such material is not necessarily of more historical value than what is found in the religiously-oriented New Testament writings, but it is less well known and serves as a basis of comparison in our quest for the historical John the Baptist. The extrabiblical data have to be scrutinized as well, over against that of the canonical. Such data are provided by the Jewish historian Flavius Josephus, who has mentioned both John and Jesus in his writings.[5] He has not, however, related one to the other and has said nothing about the relation of Jesus' ministry to that of John. In his *Antiquities of the Jews,* Josephus writes as follows about John:

> Some of the Jews thought that Herod's army had been destroyed by God and that he had been justly punished because of the execution of John called the Baptist. For Herod put to death this good man who was exhorting the Jews to live upright lives, by dealing justly with one another and submitting devoutly to God, and to join in baptism. Indeed, it seemed to John that even this washing would be unacceptable as a pardon for sins, but would only be a purification for the body, unless the soul had previously been cleansed through upright conduct. When still others had joined the crowds around John because they were quite enthusiastic in listening to his words, Herod became frightened that such persuasiveness with the people might lead to some uprising; for it seemed that they might go to any length on his advice. So before any new incident might stem from him, Herod considered it far better to seize John in advance and do away with him, rather than wait for an upheaval, become involved in a difficult situation, and regret it. As a result of this suspicion of Herod, John was sent as a prisoner to Machaerus . . . and there was put to death. This made the Jews believe that the destruction of Herod's army was a vindication of this man by God, who saw fit to punish Herod.[6]

In this testimony about John the Baptist and Herod Antipas, Josephus bears witness not only to the existence and ministry of John among first-century Palestinian Jews, but records a contemporary estimate of him "as a good man," one who exhorted his fellow Jews to live uprightly and who urged them to join in a baptism. Josephus never explains what he means by "Baptist" (*baptistēs*) or "baptism" (*baptismos*), seemingly taking it for granted that his readers would understand the terms. His testimony gives rise to a question about the origin of John's practice of baptism, about which more later. But in so speaking of John, Josephus thus lends valuable confirmation to the baptist ministry attested in the gospel tradition.

Josephus ascribes the death of John to Herod's fear and political suspicion of John, who had great influence among his contemporaries, but he is completely silent about the reason for his death that Mark gives, viz., John's criticism of Herod because he had married his brother's wife (Mark 6:14–29). Though Mark and Josephus do not agree on the reason for the execution of John, Josephus does suppport the Marcan account that John was imprisoned and put to death by Herod. Moreover, it is not that Josephus was eschewing the mention of a moral issue, because he did not hesitate to record his contemporaries' conviction that Herod's army was destroyed by God as a vindication of what Herod had done to John. The question is complicated because Josephus is not unaware of the repudiation of the first wife of Herod Antipas, the daughter of the Nabatean king Aretas IV.[7]

The extrabiblical quest for the historical John is not limited to the testimony of Josephus, for there are some data from the Qumran scrolls that bear upon it. Though no text or fragment so far discovered in the eleven caves of Qumran that have yielded written material ever mentions John, the question has often been asked whether he may have been a member of the Jewish sect to which these scrolls once belonged.[8] The identification of the Jewish community from which this Qumran literature comes with the ancient Essenes is widely admitted today,[9] and the classic descriptions of them in Philo of Alexandria, Josephus, and Pliny the Elder confirm data found in the scrolls.[10] The study of this material permits one to formulate a plausible hypothesis that the historical John may well have spent at least part of his young life "in the desert" among the Essenes of Qumran.[11] It can be neither proved nor disproved, but it plausibly explains certain aspects of the New Testament story about John that have often been left unclarified.

For instance, John, born of elderly Jewish parents, is located as a youth "in the desert" (Luke 1:80). Though born into a priestly family, he is never depicted in the Gospels following in his father's footsteps; he is never associated with the Jerusalem Temple or its cultic service. But in the account that Josephus gives of the Essenes, he tells how they took "other men's children, while yet pliable and docile . . . and molded them according to their own ways" (*J.W.* 2.8,2 § 120). After the death of his elderly parents, John may well have been so adopted; this would account for his existence in the desert, "until a message came from God to John, the son of Zechariah" (Luke 3:2). That call would have entailed a break from the esoteric and stand-offish community of the Essenes; it would have been an invitation to go forth to preach a baptism of repentance for the forgiveness of sin *to all Jews* who would come to him.

The plausibility of this hypothesis is further supported by various details in the Qumran texts and archaeology. Thus, first, as we have already noted, all four Gospels cite Isa 40:3, "the voice of someone crying out in the desert," to explain why John is ministering in the desert (Mark 1:3; Matt 3:3; Luke 3:4; John 1:23). This explanation is paralleled by the quotation of the same Isaian verse in one of the

Qumran community's rulebooks, used there to explain why the Essenes are dwelling in the desert:

> When these things come to pass for the community in Israel . . . they will separate themselves from the midst of the habitation of perverse people to go into the desert to prepare there the way of HIM, as it is written, "In the desert make ready the way of. . . . Make straight in the wilderness a highway for our God." This means the study of the law, which He has promulgated through Moses, that they may act according to all that is revealed, season by season, and according to what the prophets have revealed through His holy Spirit (1QS 8:12–16).

It may be sheer coincidence that the Essenes have invoked the same text of Isaiah to explain their existence in the desert, but that seems unlikely in view of the further items to be mentioned that support the hypothesis.

Second, the Essenes practiced daily ritual washings. This practice is known not only from Josephus (*J.W.* 2.8.5 § 129; 2.8.10 § 150), but also from references to it in their own writings. Thus they insisted, "Let one not enter into the water, to come into contact with the purity of holy men [i.e., the community], for they will not be purified unless they turn from their evil" (1QS 5:13–14). Noteworthy is the connection between a ritual washing and a turning from evil. John's preaching of a baptism of repentance for the remission of sins may not echo identically this attitude of the Essenes toward washing and upright conduct. But who can deny the generic similarity that is there (to say nothing of Josephus' description of John's "baptism"). Again, this Essene practice of ritual washing is certainly a more plausible matrix for John's baptism than the so-called proselyte baptism.[12]

Third, according to Luke 3:16 John is said to have spoken of a baptism of water and one of fire and the Spirit, as he contrasted his own ritual washing with that expected of Jesus. The juxtaposition of water, fire, and Spirit may reflect a Palestinian Jewish attitude to ritual washings that is now found in an Essene rulebook:

> Then [at the season of visitation, when the truth of the world will appear], God will purge by his truth all human deeds and will refine [i.e., by fire] for himself some of mankind in order to destroy every evil spirit from the midst of their flesh, to purify them with a holy Spirit from all wicked practices, and to sprinkle them with a spirit of truth as with water for impurity (1QS 4:20–21).

Here one notes "refining" (by fire), "holy Spirit," and "water" all used together in an act in which God will purify the community and purge it with his truth.[13] If John came from such a background, he may well have conceived his own baptism of water as a purification of Israel preparatory to the coming baptism of the Mightier One, a refinement by Spirit and fire.

Fourth, significantly the excavated area of Qumran, along the northwest shore of the Dead Sea, southeast of Jericho, where the Essenes built their community center,[14] was within walking distance of the site along the Jordan River, where tradition has normally situated the baptizing area of John, a tradition that grew up quite independently of any awareness of the Qumran site.[15] This physical proximity of the two sites is a factor to be considered. Taken together, these four items contribute to the plausibility of a temporary relationship between John, the son of Zechariah and Elizabeth, and the Essenes of Qumran.[16]

Having considered such extrabiblical data that bear on the quest for the historical John, one may turn to the biblical testimony itself and attempt to read it with form-critical eyes. In such an approach one can sift out further details about him. Possibly a detail in the Fourth Gospel, with no real counterpart in the Synoptic tradition, may be a starting-point. In John 3:25–26 disciples of John discuss purification with a Jew; eventually they come to John and report, "Rabbi, he who was with you beyond the Jordan, about whom you testified, here he is, baptizing, and all are flocking to him." This Johannine notice is not overlaid with obvious Johannine theological concerns, and yet it implies directly that Jesus began his ministry by identifying himself with John's baptism. It even depicts Jesus himself as baptizing. Later on, however, in the same Gospel this notice is corrected; someone (a redactor/editor? an early Christian censor?) adds in 4:2, "Jesus himself, however, did not baptize, only his disciples did." Such a correction makes it difficult to determine whether the historical Jesus ever did baptize, but the association of Jesus with John in the early part of the former's ministry, as attested in this passage, is to be accepted.

Moreover, in the Fourth Gospel Jesus goes up to Jerusalem at the outset of his ministry. On arriving there, he purges the Temple (2:14–22), making use of a whip of cords and overturning the tables of money changers. Of such a purging at the beginning of Jesus' ministry we read nothing in the Synoptic tradition. Rather, in Mark, Matthew, and Luke it takes place shortly after Jesus' entry into Jerusalem at the end of his journey there from his Galilean ministry. But in the Synoptics Jesus makes his way to Jerusalem only once, whereas in the Johannine story he goes several times.

The multiple attestation of the purging in the Synoptic and Johannine traditions would support the historicity of some such action of Jesus, but which date for it would be more plausible (since we cannot claim to arrive at a certain historical setting)?[17] In my opinion, the more plausible setting for it is at the beginning of Jesus' ministry, when he was associated with the reform-ministry of John. The Synoptics, aware of the tradition about the purging, changed the setting to suit their one-journey-to-Jerusalem motif that they share in common. In purging the Temple at the beginning of his ministry, Jesus thus fits into the role that the historical John expected him to play. This role is spelled out in a scene that both Matthew and Luke have inherited from "Q."

In the triple Synoptic tradition John describes Jesus as someone mightier than he, "the One Who Is to Come" (*ho erchomenos,* Mark 1:7–8; Matt 3:11; Luke 3:16; cf. also John 1:27). But the double tradition builds on that description, when it reports John sending his messengers from his imprisonment to Jesus.[18] Having been imprisoned by Herod Antipas, he sends two disciples to ask, "Are you the One Who Is to Come, or are we to look for someone else?" (Luke 7:19; Matt 11:3). His question reflects the title used by him earlier in the triple tradition. Now, apparently because he has heard of Jesus' activity, in which he seems to have turned out not to be the fiery reformer of the Elijah sort, John hesitates and queries.

The title, "the One Who Is to Come," is an echo of Mal 3:1, where Yahweh says through the prophet, " 'Look, I am sending my messenger to prepare the way before me,' and suddenly the Lord whom you seek will come to his temple— the messenger of the covenant in which you delight. Look, *he is coming,* says the Lord." In time, this saying was interpreted in the sense of an expected coming one (in Greek, *ho erchomenos*). Well before the beginning of the Christian era, an appendix had been added to that prophecy of Malachi, in which the "messenger" of 3:1 was explicitly identified as Elijah: "Look, I am sending to you Elijah the prophet before the coming of the great and awesome day of the Lord. He will turn the hearts of fathers to their children and the hearts of children to their fathers, lest I come and smite the land with a ban" (3:23; Engl. 4:5). From this appendix there emerged an expectation of the return of the prophet Elijah of old, the expectation of *Elias redivivus,* precisely as a fiery reformer (recall 1 Kgs 18:20–24). That expectation is repeated in Sir 48:9–10, "You who were taken up in a whirlwind of fire, in a chariot with fiery horses; you who are destined, it is written, to come in time to calm the ire before it becomes fury, to turn the heart of a father to his son, and to restore the tribes of Jacob." Thus, the One Who Is to Come became the precursor of "the great and awesome day of the Lord."

Reading the Synoptic tradition form-critically, we have to conclude that the historical John at first cast Jesus in the role of *Elias redivivus.* Furthermore, the activity attributed to Jesus at the beginning of his ministry in the Fourth Gospel would thus suit him in such a role. His purging of the Temple is easily understood as the act of such a fiery reformer. In thus identifying himself with John the reform-preacher, Jesus would have acknowledged the heaven-sent role of the Baptist, sanctioned his reform-preaching, and even submitted himself to his baptism. But after John was imprisoned, Jesus went off and developed his own ministry. When John in prison heard about his activity, he began to doubt, "Are you the One Who Is to Come, or are we to look for someone else?"

In answer to John's question, Jesus says, "Go and inform

John of what you have seen and heard: *Blind people recovering their sight,* cripples walking, lepers being cleansed, *deaf hearing again, dead being raised to life,* and *good news being preached to the poor"* (Luke 7:22; cf. Matt 11:4–5).[19] In other words, instead of bringing down fire from heaven as did Elijah of old, Jesus has appeared like Isaiah of old, manifesting God's mercy toward the unfortunates of humanity. Having thus identified himself, Jesus sends the messengers back to John, commenting, "Blessed, indeed, is the person who is not shocked at me," or, blessed is the one who can take me for what I am, and not according to preconceived ideas.

After John's disciples have departed, Jesus turns to the crowds around him and asks, "What did you go out to the desert to look at? A reed swaying in the wind? . . . A man dressed in fine robes? . . . A prophet? Yes, and I tell you, something greater than a prophet: He is the one about whom it is written, 'I am sending my messenger ahead of you, to prepare the way before you' " (Luke 7:25–27; cf. Mal 3:1). Thus Jesus reverses the roles, and John becomes *Elias redivivus,* as one greater than any prophet of old. In this way, John himself became the One Who Is to Come, the one sent before the great and awesome day of the Lord, for Jesus himself eventually becomes recognized as "the Lord."

From this reversal of roles, introduced by Jesus, the historical John came to be the new Elijah, and from this same reversal comes the belief that Elijah is the precursor of the Messiah. Despite claims to the contrary, there is no evidence in any extant pre-Christian Jewish writings that depicts Elijah as the forerunner of the Messiah.[20] In Mal 3:23 he is the precursor of "the great and awesome day of the Lord," and there is no mention of a messianic figure in that text; nor is there in Sir 48:9–10. The historical John, having expected Jesus to come as *Elias redivivus,* has now become that figure himself, because Jesus has reversed the roles. Apart from the tradition that is thus recorded in the Synoptics, the belief in Elijah as the precursor of the Messiah first turns up in patristic writings: in Justin Martyr, *Dialogue with Trypho,* 8.4; 49.1–7.[21] In other words, John's role as precursor of Jesus gives rise to the role of Elijah as the precursor of the Messiah, for Jesus was the Messiah. As John was to Jesus, so Elijah became to the Messiah.

This brings me to the end of the discussion of what can be sifted form-critically from the gospel tradition about the historical John. Taken together with what can be garnered from the extrabiblical data of Josephus and the Qumran literature, we have been able to paint something of a picture of the historical John and his activity in relation to Jesus of Nazareth.

II. John the Baptist in the Marcan and Matthean Gospels

Though the main concern in this chapter is a reconsideration of the Lucan picture of the Baptist's role as precursor, we have to look briefly at the Marcan and Matthean presentation of him in order to provide a proper background for the remarks on the Lucan picture.

First of all, the distinctive Marcan tradition about John. At the outset one notes that the evangelist is aware of John as the messenger mentioned in Mal 3:1. Though the evangelist quotes Isa 40:3 in 1:2, the quotation is actually conflated, joining Mal 3:1 to Isa 40:3.[22] This conflation occurs only in Mark, but it shows that this evangelist was already writing with hindsight; he too had learned of the reversal of roles that we have traced to the historical Jesus through "Q" (Luke 7:27; Matt 11:10).

Mark further describes John's clothing: of camel's hair and a leathern belt; also his food: locusts and wild honey.[23] But the main scene in the Marcan Gospel involving the Baptist is that of the baptism of Jesus: "When Jesus came out of the water, he immediately saw the heavens opened and the Spirit descending on him like a dove; a voice came from heaven, 'You are my beloved Son; with you I am well pleased' " (1:10–11). In this Gospel the opened heavens are seen by Jesus alone, and the voice addresses *him*. The purpose of this episode, however, is the identification of Jesus for the reader of this Gospel. It establishes Jesus' relation to heaven—an identification that the Marcan Gospel has had no other opportunity to present, lacking, as it does, an infancy narrative.

Later on Mark presents the elaborate story about Herod Antipas' imprisonment and execution of John, "because of Herodias, the wife of his brother Philip, since he had married her. But John had said to Herod, 'It is not lawful for you to have your brother's wife' " (6:17–18). We have already mentioned the difference in reason given by Mark from that used by Josephus for the execution of John. Josephus knows indeed of the repudiation of the daughter of Aretas IV, the first wife of Herod Antipas, but he makes no mention of John's involvement in it, nor does he mention the brother as Philip.[24] Mark has identified the "brother" as Philip, and Matthew follows him. This has always been a notorious problem in the interpretation of the Second Gospel.

Second, the Matthean Gospel repeats most of what is found in the Marcan story of John, adding to it two main things: (1) The sermon about the brood of vipers (3:7–10) that John addresses to the Pharisees and Sadducees, whom he warns to flee from the coming wrath; he calls their attention to the axe already laid to the root of the trees.[25] (2) The "Q" story about the messengers of John sent to Jesus, which we have already discussed in part I.

Four things, however, should be noted in the Matthean treatment of John the Baptist: (1) In this Gospel John is depicted as a kingdom-preacher; the message is put on his lips, "Repent, for the kingdom of heaven is at hand." This not only stands in contrast to Mark 1:4, but the message is phrased in wording identical with that which Jesus will use in 4:17. Thus, in the Matthean Gospel John becomes the explicit forerunner of Jesus in the proclamation of the kingdom. (2) When the Matthean Jesus comes to be baptized by John, the latter protests, "I ought rather to be baptized by you." Then Jesus reproves him and insists that he is submitting to John's baptism "to fulfill all righteousness" (3:15), i.e., he is fulfilling what God desires for a status of uprightness before him. It not only implies divine approval of John's mission, but it brings to completion a personal righteous relationship of Jesus with God himself. Jesus conducts himself rightly, as John has been doing.[26] (3) When Jesus has been baptized, the evangelist writes, "The heavens were opened." This differs from the Marcan account of the baptism in which Jesus himself *sees* the heavens opened. In the Matthean version it is implied that the opening of the heavens was perceptible to all. Moreover, the heavenly voice addresses not Jesus, as in Mark 1:11, but declares, "This is my beloved Son with whom I am well pleased" (3:17). Thus Matthew has retained the baptism scene from his Marcan source, but he has made of it a public heavenly proclamation about the identity of Jesus. He has already told his readers about Jesus' heavenly relationship in the infancy narrative: a child born of Mary "of the holy Spirit" (1:18). As a result the baptismal scene now plays a secondary role in this Gospel, no longer one of identification, but of inauguration of the public ministry. Lastly, (4) the reversal of roles by which John becomes Elijah returned is made explicit in this Gospel, for the evangelist adds at the end of the "Q" episode, "For all the prophets and the law have prophesied up until John; and if you are willing to accept it, he is Elijah, the One Who Is to Come" (11:13–14).[27] Thus the hindsight about the reversal of roles has become explicit. So much for the résumé of details about John the Baptist in the Marcan and Matthean Gospels.

III. The Lucan Picture of John the Baptist

The most elaborate treatment of John is found in the Lucan writings. Not only does Luke make John a foil for Jesus in the infancy narrative, which is without parallel in other Gospels, but he also refers to him nine times in the Acts of the Apostles (1:5,22; 10:37, 11:16; 13:24,25; 18:25; 19:3,4). In six of the nine instances Luke simply recalls things already described in the Third Gospel, such as the baptism performed by John or the beginning of Jesus' ministry as dating from John's baptist activity. Only in Acts 18–19 do we learn something new: the continuation of John's baptism carried on now by his disciples, even as far away as Ephesus in Asia Minor (Acts 18:24–19:3).

In chapter II I called attention to the step-parallelism of the infancy narrative, the literary construction of Luke who made use of the Baptist source that recounted the events of John's conception, birth, circumcision, and manifestation to neighbors.[28] Whether one agrees about Luke's use of such a

Baptist source or not, the step-parallelism is clear. R. E. Brown prefers to think that the Baptist-side of the parallel narrative has been created by Luke in imitation of what he has made of the Jesus-side, utilizing details from the treat-ment of John in the rest of the Lucan Gospel.[29] There is no way to be certain about this literary construction.

The important thing in the infancy narrative is the way that Luke has already depicted John as the precursor of Jesus. Verses 15–17 in chap. 1 define the Baptist's role thus: he will be "great in the sight of the Lord," a Nazirite, one filled with the holy Spirit, and one sent for the conversion of Israel like the reformer Elijah. "He will go before him [the Lord] with the spirit and power of Elijah" (1:17), where "him" in the immediate context refers to Yahweh of the Old Testament (in an allusion to Mal 3:23). But no reader of the parallel accounts fails to miss the further import of *Kyrios,* which is eventually transferred in the infancy narrative to Jesus himself. In the scene of Mary's visit to Elizabeth, the precursor motif reappears as the child in Elizabeth's womb makes known to his mother the presence of "the mother of my Lord" (*hē mētēr tou Kyriou mou,* 1:43).

In the Gospel proper, Luke is following the Marcan order, with the opening scenes about John's appearance, preaching, and baptism (3:1–22) parallel to Mark 1:2–8. Luke expands the material, giving three samples of the Bap-tist's preaching: his *eschatological* sermon (3:7–9), the brood of vipers speech known from Matt 3:7–10, now addressed not to the Pharisees and Sadducees, but to "the crowds"; his *ethical* preaching (3:10–14), the counsel he gives to the crowds, toll-collectors, and soldiers; and his *messianic* preach-ing (3:15–17), in which he admits that he is not the Messiah, but that someone mightier than he is coming. The second and third samples turn out to be distinctively Lucan. It is hard to say whether they have been derived by Luke from his private source "L" or have been freely composed by him (apart from 3:16, which is a redactional form of Mark 1:7–8).[30]

Luke's handling of the baptism of Jesus is significant. Three things are to be noted: (1) The imprisonment of John is recorded before Jesus is actually baptized. In two verses (3:19–20) Luke presents a drastic reduction of the sixteen-verse story in the Marcan source (6:14–29). It reads: "Now the tetrarch Herod, who was criticized by John because of Herodias, his brother's wife, and of all his other misdeeds, crowned them all by this—by shutting up John in prison." Luke makes no mention of Salome's dance or the enmity of her mother Herodias. Only later on in the Gospel will the reader learn that Herod has beheaded John (9:9). More significantly, Luke has not identified the "brother" of Herod. Was he aware of the Marcan mistake? Or is the name omitted only because of the drastic curtailment of the story?[31] (2) In the baptism scene itself Luke records: "Then when all the people had been baptized and Jesus too was baptized and was praying, the heavens happened to open" (3:21). In this Lucan form of the episode we are never told who baptized Jesus; the reader assumes that it was John who did so—but he has already been imprisoned in the Lucan story. Moreover, a distinctively Lucan note has been added: Jesus at prayer—a motif well known in the Third Gospel.[32] (3) The description of the sequel to Jesus' baptism runs thus: "The heavens happened to open, and the holy Spirit descended in bodily form like a dove upon him. A voice was heard from heaven, 'You are my beloved Son; in you I have taken delight' " (3:21b–22). Again, the heavenly voice makes a public proclamation, even though the words are couched in the second singular and addressed to Jesus (as they were in the Marcan version). Luke, however, adds the detail that the Spirit descended

upon Jesus like a dove "in bodily form."[33] This is one of
several instances in the Lucan writings where the evangelist is
concerned to stress the reality of the experience.[34] One wonders how else a dove would descend but "in bodily form."

Two other aspects of the baptism of Jesus in the Lucan
presentation should be noted. First, R. Bultmann labels the
scene as "Jesus' consecration as messiah,"[35] and he has
often been followed in this messianic interpretation of Jesus' baptism. Others have gone so far as to maintain that it
was at his baptism that Jesus became aware of himself as
Messiah. Yet if one scrutinizes the text, neither the descent
of the Spirit upon Jesus, nor the recognition of him as
"Son," nor the implication of his being Yahweh's Servant
(by the allusion to Isa 42:1, "In you I have taken delight")
connotes a messianic function—a view of Jesus as an
anointed agent of God for the deliverance of his people.
There is simply no evidence in pre-Christian Palestinian
Judaism that the titles "Son (of God)" and "Servant of
Yahweh" were regarded as *messianic*.

However, Luke himself has interpreted Jesus' baptism as
messianic—not in the Gospel scene of the event, but in Acts
10, in the speech of Peter at the conversion of Cornelius.
There Peter gives a résumé of the message sent by God to
Israel through Jesus Christ, "the word proclaimed throughout
all Judea, beginning from Galilee after the baptism which
John preached: how God anointed Jesus from Nazareth with
a holy Spirit and with power, who went about doing good and
healing all who were oppressed . . ." (10:37–38).[36] In this
comment Luke looks on the descent of the Spirit on Jesus at
his baptism as an "anointing"; thus in Acts he gives the event a
"messianic" nuance, which it does not bear in itself in the
Third Gospel.

Second, in depicting John imprisoned by Herod even

before the baptism of Jesus takes place, Luke has in effect finished off the story of John's ministry and removed him from the scene before the ministry of Jesus itself begins. This mode of presenting the Baptist and his role has been used by H. Conzelmann to separate John from Jesus, to make John a figure solely in the Period of Israel, and to distance John both historically and geographically from the Period of Jesus and the area in which Jesus' ministry takes place.[37] Much of Conzelmann's understanding of John depends on his interpretation of Luke 16:16, "Up until John it was the law and the prophets; from that time on the kingdom of God is being preached. . . ." Conzelmann understands the first words, "up until John," in an inclusive sense, thus making John a figure in the Period of Israel. He also maintains that Luke has clearly demarcated the geographical locales of John and Jesus: the desert and all the region about the Jordan form the locale of John, who has nothing to do with Galilee, Judea, or Jerusalem. Moreover, John is not depicted in the Lucan Gospel as a kingdom-preacher; his reform preaching and ministry differ entirely from that of Jesus. As a result, Conzelmann denies to John the role of precursor or forerunner of Jesus. Instead, John is for him "the greatest of the prophets," a figure in the Period of Israel. W. Wink has modified Conzelmann's position somewhat, but he too admits that Luke "has retained *nothing* of John's role of Elijah."[38] Much of the denial of John's role as precursor depends on the Lucan omission of the post-transfiguration conversation of Jesus with the disciples about Elijah's coming first (Mark 9:11–13—omitted at Luke 9:36–37) and on the lack of an explicit identification of John as Elijah, such as one finds in Matt 17:13.

However, I have some misgivings about such an interpretation. It is far from certain that Luke in 16:16 intends the phrase, "*up until John* it was the law and the prophets," to be understood in the inclusive sense. I would not insist on the exclusive sense either; that would create further difficulties. Rather, John is to be taken as a transitional figure, acting as the caesura between the Period of Israel and the Period of Jesus. He basically belongs to the Period of Israel because of his circumcision and incorporation into the Israel of God; but he is a figure of the period chosen by God to inaugurate the Period of Jesus, when salvation would be accomplished. Indeed, John serves as more of a transitional figure than Mary, because he appears in the episodes that inaugurate the public ministry of Jesus himself. How one can say that John plays no role in the Period of Jesus, when one reads Luke 3:1–18, is puzzling indeed. Luke links Jesus' own ministry to Roman and Palestinian history precisely by making John appear on the scene in the fifteenth year of Tiberius Caesar and in the priesthood of Annas and Caiaphas, not to mention all the other details of the sixfold synchronism in 3:1–2.

In the Lucan Gospel John does not play the role of a kingdom-preacher (as we saw he does in Matthew); that is reserved for Jesus himself. But that does not mean that John's reform-preaching is not a preparation for the kingdom-preaching of Jesus.

Moreover, John is not the only one who appears "in the desert." After Jesus' baptism, the Lucan story recounts that he, "filled with the holy Spirit, departed from the Jordan and was led about by the Spirit for forty days in the desert" (4:1–2). It may be an episode preliminary to Jesus' ministry, but it is clearly intended to make the transition from John's ministry to that of Jesus.

For these reasons I should not put the caesura between the Period of Israel and the Period of Jesus precisely at the imprisonment of John. Following the lead of Luke 16:16, I prefer to use the phrase, "up until John," as the demarcation of the first Period, but recognize him also as the inaugurator of the Period of Jesus, as the first episodes of Luke 3 suggest. He is thus a transitional figure, functioning in both periods of Lucan salvation history.[39]

Part of the reason why interpreters have had difficulty with John as the precursor of Jesus in the Lucan Gospel is that this role is never made explicit there. In the post-transfiguration conversation of Jesus with his disciples, as they come down from the mountain, the disciples ask Jesus, "Why do the scribes say that Elijah must come first?" (Mark 9:11). Jesus not only affirms that Elijah must come first "to restore all things" (a reference to either Mal 3:23 or Sir 48:10), but he continues, "I tell you, Elijah has come, and they did to him what they wanted" (9:13). The Marcan Jesus never further identifies this Elijah who has come, but in the Matthean parallel the vague identification becomes explicit, as the evangelist comments, "The disciples then understood that he was telling them about John the Baptist" (Matt 17:13). Luke, however, in omitting the post-transfiguration conversation completely, has avoided both the vague (Marcan) identification of this Elijah who has come and the explicit (Matthean) one. But has he omitted this scene because he denies to John a precursor role? So it is apparently often understood.

When, however, one reads the Lucan form of the "Q" story about the messengers sent by John to Jesus (7:18–30), to which I have already referred,[40] one gets a different impression from the end of it, for v. 27 does identify John as the precursor of Jesus. Jesus asks the people what they went out into the desert to see, and he eventually answers his own question by admitting that they went to see "something greater than a prophet!" He continues, "He is the one about whom it is written, 'I am sending my messenger ahead of you, to prepare your way before you' " (Luke 7:26c–27; with reference to Mal 3:1). *Pace* H. Conzelmann, Jesus has not made of John "the greatest prophet,"[41] i.e., the greatest of the figures of the Period of Israel. Rather, the Lucan Jesus says of him that he is "something greater than a prophet." Then he identifies John (without naming him) as "the one about whom it is written" in Mal 3:1. It may be no more explicit a reference to John than the vague identification of Elijah who "has come" in Mark 9:13. One suspects that the trouble comes from the Matthean parallel, where Jesus continues and names John the Baptist and says of him, "If you are willing to accept it, he is Elijah who is to come" (Matt 11:14). Yet that has been added to the "Q" passage by Matthew, just as he added the reference to the Baptist in 17:13. It is not that Luke has suppressed something that was in "Q," i.e., the explicit identification of John as *Elias redivivus*. No, for Luke the reference was sufficiently clear in the words of Jesus, "This is he about whom it is written." Thus for Luke John is indeed the precursor of the Lord, just as much as he was in the pre-Lucan tradition. This identification may not be in the Lucan Gospel as explicit as it is in the Matthean, but it is there.

Moreover, this is the real reason why Luke has presented John as the precursor of Jesus even in the infancy narrative: the one who would go before him in the spirit and power of Elijah (1:17). True, one may not begin with the precursorship of John as it is presented in the infancy narrative, because that has been written with hindsight—with the hindsight generated by the idea of his precursorship in the tradition that came to Luke about the relation of the historical John to the historical Jesus. Part of the problem that H. Conzelmann has with John as the precursor of Jesus has to do with his understanding of the infancy narrative; for him this narrative is not really part of authentic Lucan writing.[42] This is why I have tried to show from other parts of the Lucan Gospel that John is indeed considered as a precursor. Once that is established, one can see that the picture of him as such in the infancy narrative only serves to confirm what is found elsewhere.

As a result, one must continue to say that Luke in his Gospel and Acts has his own way of presenting John the Baptist, even as precursor of the Lord. The idea was already present in the pre-Lucan tradition. Luke has picked it up and handled it in his own way, but he has not suppressed the idea. He is the chosen figure of the Period of Israel, chosen to inaugurate the Period of Jesus itself, wherein salvation for humanity is achieved in a new way.

Notes

¹ In general, see C. H. Kraeling, *John the Baptist* (New York: Scribner, 1951). T. W. Manson, "John the Baptist," *BJRL* 36 (1953–54) 395–412. A. S. Geyser, "The Youth of John the Baptist: A Deduction from the Break in the Parallel Account of the Lucan Infancy Story," *NovT* 1 (1956) 70–75. A. R. C. Leaney, "The Birth Narratives in St Luke and St Matthew," *NTS* 8 (1961–62) 158–66. J. Bergeaud, *Saint John the Baptist* (New York: Macmillan, 1963). C. H. H. Scobie, *John the Baptist* (London: SCM, 1964).

² See pp. 43–44 above.

³ On the stages of the gospel tradition, see p. 64 above.

⁴ The terms are borrowed from J. A. T. Robinson, *Can We Trust the New Testament?* (Grand Rapids, MI: Eerdmans, 1977) 13–16.

⁵ See *Ant.* 20.9.1 § 200; also the controverted passage in *Ant.* 18.3.3 § 63–64. On the latter, see the important study of S. Pines, *An Arabic Version of the Testimonium Flavianum and its Implications* (Jerusalem: Israel Academy of Sciences and Humanities, 1971).

⁶ *Ant.* 18.5.2 § 116–19. See further J. M. Creed, "Josephus on John the Baptist," *JTS* 23 (1922) 59–60. E. Nodet, "Jésus et Jean-Baptiste selon Josèphe," *RB* 92 (1985) 321–48, 497–524.

⁷ See *Ant.* 18.5,1 § 109–15. This passage explains how Aretas IV used the repudiation of his daughter as the excuse to mount an expedition against Herod, whose army he defeated. This is undoubtedly the defeat to which Josephus refers in the passage quoted above. This, however, makes his silence about the execution of John for criticizing Herod

for his second marriage all the more puzzling. See further p. 100 below.

⁸ See W. H. Brownlee, "John the Baptist in the New Light of Ancient Scrolls," *Int* 9 (1955) 71–90. J. A. T. Robinson, "The Baptism of John and the Qumran Community: Testing a Hypothesis," *HTR* 50 (1957) 175–91; repr., *Twelve New Testament Studies* (SBT 34; London: SCM; Naperville, IL: Allenson, 1962) 11–27. K. Smyth, "St John the Baptist and the Dead Sea Scrolls," *Month* 20 (1958) 352–61. P. Benoit, "Qumran and the New Testament," *Paul and Qumran: Studies in New Testament Exegesis* (Chicago: Priory, 1968) 1–30, esp. 6–9. N. S. Fujita, *A Crack in the Jar: What Ancient Jewish Documents Tell Us about the New Testament* (New York/Mahwah, NJ: Paulist, 1986) 112–17.

⁹ See the forthcoming publication of T. S. Beall, *Josephus' Description of the Essenes Illustrated by the Dead Sea Scrolls* (SNTSMS 58; Cambridge: University Press, 1988). This is a revision of a dissertation written under my direction at the Catholic University of America.

¹⁰ See A. Adam, *Antike Berichte über die Essener* (Kleine Texte 182; 2d ed.; Berlin: de Gruyter, 1972).

¹¹ See J. A. T. Robinson, "The Baptism" (n. 8 above); *Luke*, 453–54.

¹² The origin of John's baptism has often been explained against the background of proselyte baptism, but the biggest difficulty that this explanation encounters is to show that such a practice was in use among Palestinian Jews in the first century A.D. The earliest evidence for it is derived from Tannaitic sources. See J. Jeremias, "Der Ursprung der Johannestaufe," *ZNW* 28 (1929) 312–20; "Proselytentaufe und Neues Testament," *TZ* 5 (1949) 418–28. H. H. Rowley, "Jewish Proselyte Baptism and the Baptism of John," *HUCA* 15 (1940) 313–34. T. F. Torrance, "Proselyte Baptism," *NTS* 1

(1954–55) 150–54. W. Michaelis, "Zum jüdischen Hintergrund der Johannestaufe," *Judaica* 7 (1951) 81–120. T. M. Taylor, "The Beginnings of Jewish Proselyte Baptism," *NTS* 2 (1955–56) 193–98. O. Betz, "Die Proselytentaufe der Qumransekte und die Taufe im Neuen Testament," *RevQ* 1 (1958–59) 213–34. E. F. Sutcliffe, "Baptism and Baptismal Rites at Qumran?" *HeyJ* 1 (1960) 179–88. J. Gnilka, "Die essenischen Tauchbäder und die Johannestaufe," *RevQ* 3 (1961–62) 185–207. D. Smith, "Jewish Proselyte Baptism and the Baptism of John," *ResQuart* 25 (1982) 13–21. K. Pusey, "Jewish Proselyte Baptism," *ExpTim* 95 (1983–84) 141–45.

[13] See further P. A. Hamman, "Le baptême par le feu," *Mélanges de science religieuse* 8 (1951) 285–92. E. Best, "Spirit-Baptism," *NovT* 4 (1960) 236–43. J. D. G. Dunn, "Spirit-and-Fire Baptism," *NovT* 14 (1972) 81–92. S. Brown, " 'Water-Baptism' and 'Spirit-Baptism' in Luke–Acts," *ATR* 59 (1977) 135–51.

[14] See R. de Vaux, *Archaeology and the Dead Sea Scrolls* (Schweich Lectures of the British Academy, 1959; London: Oxford University, 1973).

[15] See C. Kopp. *The Holy Places of the Gospels* (New York: Herder and Herder, 1963) 96–103. D. Baldi, *Enchiridion locorum sanctorum: Documenta s. evangelii loca respicientia* (2d ed.; Jerusalem: Franciscan Press, 1955) 169–88.

[16] For another view of this matter, see R. E. Brown, *Birth,* 376 n. 2. Is it really "pure fiction," when the hypothesis explains many things that are otherwise unaccounted for? That the Qumran group was vigorously opposed to worship conducted at the Temple of Jerusalem and to the priesthood that functioned there may be granted. But does it follow *eo ipso* that "the fact that JBap was the son of a loyal Temple priest would not have been a recommendation for membership" in the Essene community? Josephus knew of both John

and the Essenes, indeed, but he "never connects them." Nor does he connect John and Jesus, both of whom he knew.

[17] See further R. E. Brown, *The Gospel According to John* (AB 29, 29A; Garden City, NY: Doubleday, 1966–70) 116–18. J. A. Fitzmyer, *Luke,* 1262–67. Cf. W. W. Watty, "Jesus and the Temple—Cleansing or Cursing? *ExpTim* 93 (1981–82) 235–39. E. Spiegel, "War Jesus gewalttätig? Bemerkungen zur Tempelreinigung," *TGl* 73 (1985) 239–47.

[18] Here I am following the important form-critical analysis of the gospel tradition about the relation of John to Jesus proposed by J. A. T. Robinson, "Elijah, John and Jesus: An Essay in Detection," *NTS* 4 (1957–58) 263–81; repr., *Twelve New Testament Studies* (n. 8 above) 28–52.

[19] Jesus' words echo Isa 61:1; 35:5; 26:19.

[20] See M. Faierstein, "Why Do the Scribes Say that Elijah Must Come First?" *JBL* 100 (1981) 75–86. Cf. D. C. Allison, Jr., " 'Elijah Must Come First,' " *JBL* 103 (1984) 256–58. J. A. Fitzmyer, "More about Elijah Coming First," *JBL* 104 (1985) 295–96.

There is a small papyrus fragment from Qumran Cave 4, dated about 50–25 B.C., which contains the beginnings of two lines one of which begins, *lkn 'šlḥ l'lyh qd[m   ],* "to you I shall send Elijah be[fore   ]." Unfortunately, the fragment is broken and, though it alludes to Mal 3:23, there is no evidence that that verse of Malachi was already being interpreted in terms of a Messiah (see J. Starcky, *RB* 70 [1963] 481–505, esp. 498). When Mal 3:23 begins to be quoted or alluded to in the Mishna (*m. Eduyot* 8:7; *m. Baba Meṣi'a* 1:8; *m. Šeqalim* 2:5), it is not used in the sense of a forerunner of a messianic figure.

[21] It eventually emerges in the rabbinic tradition (see Str-B, 4.784–89, 872–74). Cf. R. B. Y. Scott, "The Expecta-

tion of Elijah," *CJRT* 3 (1926) 1–13. A. J. B. Higgins, "Jewish Messianic Belief in Justin Martyr's *Dialogue with Trypho,*" *NovT* 9 (1967) 298–305. J. A. T. Robinson, "Elijah, John" (n. 8 above) 276.

22 For details on this conflated verse, see M.-J. Lagrange, *Evangile selon saint Marc* (EBib; 5th ed.; Paris: Gabalda, 1929) 3–4.

23 Cf. CD 12:13–24, for a similar diet in one of the Essene community's rulebooks: strained honey and boiled or roasted locusts.

24 See pp. 90–91 above. Philip the tetrarch was actually married to Salome, the daughter of Herodias, and was the half-brother of Herod.

25 This eschatological sermon Matthew has derived from "Q"; it has its counterpart in Luke 3:7–9.

26 See further J. Reumann, *"Righteousness" in the New Testament* (Philadelphia: Fortress; New York: Paulist, 1982) 127 § 230. B. Przybylski, *Righteousness in Matthew and His World of Thought* (SNTSMS 41; Cambridge: University Press, 1980) 91–94. For Przybylski, ". . . in 3:15 righteousness does not refer to the gift of God but to God's demand upon man" (p. 94).

27 Contrast Luke 7:27–28; 16:16 (see pp. 108–9 below).

28 See p. 35 above.

29 *Birth,* 244–47, 265–66. Cf. his article, "Luke's Method in the Annunciation Narratives of Chapter One," *No Famine in the Land: Studies in Honor of John L. McKenzie* (eds. J. W. Flanagan and A. W. Robinson; Missoula, MT; Scholars, 1975) 179–94.

30 See *Luke,* 463–75.

31 Ibid., 476–87.

32 Ibid., 244.

[33] See P. Seethaler, "Die Taube des Heiligen Geistes," *BibLeb* 4 (1963) 115–30. L. E. Keck, "The Spirit and the Dove," *NTS* 17 (1970–71) 41–67.

[34] See Luke 24:41–42; Acts 1:3–4; 10:41; cf. *Luke,* 1574.

[35] *HST,* 248.

[36] See further R. F. Collins, "Luke 3:21–22, Baptism or Anointing," *TBT* 84 (1976) 821–31. I. de la Potterie, "L'Onction du Christ: Etude de théologie biblique," *NRT* 80 (1958) 225–52.

[37] *Theology,* 19–27.

[38] *John the Baptist in the Gospel Tradition* (SNTSMS 7; Cambridge: University Press, 1968) 42 (my italics).

[39] This detail has also been noted by E. Käsemann: ". . . the Old Testament epoch of salvation history concludes with the Baptist, who himself already belongs to the new epoch and is not to be counted among the prophets" (*Essays on New Testament Themes* [SBT 41; London: SCM, 1964] 42–43).

[40] See p. 97–99 above.

[41] *Theology,* 25.

[42] See *Theology,* 118: "The authenticity of the first two chapters is questionable." Cf. *Luke,* 310.

5

Discipleship in the Lucan Writings

      If a person in the twentieth century were to be asked, "Why are you a Christian?" his or her answer might well be, "Because I consider myself a *disciple* of Jesus of Nazareth and a *follower* of the tradition he initiated." Discipleship or the following of Christ has been for centuries a way of characterizing the Christian commitment. It is a commitment based on allegiance to a Palestinian Jew, Jesus of Nazareth, who more than nineteen centuries ago made an impact on human history that has echoed ever since. Discipleship, of course, can mean many things to many people, and even twentieth-century Christians have to scrutinize their commitment to Jesus the Christ and assess their degree of involvement.

      Part of that scrutiny and assessment has to be measured by the biblical roots of such commitment. Twentieth-century Christians are no longer contemporaries of Jesus of Nazareth; his impact on them differs from that made on those who were his privileged contemporaries. What we know of him as a Palestinian religious teacher who revitalized a form of Judaism by his "teaching with authority" (Mark 1:27) comes to use in neither stenographic nor cinematographic reports. For nineteen centuries Christians have had to depend on the testimony of his contemporaries who became his followers and propagated his teaching. Moreover, the allegiance to Jesus of twentieth-century disciples has to cope with the portraits of him left in four New Testament writings and the interpretations of him and his impact in other writings of that same collection. These diverse portraits and interpretations may have been composed under the inspiration of the holy Spirit, but they were drawn and composed more than a generation after his departure from the primitive nucleus of his followers. As a result, we have in the four canonical Gospels portraits of Jesus with lines, shadows, colors, and *chiaroscuro* that differ. The Marcan Jesus acts differently from the Lucan Jesus; the Matthean Jesus speaks differently from the Johannine Jesus. Corespondingly, the role of discipleship differs in the four Gospels and this brings us to the topic of this chaper: to consider how the evangelist Luke has sketched discipleship in his Gospel and Acts. Luke's treatment of this topic is unique, because he alone among New Testament writers has left us not only an account of Jesus' ministry, but also a narrative sequel to that account. Hence the Lucan teatment of discipleship is more developed than that in other evangelists.

How, then, does Luke depict Jesus' immediate disciples? How does he present discipleship? How do the Lucan writings help a twentieth-century Christian evaluate or assess his or her allegiance to Christ? My answer to such questions will entail a discussion of three main topics: (1) discipleship as a Christian phenomenon? (2) the Lucan picture of Jesus' immediate disciples; and (3) the Lucan demands of Christian commitment.

I.   Discipleship as a Christian Phenomenon?

In ordinary language a "disciple" is someone who learns from a teacher. The word comes into English from Latin *discipulus,* "pupil," related to the verb *discere,* "learn." In a secular sense the word was quite common in the ancient cultures in which the Bible was compiled, but in a religious sense, "disciple" seems to have been almost a Christian development.

In each of the canonical Gospels followers of Jesus of Nazareth are referred to as his "disciples," *mathētai.*[1] The name *mathētai* is further used in Acts as one of the early designations for members of the Christian community that came into being after the death and resurrection of Jesus, used of those who lived either in Jerusalem, Damascus, or Antioch. Luke is the only New Testament writer who uses the feminine form *mathētria,* a description of Tabitha of Joppa, whom Peter raises from the dead (Acts 9:36). Outside of the Gospels and Acts the term *mathētai* never occurs in the New Testament.

What is even stranger is that the word *mathētēs* occurs in the Greek translation of the Old Testament only three times (LXX Jer 13:21; 20:11; 46:9), and in each case there is a variant reading in important manuscripts.[2] In other words, its occurrence in the LXX is quite uncertain.

There were, of course, "followers" of the prophets in Old Testament times. One thinks of "the sons of the prophets" (1 Kgs 20:35; 2 Kgs 2:3,5,7,15; 4:1,38; 5:22; 6:1; 9:1), but they are really members of a prophetic guild or order. More specifically one thinks of Elisha, who offers to "follow after" Elijah (1 Kgs 19:20; in the LXX, *akolouthein opisō*), or of Baruch in relation to Jeremiah. Yet the relationship of such followers to their leaders seems never to have been expressed in terms of "discipleship"; they were rather servants of the prophets. The verb *akolouthein,* "follow," occurs elsewhere in the LXX a mere thirteen times, either in the neutral sense of physical following (Num 23:20, Ruth 1:14; 1 Kgs 16:22; Jdt 12:2; Hos 2:5; Isa 45:14; Sir prol. 2), or

in the sense of accompanying, as would attendants (1 Sam
25:42; Jdt 15:13), or even in the sense of obeying a person or
a law (Jdt 2:3; 5:7; 2 Macc 8:36—but, strikingly enough,
only in late deuterocanonical writings). Consequently, one
realizes that the religious sense of "following" or "discipleship" is practically non-existent in the Old Testament.[3]

In the later rabbinic literature of the Jews (after A.D.
200) one finds the word *talmîd,* "pupil, disciple," used of a
follower of a rabbi.[4] This very word *talmîd,* occurs only once
in the Hebrew Old Testament, in a passage which recounts
David's activity in organizing musicians for the temple cult (1
Chr 25:8): "They cast lots for their service, small and great
alike, master along with pupil." The Greek Old Testament
renders the last phrase as *teleiōn kai manthanontōn,* "profi-
cient and learners." Even though the term is used here in
relation to the Temple's musical cult, it is still an expression
of secular usage; it has nothing to do with allegiance to a
religious teacher. The closest one comes to a word for "disciple" in the Old Testament is *limmûd,* which is not without its
problems and is not certainly so translated.[5]

Furthermore, the Semitic word *talmîd* never occurs in
any of the Hebrew or Aramaic texts of Qumran literature. In
this case, it is surprising because some of these Palestinian
Jews, usually identified as Essenes, were contemporaries of
early Christians, and lived a closed, ascetic, communal life in
which their candidates had to learn the way of life before full
membership was accorded them.[6] One might expect that
such candidates would have been regarded as *talmîdîm* of
the sect's Teacher of Righteousness. One of the Qumran
texts comments on Hab 2:4, "the righteous one shall live by
his fidelity," explaining it thus: "The interpretation of it
concerns the observers of the law in the house of Judah,
whom God shall deliver from the house of judgment because

of their struggle and their fidelity to the Teacher of Right-eousness" (1QpHab 8:1–3).[7] Yet such allegiance to this teacher makes no mention of a *talmîd*. Though the phenome-non of allegiance to a teacher is found here, it is not spoken of in terms of "following" or "discipleship."[8]

Each of the evangelists mentions once "disciples of the Pharisees" (Mark 2:18; Matt 22:16; Luke 5:33). This might suggest that at least this group of Palestinian Jews did have followers who adhered to their tenets. Yet the earliest refer-ence to such disciples is found in Mark 2:18, itself a Christian writing. One has no way of being sure that the phrase "disci-ples of the Pharisees" is anything more than an early *Chris-tian* way of referring to such adherents of Pharisaism.[9] The same would have to be said about "the disciples of John the Baptist" (Mark 2:18; 6:29; Matt 9:14; 11:2; 14:12).[10]

When one considers the abundant use of *mathētēs* in the Gospels and Acts over against this evidence from the Pales-tinian Jewish situation, one begins to see why "discipleship" in a religious sense may have emerged as a Christian phe-nomenon. But how did it emerge? Under what influence? Here we may have to turn to the Greek world of the time.

From at least the fifth century B.C. on, one finds references to disciples of famous Greek teachers, of the Sophists, of the Stoic philosophers, of Pythagoras, of Epicu-rus (to name only a few). Though Socrates never wanted to be called *didaskalos,* "teacher," and refused to allow his companions to be designated his *mathētai,*[11] other philo-sophical teachers did encourage teacher-disciple relation-ships, which often connoted the "imitation" (*mimēsis*) of the teacher.[12] Aristotle and Xenophon were affected by the negative Socratic-Platonic notions about such a relation-ship, but it did exist in other philosophical schools. Prota-goras of Abdera, one of the first Sophists, is said to have taken disciples "in exchange for payment," indeed, for a high sum of money.[13] As this relationship of master-disciple took shape in the philosophical schools of the Hellenistic world, it developed in time not only with the imitation of the master, but even with the veneration of him, seemingly in a quasi-religious sense. Moreover, the master-disciple relationship existed also in some of the mystery religions of the Greco-Roman world.[14] In such movements the "initiate needs the master to introduce him to the mysteries of the god and the cultus in order that he may become a member of the society gathered around the god."[15] Also closely associated with this relationship in the Hellenistic world was the principle of tradition, which saw to the continuation and propagation of the master's teaching.

This Hellenistic influence seems to have made itself felt in the way that the evangelists depict the relation of Jesus of Nazareth to his followers. This religious relationship is clearly found in the Gospels and Acts, none of which, it must be recalled, was composed on Palestinian soil. Even if one detects the emergence of this sort of relationship between the *rabbi* and the *talmîd* in the later rabbinic tradition, it may well be emerging under the same Hellenistic influence.[16]

Hence whereas one may point to the relationship of Elijah and Elisha in 1 Kgs 19:20, to a prophet and his "follower," as the Palestinian Jewish background for the relationship of Jesus to his "followers," one may rather have to look to the contemporary Hellenistic world for the background of that relationship expressed as "discipleship," which is so frequently used in the Gospels and Acts. For this reason the special *religious* sense of the discipleship that one finds expressed there may have assumed the aspect of a Christian phenomenon.

II. The Lucan Picture of Jesus' Immediate Disciples

When Luke depicts Jesus gathering followers, he is in many respects dependent on his Marcan source.[17] As in Mark, the Lucan Jesus is constantly surrounded by such companions, whom he has summoned to himself and whom he sends out with instructions to preach and with power to heal (Luke 6:13; 9:1–6). They witness his wondrous and mighty deeds (Luke 4:31–44). As in Mark, the disciples are given privileged instructions (Luke 8:9–10). But more specifically Luke uses his lengthy travel account (9:51–19:27) as a means whereby Jesus instructs these companions from Galilee, who become in time the foreordained "witnesses chosen by God" (Acts 10:41), who bear testimony "to all that he did in the country of the Jews and in Jerusalem" (10:39), beginning from Galilee (10:37). These companions fail to understand Jesus' dire forebodings about what awaits him in Jerusalem (Luke 9:45), but he tolerates them and uses them nonetheless, as in the Marcan Gospel, to administer his bounty to the crowds in the multiplication of the loaves (Luke 9:16).

Yet there are differences in the treatment of Jesus' immediate disciples in the Marcan and Lucan accounts of his ministry. The most notable of them are the following six:[18]

(1) The Lucan Jesus sends out to preach and to heal not only the Twelve (9:1–6), as in Mark 6:6b–13, but also Seventy(-two) others (10:1–16), and at the end of the commission to the latter he solemnly states, "Whoever listens to you listens to me; whoever rejects you rejects me; and whoever rejects me rejects him who sent me" (10:16).[19] This utterance clearly manifests the closeness of the relationship of the disciples to Jesus, of which Luke is so conscious.

(2) Luke obviously did not care for the abrupt beginning of the Marcan Gospel and of Mark's account of the call of the first followers. In Mark 1, after Jesus' baptism by John in the Jordan and his forty-day temptation in the desert, and after John's imprisonment, Jesus is depicted coming to Galilee and passing along the Sea, where he catches sight of Simon and Andrew. Without a hint as to why they should do so, the Marcan Jesus simply calls to these fishermen, "Follow me; I will make you fishers of men" (Mark 1:17). Though they know nothing about Jesus and nothing about the experiences he has just had in his baptism and temptation,[20] and though they have not yet witnessed any of his ministry, "immediately they left their nets and followed him" (1:18). The same thing happens to James and John, the sons of Zebedee (1:19–20). No explanation is given by Mark why these four should have followed Jesus. But Luke, with the finesse of the story-teller, first recounts some of Jesus' own ministry after his baptism, genealogy, and temptations by the devil. In chap. 4, Luke portrays Jesus teaching, preaching in the Nazareth synagogue, and healing a possessed person, and even Simon's mother-in-law (4:1–44). The last verse of that chapter summarily records, "And he went on preaching in the synagogues of Judea." After such a period of ministry Luke introduces the call of Simon, James, and John (5:1–11). It is one of the famous Lucan transpositions of Marcan material in his Gospel; he has transposed Mark 1:16–20 to this later position in the ministry and conflated it with a tradition known to us otherwise only from the Johannine Gospel about the wondrous catch of fish (21:1–11). The reason for all this is clear: Luke was concerned to offer some psychological background and explanation for why such fishermen would abandon their fishing nets and follow Jesus, the teacher and healer. By recounting a bit of

Jesus' ministry first, Luke has subtly prepared the reader for
the call of the disciples. Luke 5:11 concludes, "Once they
had brought the boats to shore, they left everything and
followed him." Whether one refers to the abrupt Marcan
story or to the well-constructed Lucan form, one cannot fail
to note the nature of this following of Jesus; it is rooted in his
own initiative and his invitation to followers, explicitly expressed in Mark 1:17, "Follow me!" and subtly implied in
Luke 5:10b, "From now on you shall be catching human
beings." Note too that, in this earliest episode involving a
gracious call of Jesus, it is expressed in terms of "following,"
as in the Old Testament story of Elisha and Elijah, and not
yet in terms of discipleship.[21]

(3) The next time the Lucan Jesus calls a disciple occurs
in 5:27–28, where Levi the toll-collector is accosted, " 'Follow me!' Levi got up, left everything behind, and followed
him." Again, the call is expressed in terms of following; but
in the sequel to it, at the banquet that Levi gives in Jesus'
honor, the first use of *mathētai* for Jesus' "disciples" is encountered (5:30). Here the influence of the Hellenistic terminology begins to enter the Lucan story, for by the time that
Luke writes his Gospel and Acts (A.D. 80–85) that term has
become the ordinary Greek word for a Christian follower of
Jesus.

(4) The next significant Lucan presentation is met in
chap. 6 of his Gospel, where Jesus chooses the Twelve. In
typically Lucan fashion he first depicts Jesus at prayer during
the night before the summoning of "his disciples" to himself,
and the narrative continues, "He chose twelve of them
whom he also named apostles" (6:13). Only Luke has added
the last clause, "whom he also named apostles." In the New
Testament in general "apostle" is a title given to persons
more numerous than the Twelve, persons "sent out" as com-

missioned emissaries.[22] Luke, however, here equates the Twelve with the "apostles" and the apostles with "the Twelve." This is further implied by him at the beginning of Acts, when he portrays Peter standing up before the others to supervise the casting of lots for the one who is to take Judas' place in the Twelve that must be reconstituted to confront Israel on Pentecost.[23] Yet for all Luke's concern to identify the apostles with the Twelve, it is a detail that he does not pursue; once the Twelve so reconstituted confront the Jews assembled in Jerusalem on Pentecost and provide for restructuring of the Jerusalem Christian community by imposing hands on the Seven chosen to "wait on tables" (Acts 6:2–6), the Twelve disappear from his story. Though lots were cast to choose a replacement for Judas to reconstitute the Twelve, no attempt is made to do this again after the death of James, the son of Zebedee, under Herod Agrippa (Acts 12:2). Though "the apostles" are mentioned at the so-called Council of Jerusalem (Acts 15:2,4,6,22–23) and their decisions are passed on (16:4), they too disappear from the Lucan story after that verse.

(5) Even though all the evangelists tell of the threefold denial of Jesus by the leader of the disciples, Simon Peter, only Luke presents Jesus at the Last Supper praying for Peter: "Simon, Simon, beware! Satan has sought you all out to sift you like wheat. But I have prayed for you (sing.) that your faith might not give out. Indeed, you yourself will turn back, then reinforce your brothers" (22:31–32). The scandal of Peter's denial is thus tempered somewhat in Luke's story. He could not gloss over the historic denials; so he makes Peter a disciple on behalf of whom Jesus has specially interceded with his heavenly Father. He singles out Peter for the role of strengthening other disciples.

(6) Luke departs from the Marcan tradition that re-

cords the dereliction of Jesus by his disciples at the time of his arrest on the Mount of Olives. For Mark ominously notes, "They all forsook him and fled" (14:50). Then to heighten the reader's sense of the absolute dereliction Mark adds the scene about the young man who was "following" him, clothed only in a linen cloth; when he was seized, he let go of the cloth and ran away naked (14:51–52). Letting go of the cloth thus symbolically encapsulates the utter abandonment of Jesus by those who were supposed to be his followers. So runs the Marcan form of the story of Jesus' arrest, but Luke has none of this. He has no counterpart of the Marcan notice that they *all* fled (14:50), nor of the episode about the young man fleeing naked. Mere omission, however, is not enough for Luke, who is thus silent about the desertion of the disciples, for he even goes so far as to include them with "the women from Galilee" in the group that stood watching the crucifixion at a distance: "All his acquaintances (*pantes hoi gnōstoi,* masculine plural!) and the women who had come with him from Galilee stood at a distance, looking on" (23:49). In this detail of the Lucan story one can detect the later generation of Christian disciples seeking to reinterpret the great scandal of the defection of Jesus' immediate disciples at the moment of his arrest. It was a hard pill to swallow. Mark minced no words about it, but Luke sought to color it otherwise.

These, then, are six of the notable details in which the Lucan picture of the immediate disciples of Jesus differs from that of the Marcan story. They all occur in the Lucan Gospel, but to it we should add a further scene from the beginning of Acts. At the end of the Gospel the risen Christ commissions "the Eleven and those who were with them" (24:33) to be "witnesses of all these things" (24:48). They are further to wait in Jerusalem itself for "the promise of my

Father" (24:49), which in Acts 1:4–5 is eventually explained as the outpouring of the holy Spirit upon them. Then in Acts we are told of the Eleven gathered in the upper room, waiting and devoting themselves with one accord to prayer, "together with the women and Mary, the mother of Jesus, and with his brothers" (1:14). This is the picture of the first believing community, eventually numbered by Luke as a hundred and twenty (Acts 1:15). But they are called neither "disciples" nor "followers," but rather *adelphoi,* "brethren" (1:15). For Luke this is the nucleus Christian community. It will be a while yet in his story before he records that "in Antioch the disciples were for the first time called Christians" (11:26).

So much, then, for Luke's portrayal of Jesus' immediate disciples. Jesus himself has passed on, and the Christian community now begins its Spirit-guided existence, proclamation, and missionary activity. This leads to our third topic.

III.   The Lucan Demands of Christian Commitment

As I already intimated at the beginning of this chapter, we have to read the Lucan writings not only from the standpoint of what they might be able to tell us about the historical Jesus of Nazareth and his disciples, but also with the awareness that the evangelist has colored his portrait of the disciples with didactic strokes. In Luke 1:4, the evangelist states his purpose in writing his two-volume work: to make Theophilus, and others like him, realize "what assurance you have for the instruction you have received." *Asphaleia,* "assurance," is put in emphatic position at the end of the periodic sentence, which makes up the prologue, to bring out an aspect of the teaching of the Christian community in Luke's own day. In tracing such matters to their beginning, Luke discloses the solidity of the early community's catechetical instruction. He is concerned to show that what the community of disciples was teaching in his day was rooted in the very teaching of Jesus himself. Now those who were his disciples have become teachers, and he who was the teacher and proclaimer has become the one taught about and proclaimed. Consequently, we must try to cull from the Lucan account those details that express the nature of the relation of disciples or followers of Jesus, for such details characterize what is expected not merely of his contemporaries, but also of disciples of subsequent generations. The Lucan demands of Christian commitment are merely another way of speaking about how Luke would see other followers of Jesus respond, those to whom the Word of the Lord is being carried by the immediate disciples and their successors, who have become the witnesses of the risen Christ. How, then, does one respond when confronted or challenged by the Christian proclamation?

Before trying to answer that question, I must introduce, by way of digression, a few remarks about a generic problem in the Lucan account that bears on the demands of Christian commitment. It has to do with Luke's eschatology. It is often said that Luke has shifted the emphasis in Jesus' message from the *eschaton* to the *sēmeron,* from the "end" to the "today."[24] With interest no longer so clearly concentrated on the imminent parousia, Luke has become more interested than other evangelists in the day-to-day reaction of human beings to the preaching of disciples chosen and commissioned as witnesses to go forth and proclaim in Jesus' name the forgiveness of sins. Luke has by no means completely eliminated all consideration of the parousia from his story (cf. Acts 1:11), but he has moved it off center, as it were. His sketch of the early community in Acts depicts, somewhat idyllically, the spread of the Word of God from Jerusalem to the end of the earth. This Lucan geographical perspective is linked to a sense of history that blunts somewhat the imminence of the expected parousia found in other New Testament writers. Luke has done this so that his story may better serve a hortatory concern.

Given such a shift in emphasis in the Lucan writings, one that reveals an everyday concern for discipleship, the Lucan demands of Christian involvement can be summed up under three main headings: (1) the response expected from people to the Christian kerygma; (2) the demands of Christian living; and (3) the community aspects of Christian life.

(1) *The Response Expected from People to the Christian Kerygma.* The response expected of disciples consists of three things: faith, repentance and conversion, and baptism.

(a) *Faith.* In Acts 16:31 Luke depicts Paul saying to the jailer at Philippi, "Believe in the Lord Jesus, and you and your household will be saved." The connection between faith and salvation is thus made clear; it is the only route for the disciple to the latter. Again, in the parable of the sower the disciples are "those who listen to the word and hold on to it with a noble and generous mind; these yield a crop through their persistence" (Luke 8:15). Such faith involves a listening to the word proclaimed, an allegiance of openness ("a noble and generous mind"), and a persistence that is subject to neither uprooting, nor apostasy, nor worldly distraction. For Luke, "the faith" can at times mean Christianity itself: many of the (Jewish) priests "submitted to the faith" (Acts 6:7); and "believers" and "those who came to believe" are some of his ways of speaking of Christians (Acts

2:44; 4:4,32, etc.). On one occasion Luke even links "faith" with "justification," as he depicts Paul preaching in the synagogue of Antioch in Pisidia: "Through him [i.e., Jesus] the forgiveness of sins is proclaimed to you, and in all those things in which you could not be acquitted in the Mosaic law everyone who has faith is (now) acquitted through him" (Acts 13:38–39). This, however, is the sole passage in the Lucan writings where such a link is made.[25] Much more frequently he links "faith" with "salvation": "Your faith has brought you salvation" (Luke 7:50; 8:48; cf. Acts 14:9).

(b) *Repentance and Conversion.* Another Lucan way of describing the ideal disciple's reaction to the Christian proclamation is "repentance and conversion." *Metanoia* literally means "a change of mind," but in the New Testament it almost always connotes a religious turning from sin, a new beginning in moral conduct, a "repentance." Closely related to such repentance is "conversion" (*epistrophē*), i.e., a turning of the human being to God (from paganism or sinful conduct). Thus, in Acts 26:20 Paul tells of his experience near Damascus and of his call to preach to Jews at Damascus and Jerusalem and also to Gentiles that "they should repent and turn to God and do deeds worthy of repentance." Both repentance and conversion, two sides of the same coin, are complementary to faith for Luke, and they are God-given (Acts 18:27). Luke never quite brings himself to speak of the Christian disciple as one empowered by the Spirit in the manner of Paul. But repentance and the forgiveness of sins are linked in the commission by the risen Christ to the Eleven who are to go forth and bear testimony to him and preach in his name (Luke 24:47; cf. Acts 5:31). Thus repentance and conversion sum up a further reaction of the disciples to the proclamation of forgiveness.[26]

(c) *Baptism.* Faith and repentance and conversion lead

to the baptism of the disciple. As in the case of Paul before him, for Luke this early Christian requirement initiates the new believer and convert into the community. Such a one had not only to believe in Jesus Christ and his role in the Father's plan of salvation, but also had to be baptized in his name. This ritual washing is never described by Luke; it is simply taken for granted as known. It is never said, moreover, to stem from an action performed by Jesus himself; nor does it feature in the great commission given by the risen Christ to the Eleven in Luke 24 (in contrast to Matt 28:19 and Mark 16:16). However, Luke takes pains to distinguish Christian baptism from that administered by John the Baptist, for he knows of the former as Spirit-related, whereas the latter is not: "Repent, and let each of you be baptized in the name of Jesus Christ for the forgiveness of your sins; and you shall receive the gift of the holy Spirit." So Peter concludes his proclamation on Pentecost to the Jews assembled in Jerusalem (Acts 2:38).

Three texts in Acts mentioning baptism, however, call for special comment. In 8:16 Samaritans baptized by Philip the evangelist in the name of the Lord have not yet received the Spirit; to this end Peter and John have to be sent by the apostles in Jerusalem to Samaria. In 10:44–48 the Spirit falls upon Cornelius and his Gentile household while Peter was still addressing it; then Peter orders the people to be baptized in the name of Jesus Christ. In 19:1–6 Paul on his arrival at Ephesus finds "disciples" (apparently Christian neophytes) who have received only John's baptism and know nothing of the Spirit; they are then baptized in the name of the Lord Jesus and receive the Spirit, as Paul imposes hands on them.

Despite attempts to read these three texts as the basis for different sacraments (baptism and confirmation) or as the basis for two kinds of early Christian baptism (e.g., a Christ-baptism and a Spirit-baptism), such attempts do not cope with the real thrust of the Lucan story. The reception of the Spirit by Christian disciples is paramount for Luke; he mentions the reception of it first, prior to the act of baptism, not only in the case of Cornelius' household (Acts 10), but even in the case of Paul himself (Acts 9:17–18). Again, he singles out the reception of the Spirit as the way of incorporating converts into the community of disciples. The Spirit is the Father's promised gift to the Christian church, and Luke insists that it is given only through the church, and especially through the Twelve or members of the Twelve (e.g., Peter and John in chap. 8, or Peter in chap. 10) or their delegate (e.g., Paul in chap. 19).[27] For in Acts the body of the disciples becomes the Spirit-guided institutional church.

These three things, then, make up for Luke the fundamental response of a disciple to the Christian kerygma: faith, repentance and conversion, and baptism.

(2) *The Demands of Christian Living.* To the foregoing three fundamentals Luke adds further demands that should guide Christian life and conduct, four of them: the following of Jesus, testimony, prayer, and the right use of material possessions. A few comments may be made on each of these demands.

(a) *The Following of Jesus.* Even though "following" is merely another way of saying "discipleship," there is a special nuance given to the former in the Lucan writings. These two volumes are dominated by a geographical perspective with Jerusalem as its central focus. In the Gospel itself Luke depicts Jesus en route, moving without distraction from Galilee where his ministry begins to Jerusalem, the city of destiny. In that city Jesus' *exodos,* his transit to the Father through passion, death, burial, and resurrection, takes place. In the Acts of the Apostles Jerusalem becomes the place from which the Word of the Lord must be carried forth by his witnesses to all Judea, Samaria, and even "to the end of the earth" (1:8; cf. Luke 24:47). In dependence on this perspective the Christian disciple in Luke's view must be a follower on the road that Jesus treads. Thus, even though Luke has taken over from his Marcan source the challenge, "Follow me!" as disciples are called, that call and challenge are now colored by the Lucan geographical perspective. The disciples must not only walk behind him, but in his very footsteps. As the distinctively Lucan travel account begins (Luke 9:51), three would-be followers offer to come along, and they are further challenged by Jesus (9:57–62); all of this takes place "as they moved along the road." Thus for Luke, Christian discipleship is not merely the acceptance of the master's teaching, but an identification of the person with the master's very way of life and destiny, a following that involves intimacy and imitation. The conditions of such following are made clear. Immediately after the first announcement of the passion (9:22), the Lucan Jesus proclaims, "If anyone wishes to come with me, let him disregard himself, take up his cross each day, and follow me" (9:23). Though Luke has derived this saying from Mark (8:34), he has significantly modified it, by adding "each day" to his form of the proclamation. He calls for daily self-denial, daily carrying of one's cross, and a daily following in the footsteps of the master.

For Luke salvation itself is "a way" (*hē hodos*) that is revealed; it consists not merely in a manifestation of power in healings and exorcisms. All these may pertain to salvation, but they must be seen as part of a pattern, the realization of the Father's plan conceived of by Luke as *hodos*. He plays on the compounds of that word and aspects of "the way." Jesus has entered on that course (*eisodos,* Acts 13:24);

he moves along it (*poreuesthai,* passim); and he heads for its outcome (*exodos,* the transit to the Father, Luke 9:31). This idea of salvation as a "way" leads in time in Acts to the calling of the Christian community "the Way" (9:2; 19:9,23; 22:4; 24:14,22), a primitive designation or title for the organized community of disciples, which eventually is known as "the church."[28] Thus, disciples must trudge along that Way in the footsteps of the Savior.[29]

(b) *Testimony.* The Christian disciple is so to live as to bear witness to the risen Christ and his teaching. Such testimony becomes a major motif in Acts:

> We are witnesses of all that he did in the country of the Jews and in Jerusalem. Him whom they did away with, in hanging him on a tree, God raised up on the third day and made manifest, not to all the people, but to witnesses fore-ordained by God, to us who ate with him and drank with him after he rose from the dead. He commissioned us to preach to the people and to bear witness that he is the one appointed by God to be the judge of the living and the dead" (10:39–42).

Such testimony plays an important role at the beginning of Acts, when Matthias is chosen by lot to take the place of Judas in the Twelve; it had to be reconstituted for the initial proclamation of the word of testimony to the Jews assembled in Jerusalem on Pentecost;[30] the one chosen had to be a witness to the risen Christ (1:22). Even Paul, who was not one of the Twelve and had not been with Jesus during his earthly ministry, is cast by Luke as a witness to the same Christ (22:15; 26:16). Thus this notion becomes one that must mark the life of every Christian disciple in every generation—testimony to the risen Lord.

(c) *Prayer.* Another important aspect of Christian discipleship in Luke's view is one's ongoing communion with
God. It has always been noted how preoccupied this evangelist is with prayer in both his Gospel and Acts. The chord is
struck in the infancy narrative itself, where in the very first
episode Zechariah enters the sanctuary to offer incense,
while the people stand outside in prayer (1:10); in the sanctuary Zechariah learns that his prayer has been answered
(1:13). Major episodes in Jesus' ministry are linked with his
own prayer: his baptism (3:21), his choosing of the Twelve
(6:12), the acknowledgement of him by Peter (9:18), his
transfiguration (9:28), his intercession for Peter at the Last
Supper (22:32), his agony on the Mount of Olives (22:41),
and his prayer on the cross (23:46). The Lucan Jesus not
only prays himself, but teaches his disciples to pray (11:2–4)
and inculcates "the need to pray always and never give up"
(18:1). When the Seventy(-two) are sent out, they are not
only to preach and heal, but also to "pray" that "the owner
of the harvest may send out laborers enough for his harvest"
(10:2). The parable of the persistent friend (11:5–8) is followed by sayings on the efficacy of prayer (11:9–13). In Acts
the nucleus community, awaiting the promise of the Father,
is portrayed at prayer (1:14). Peter and John go up to the
Temple to pray at the ninth hour (3:1), and when the Seven
are appointed to serve tables, it is to allow the Twelve to
engage in "prayer and the ministry of the word" (6:4). Two
features of Jewish piety are taken over by Christian disciples, prayer and almsgiving, and Luke interprets them as
rising before God as a memorial (Acts 4:24–30), when the
community supplicates God, the sovereign Lord, on behalf
of Peter and John who have been arrested and forbidden to
speak again in Jesus' name. It is a petition for courage and
boldness that these disciples may carry out the roles ex-

pected of them. This prayer becomes the context of their being filled with the holy Spirit (4:31). In all of this one notes Luke's concern to join to the disciples' ministering activity the need for ongoing communion with God himself. That has to be the source of vitality in the activity of the disciples.

(d) *The Right Use of Material Possessions.* No other New Testament writer, save perhaps the author of the Epistle of James, speaks out so forthrightly as does Luke about the use of material possessions by Christian disciples. More than the other evangelists Luke either preserves sayings of Jesus about this topic or puts on his lips statements that concern wealth, money, and material goods in general. In Acts Luke further sketches an idyllic picture of the early Jewish Christian community in Jerusalem with its common ownership of property and the sharing of wealth and possessions as a model for the community of his own day. Luke was clearly not happy about what he had seen of the use of wealth and possessions by Christian disciples.

So he portrays Jesus speaking about this matter both in sayings that he has taken over from Mark and "Q" and also in a number of sayings that he has composed himself or derived from his own source "L." For instance, in Mark Jesus tells a rich young man to sell what he possesses, give the proceeds to the poor, and come, follow him (10:21), whereas in Luke Jesus tells "the magistrate": "Sell *all* that you have" (18:22). Again in Mark, the first disciples called leave their nets to follow Jesus (1:18,20), but in Luke they leave "everything" to do so (5:11).

The contrast between the rich and the poor surfaces often in the Lucan story, e.g., in Mary's Magnificat (1:53), in the instruction of John the Baptist to the people (3:11,14), in Jesus' interpretation of Isa 61:1–2 in his Nazareth synagogue sermon (4:18), in the first beatitude and first woe (6:20,24), in the story of the rich man and Lazarus (16:19–31), and in Jesus' advice to "invite the poor" to dinner instead of rich neighbors who might reciprocate (14:13),

In the special Lucan material, in particular, one detects a twofold attitude toward material possessions: (i) a moderate attitude, in which the Lucan Jesus advocates a prudent use of such possessions to give assistance to human beings who are less fortunate: "Give to everyone who begs from you" (6:30), as well as in the story of the dishonest manager (16:1–8a); (ii) a radical attitude, which recommends the absolute renunciation of all wealth: "Everyone of you who does not say goodbye to *all* he has cannot be a disciple of mine" (14:33); or "No servant can serve two masters; either he will hate the one and love the other, or he will be devoted to the one and despise the other. You cannot serve both God and mammon" (16:13). For Luke all of this is not merely a question of haves and have-nots, since there is an eschatological dimension to the topic, which the first beatitude and the first woe make clear (6:20,24), as well as does Mary's Magnificat. Having and not having material possessions ultimately symbolize an important aspect of the disciple's inner response to the call of God and to his visitation of his people in and through the ministry of Jesus. Material possessions are liable to stand in the way of the proper response, and Luke is concerned that they do not.

(3) *Community Aspects of Christian Life.* Finally, we turn to the ecclesial dimension of Christian discipleship, a topic already touched on in a few earlier minor comments. It is best summed up in the first of Luke's major summaries in Acts:

> They continued to adhere to the teaching of the apostles, to community (*koinōnia*), to the breaking of the

bread, and to prayers. Awe was characteristic of everyone, and many were the signs and wonders wrought by
the apostles. All who came to believe lived together and
held all things in common; their possessions and their
substance they sold and distributed to each as had need.
Day by day, they continued to frequent the Temple,
breaking bread in their homes, and partaking of food
with joy and simplicity of heart, praising God and enjoying favor with all the people (2:42–47).

Such a *koinōnia* comes in the course of Acts to be called
ekklēsia; but it is not yet so named at this very early stage of
the community described in Acts 2. No one knows how long
the idyllic common life thus described persisted; after chap.
5, in which Luke recounts the scandal that the conduct of
Ananias and Sapphira caused, we never hear of it again.

Then, once the story of Paul begins (8:1), the community of the disciples becomes known as "the church" and
continues to be so called until the end of Acts.[31] *Ekklēsia* is
significant, since it is used in a religious sense and is derived
from the LXX, where it designates the Israelites in their
religious and cultic groupings in the desert of Sinai (Deut
23:2; Judg 20:2; cf. Acts 7:38). Etymologically, the name
stresses the "called" aspect of the Christian community. Together, the disciples have become the people of God, reconstituted Israel, *called* to a destiny that they continue to share
in common as the Word of the Lord is carried from Jerusalem to the end of the earth. Though Luke never thinks of the
church as the body of Christ (a typically Pauline notion),[32] it
is for him the reality in which one shares in the Spirit of God.
"Church" is for Luke the Spirit-guided organized Christian
community; through it the Spirit is given, is poured out, and
acts as the substitute for Jesus of Nazareth, who began the

whole movement and initiated the teacher-disciple relationship that is the basis of it all. Luke is concerned to teach
disciples of his own generation, toward the end of the first
Christian century, that Jesus is present to them in two ways:
in the promise of the Father (or the Spirit poured out from
on high) mediated through the community and in the breaking of bread. The latter is the meaning of the great Emmaus
scene, the climax of which is summed up in the words of the
disciples who report to those in Jerusalem "what had happened to them on the road, and how he was known to them
in the breaking of the bread" (Luke 24:35). For the main
point of Luke's story about the church is that it is the body of
disciples whose allegiance to Jesus of Nazareth is manifest in
his day. It is, moreover, manifest throughout the centuries
ever since, because the church is the locus where the "promise of the Father" is experienced and where the "breaking of
the bread" is celebrated.

Such Lucan ideas on discipleship may also serve to help
Christians in the twentieth century to assess and evaluate
their allegiance to Jesus of Nazareth. For Luke's ideas on
this topic are an important part of the biblical roots of Christian discipleship.

Notes

¹ The noun *mathētēs* occurs 73 times in Matthew, 46 times in Mark, 37 times in Luke, 78 times in John, and 28 times in Acts. The verb *mathēteuein*, "be/become a disciple," occurs three times in Matthew and once in Acts, but in no other New Testament writing. It is, moreover, unknown in pre-Christian extrabiblical Greek. As a term referring to the followers of Jesus, *mathētēs* occurs in Matthew 69 times, in Mark 43 times, in Luke 34 times, and in John 74 times; for Acts, see above.

² See J. Ziegler, *Jeremias, Baruch, Threni, Epistula Jeremiae* (Septuaginta, Vetus Testamentum graece 15; 2d ed.; Göttingen: Vandenhoeck & Ruprecht, 1976) 216 (codex A reads *mathētas* instead of *mathēmata* in 13:21), 251 (codex A reads *mathētēs* instead of *machētēs*, "warrior" in 20:11), 277 (codex A and ms. 710 read *mathētai* instead of *machētai* in 26:9 [= MT 46:9]). Cf. K. H. Rengstorf, "*Manthanō . . . mathētēs . . . ,*" *TDNT* 4. 426–31.

³ See, however, G. Kittel, "*Akoloutheō . . . ,*" *TDNT* 1. 210–16, which needs some correction. Certainly, the Old Testament phrase, *hālak 'aḥărê*, "go/walk after," sounds similar to the New Testament sense of "following," but "the following of God/the Lord" (Deut 1:36; 1 Kgs 14:8; 2 Kgs 23:3), while expressing adherence, has other connotations. Moreover, the use of this expression, when other gods are the object of adherence, denotes apostasy—hardly the same connotation. The only example that Kittel cites of "following" in the Old Testament, which would be similar to the New Testament usage, is that of Elisha-Elijah (1 Kgs 19:20–21).

⁴ E.g., *m. 'Abot* 1:1. Cf. K. Rengstorf, "*Manthanō*" (n. 2 above), 431–37.

⁵ It seems to mean "disciple" in Isa 8:16, but compare the LXX (*tou mē mathein!*). In Isa 50:4 it occurs twice in the

plural, and the *RSV* translates it "the tongue of those who are taught," whereas the LXX more correctly renders it *glōssan paideias,* "a tongue of education," since the noun-type *qittûl* usually expresses an abstract notion. In Isa 54:13 *limmûdê yhwh* means "taught by the Lord" (*RSV;* LXX: *didaktous theou*). Cf. Jer 13:23, *limmûdê hārēaʿ,* "accustomed to evil." See *HALAT,* 505.

⁶ See Josephus, *J.W.* 2.8.2 § 120.

⁷ See M. P. Horgan, *The Pesharim: Qumran Interpretations of Biblical Books* (CBQMS 8; Washington; Catholic Biblical Association, 1979) 40. W. H. Brownlee, *The Midrash Pesher of Habakkuk* (SBLMS 24; Missoula, MT: Scholars, 1979) 125–30.

⁸ Though the Old Testament phrase *halak ʾaḥărê,* "walk after/behind," is used occasionally in Qumran literature (CD 4:19 [of followers of Ṣaw]; 19:32; 11QTemple 54:13–14), it is never used of members of the Essene community following their Teacher of Righteousness.

Though P. Nepper-Christensen (*"Mathētēs," EWNT* 2. 916) speaks of teachers in the Palestine of Jesus having *talmîdîm,* he does not document this statement. So far I have failed to uncover any evidence of the use of this term in first-century Aramaic or Hebrew.

⁹ Josephus speaks of Hyrcanus as having been at one time a "disciple" (*mathētēs*) of the Pharisees (*Ant.* 13.10.5 § 289). But Josephus, writing toward the end of the first century A.D., is trying to explain Jewish history to Roman readers; that he would use *mathētēs,* a term current in the Greco-Roman world of his time, to express such adherence of Hyrcanus to the Pharisees is not surprising. He also casts Elisha as "both a disciple and servant" of Elijah (*Ant.* 8.13,7 § 354; cf 9.2.2 § 28; 9.3.1 § 33), whereas there is no word in the biblical Hebrew text to correspond to such a designation.

Indeed, the "elders" with whom Elisha was sitting in his house (2 Kgs 6:32) become Elisha's "disciples" (*Ant.* 9.4.4 § 68), as do the "sons of the prophets" of 2 Kgs 9:1 (*Ant.* 9.6.1 §106). Similarly, Joshua becomes a "disciple" of Moses (*Ant.* 6.5.4 § 84), and Baruch a "disciple" of Jeremiah (*Ant.* 10.9.1 § 158); cf. 10.9.6 § 178). In all these instances Josephus is casting the varying degrees of allegiance in terms of "discipleship," a later term commonly used in the Greco-Roman age in which he lived.

¹⁰ Philo uses the word *mathētēs* in a generic (secular) sense of "learner," "pupil," often in juxtaposition with *gnōrimos* (*Quod det.* 18 § 66; 36 § 134; *De post. Caini* 39 § 132; 41 § 136; 44 § 146; *De agric.* 13 § 51; *De mut. nom.* 48 § 270[bis]; *De spec. leg.* 2.39 § 227; 4.26 § 140; *Quod Deus immut.* 2 § 5 [fem. *mathētris*]). In three instances *mathētēs* occurs in the sense "pupil of God" (*De sacr. Ab.* 2 § 7; 17 § 64; 23 § 79), which is a recasting of the Old Testament expression, "taught by God" (Isa 54:13; Jer 31:33–34). But there is no clear instance of "disciple" used of a member of a religious group.

¹¹ See Plato, *Apol.* 33a (cf. Isocrates, *Or.* 11.5); *Laches* 186e; *Sympos.* 217a–b; and with irony, *Euthyphro* 5a.

¹² See H. D. Betz, *Nachfolge und Nachahmung Jesu Christi im Neuen Testament* (BHT 37; Tübingen: Mohr [Siebeck], 1967) 48–136.

¹³ See Plato, *Protag.* 315a, 316b, 349a; Xenophon, *Mem.* 1.6,3; *Cyrop.* 1.4,20; Dio Chrysostom 12.5; 55.3–5. Cf. further E. Zeller, *A History of Greek Philosophy* (2 vols.; London: Longmans, Green & Co., 1881) 2. 409. W. K. C. Guthrie, *A History of Greek Philosophy* (5 vols.; Cambridge: University Press, 1962–78) 3. 35–38. H. I. Marrou, *Histoire de l'éducation dans l'antiquité* (new ed.; Paris: Editions du Seuil, 1948) 83–106.

[14] See R. Reitzenstein, *Hellenistic Mystery-Religions: Their Basic Ideas and Significance* (Pittsburgh Theological Monograph Series 15; Pittsburgh: Pickwick, 1978) 237–67. Though the relationship seems to have existed in these cults, the disciple was usually called *mystēs* or *myoumenos*, "initiate(d)," and the master *mystagōgos*.

[15] See K. H. Rengstorf, "*Manthanō*" (n. 2 above), 421.

[16] Ibid., 438–40.

[17] Cf. E. Best, "The Role of the Disciples in Mark," *NTS* 23 (1976–77) 377–401. J. R. Donahue, *The Theology and Setting of Discipleship in the Gospel of Mark* (Marquette Lecture 1983; Milwaukee, WI: Marquette University, 1983).

[18] See further R. Ryan, "The Women from Galilee and Discipleship in Luke," *BTB* 15 (1985) 56–59. D. M. Sweetland, "Discipleship and Persecution: A Study of Luke 12:1–12," *Bib* 9 (1982) 237–49.

[19] This saying is peculiar to Luke in the Synoptic tradition, but it resembles sayings in the Johannine tradition (especially 5:23; cf. 12:48; 15:23).

[20] The reader of Mark's Gospel thus has an advantage over them.

[21] See further C. Coulot, "Les figures du maître et de ses disciples dans les premières communautés chrétiennes," *RevScRel* 59 (1985) 1–11.

[22] This title is given to Barnabas and Saul (Acts 14:4,14), to Matthias (by implication in Acts 1:26), possibly to Junia(s) and Andronicus (Rom 16:7, depending on how v. 7b is interpreted), and to unnamed "brethren" (2 Cor 8:23). Paul insists on his right to the title (1 Cor 9:1; Gal 1). Cf. 1 Cor 15:7, where "all the apostles" seems to be a group distinct from "the Twelve" (15:5).

[23] See K. H. Rengstorf, "The Election of Matthias," *CINTI,* 178–92.

²⁴ For the role of the Spirit as the *Ersatz* for the delayed parousia, see H. Conzelmann, *Theology*, 95–136. Cf. *Luke*, 231–35.

²⁵ See p. 6 above. "Forgiveness of sins" occurs in the Pauline corpus only in Col 1:14; cf. Eph 1;7; these letters, however, are Deutero-Pauline.

²⁶ See further J. Dupont, "Repentir et conversion d'après les Actes des Apôtres," *ScEccl* 12 (1960) 137–73. R. Michiels, "La conception lucanienne de la conversion," *ETL* 41 (1965) 42–78.

²⁷ For Paul's indirect delegation by the church of Jerusalem, recall Acts 9:26–30; 11:22–26; 13:1–3.

²⁸ The designation "the Way" may echo the Qumran designation of its community as *derek/had-derek*, "Way, the Way" (1QS 9:17–18; CD 1:13; cf. 21). Cf. *ESBNT*, 281–84.

²⁹ See further C. H. Talbert, "The Way of the Lukan Jesus: Dimensions of Lukan Spirituality," *PerspRelStud* 9 (1982) 237–49.

³⁰ See n. 23 above.

³¹ The expression, "the whole church," occurs at the end of the Ananias and Sapphira incident (5:11), but that is in a comment of Luke who makes use of *ekklēsia*, a term well in use by the time he writes, to record the early community's reaction to that scandal.

³² This notion is not to be read into the sayings of the risen Christ who appears to Saul on the road near Damascus ("I am Jesus, whom you are persecuting," Acts 9:5; 22:8; 26:15).

6

Satan and Demons in Luke-Acts

Among the words and deeds of Jesus of Nazareth preserved for us in the Synoptic Gospels are his *dynameis,* "mighty deeds" (Mark 6:2,14; Matt 11:20–21; 13:54; Luke 10:13; 19:37). It has often been noted that this term *dynameis* better expresses the activity of Jesus in curing and exorcising than the Latin-derived, commonly-used expression "miracles," because in most instances the emphasis in the New Testament falls not on the wondrous aspect of Jesus' deeds, but on the manifestation of the power that was his. Luke, in particular, goes out of his way to relate that power to "the Spirit" (4:14, with an allusion to the reception of it at the baptism in 3:22) or to Yahweh himself (5:17, "the power of the Lord happened to be with him that he might heal people"). This power that Jesus enjoys is used toward those afflicted with diseases or unclean spirits in the various Synoptic accounts. Luke has his share of such episodes, and his writings present their own emphases in recounting the confrontation of Jesus and his disciples with the forms of evil that afflict human beings.

Jesus and his disciples carried on their ministry in a world haunted by Satan and his minions, which were all regarded as the cause of evil affliction. In referring to such preternatural beings, Luke makes use of five different terms or names: (1) *ho diabolos,* "the devil," (2) *Satanas,* "Satan," (3) *Beezeboul,* "Beelzebul," (4) *daimonion,* "demon," and (5) *pneuma akatharton* or *pneuma ponēron,* "unclean spirit" or "evil spirit." Each term calls for a few introductory remarks.

(1) *Ho diabolos.* Whereas the expression "the devil" is never found in Philo or Josephus or in extrabiblical Greek papyri of pre-Christian times, it is used in the Lucan Gospel in the temptation scenes (4:2,3,6,13) and in the explanation of the parable of the sowed seed (8:12: the devil comes and snatches away the word sowed among those represented by seed strewn "along the footpath"). In the temptation scene Luke has taken over "the devil" from the source "Q" (cf. Matt 4:1,5,8,11), whereas in the explanation of the parable he substitutes it for the Marcan *ho satanas* (4:15). Why Luke substitutes *ho diabolos* for the Semitic *satanas,* which he uses elsewhere, is anyone's guess.[1] *Ho diabolos* further occurs in Acts 10:38, where Peter at the conversion of Cornelius summarizes Jesus' career and speaks of him as one anointed by God with the holy Spirit and power, who went about doing good and curing all those caught in the grip of "the devil." Again, in Acts 13:10 Paul on the island of Cyprus addresses Elymas the magician as "Son of the devil, enemy of all uprightness"; Elymas has just been described as "full of all deceit and villany." In each of these instances *diabolos* is scarcely meant in its etymological sense of "calumniator, (false) accuser," but denotes rather the personification of evil, a being who sums up all opposition to the good that comes in Jesus, his word, his disciples or their mission. This generic designation yields in the Lucan story to two specific proper names.

(2) *(Ho) Satanas.* The first name encountered in the Lucan writings is "Satan," which occurs five times in the

Gospel: 10:18, when Jesus comments on Satan's fall; 11:18, when Jesus speaks of the Satanic kingdom as divided; 13:16, when Jesus cures a crippled woman bound by Satan for eighteen long years; 22:3a, when Satan is said to enter Judas at the beginning of the passion; and 22:31, when Satan is said to have sought out the disciples to sift them as grain. Of these five instances, only one (11:18) is derived from "Q" (cf. Matt 12:26), whence Luke gets the whole Beelzebul controversy in which it occurs. All the other instances are in episodes peculiar to Luke, undoubtedly derived from his source "L." In these instances he did not take the pains to change the Semitic name for the generic Greek expression *diabolos*. Unknown in the writings of Philo, Josephus, or extrabiblical papyri of pre-Christian times, "Satan" is derived from a Palestinian Jewish tradition. In the Greek Old Testament it is transliterated as *satan(as)* and occurs in the generic sense of "adversary" (1 Kgs 11:14,23; Sir 21:27); but, strikingly enough, in those passages where Hebrew *śāṭān* appears as the name of the prosecutor or arch-adversary in the heavenly court (Job 1:6,7bis,9,12bis; 2:1,2bis,3–4,6–7; Zech 3:1,2; 1 Chr 21:1), it is always translated into Greek as *diabolos*.[2] Luke himself continues to use "Satan" in Acts. In the story of Ananias and Sapphira he depicts Peter querying Ananias, "Why has Satan filled your heart to lie to the holy Spirit?" (5:3). Again, when the risen Christ appears to Saul near Damascus in the third conversion account, he commissions him to go to the Gentiles "to open their eyes that they may turn from darkness to light and from the power of Satan to God" (26:18).

(3) *Beezeboul.* Another proper title for the devil in the Lucan Gospel is "Beelzebul" (11:15,18,19). In this sole episode in which it occurs, it comes to Luke from "Q" (cf. Matt 12:24–27).[3] In both the Matthean and Lucan forms of the

episode *ho satanas* also occurs (Luke 11:18; Matt 12:26) so that "Beelzebul" becomes clearly only another specific name for the same archadversary. The name *Beezeboul* is not used by Philo or Josephus, but it preserves that of an old Canaanite deity, "Baal the Prince," or "Baal of the Exalted Abode," a title once given to *Bĕʿel šĕmayin*, "Lord of the heavens" considered to have been a rival of Yahweh in Hellenistic times (who is also called in Dan 5:23 *mārê' šĕmayyā'*, "Lord of the heavens").[4] "Beelzebul" was applied to Satan in this period, probably because of Ps 96:5, "All the gods of the nations are idols," which became in the Septuagint, ". . . are demons" (*daimonia*).

(4) *Daimonion*. In the "Q" passage just referred to (Luke 11:15; Matt 12:24) Beelzebul is identified as "the prince of demons" (*archōn tōn daimoniōn*), which may mean that Beelzebul was himself considered to be a demon, but may also mean only that demons were under his control. In any case, in Luke *daimonion* is clearly a Greek designation for some sort of evil preternatural being, sometimes described as *akatharton*, "unclean," whereas in pre-Christian Greek texts it often designates a heavenly or other-worldly being, either neutral or good. In Acts 17:18 (the episode of Paul on the Areopagus), *daimonion* is used in the neutral sense, perhaps meaning "divinity" (as the *RSV* renders it); Epicurean and Stoic philosophers think that Paul is a "preacher of foreign divinities." But in the Lucan Gospel *daimonion* is otherwise always used in the negative sense of an evil "demon" (4:33,35,41; 7:53; 8:2,27,29–30,33,35,38; 9:1,42,49; 10:17; 11:14–15,18–20; 13:32), twenty-one times in all. Noteworthy is Luke 11:14–20, where Satan, Beelzebul, and demons all appear together in one episode.

(5) *Pneuma akatharton* or *pneuma ponēron*. Related to the use of *daimonion* is that of *pneuma* alone, "spirit" (in a

negative sense), or *pneuma akatharton* "unclean spirit," or *pneuma ponēron,* "evil spirit." In one instance it is even joined with *daimonion* (4:33, *pneuma daimoniou akathartou;* cf. 8:29). Though Luke uses *pneuma* both in a neutral sense (Acts 25:8,9) and in a good sense (Luke 8:55), especially of the "holy Spirit," the negative sense ("evil spirit") occurs fourteen times in his Gospel (4:33,36; 6:18; 7:21; 8:2,29; 9:39,42[55]; 10:20; 11:24,26; 13:11) and at least eight times in Acts (5:16; 8:7; 16:16,18; 19:12–13,15–16). In one instance (Acts 16:16) it is *pneuma pythōn,* "a spirit of divination" (*RSV*), the spirit that Paul drives out of the Philippian slave-girl.

In this fifth and last category two aspects of the negative *pneuma* are to be noted: (a) Not just Jesus in the Gospel, but Peter, Philip, and Paul in Acts are also portrayed exercising "power and authority" over such beings—that power given to the Twelve in Luke 9:1. (b) In these passages *pneuma* (in the negative sense) is often linked with "disease" or "infirmity." Thus in Luke 13:11, a crippled woman is described at first as "having a spirit of infirmity" (*pneuma echousa astheneias,* which is most likely a genitive of apposition), and later on as having been bound by Satan for eighteen years (13:16). One may wonder just what is meant. Again, the women followers of Jesus were "cured of evil spirits and infirmities" (8:2, which is most likely a hendiadys). The exegetical problem one encounters in such instances is whether one is dealing with a mode of speech, a disease figuratively described as *pneuma* or *daimonion,* or with a distinct preternatural being. In this regard, the episode of the epileptic boy is instructive. Whereas Luke ascribes his condition to a *pneuma* (9:39) or *daimonion* (9:42) and Mark says, "having a dumb spirit" (9:17, *echonta pneuma alalon*), Matthew says of the boy, "he is moonstruck" (17:15, *selēnizetai*). In such instances we are faced with what might be called "demon-sickness," wherein proto-logical thinking is operative. Ancient folk, unable to diag-nose properly an illness or discern its secondary, natural causality, ascribed it to a preternatural being, a spirit or a demon. The standard title for the episode in Mark 9:14–29 par., to which I have just referred, is "An Epileptic Child Healed."[5] That, of course, is a title put on the episode from a modern analysis of the details in it.

With such preliminary remarks, I may now turn to three aspects of the Lucan treatment of Satan or the devil. I shall concentrate on (1) the temptation of Jesus by the devil in the Lucan story; (2) the alleged Satan-free Period of Jesus that follows the temptation; and (3) Jesus' comment about Sa-tan's fall in Luke 10:17–20.

I.   The Temptation of Jesus by the Devil in the Lucan Story

The programmatic aspect of the temptation scene in each Synoptic Gospel is obvious and has often been noted.[6] Following closely on the baptism of Jesus, in which he has been identified by the heavenly voice as "my beloved Son" and invested with the Spirit, it introduces another, adversar-ial aspect of Jesus' ministry that is about to be inaugurated. The good that he has been sent by heaven to bring to human-ity will be countered by evil of no small proportion. Thus the temptation episode is the last of the preparatory scenes in the Lucan Gospel introducing the public ministry and encap-sulates a programmatic aspect of it. Closely related to the foregoing baptism and genealogy, it depicts Jesus as being tested precisely in his character as God's Son.

In the Lucan Gospel the order of the preparatory episodes is derived from Mark (preaching of John the Baptist, baptism of Jesus, temptation), except for the genealogy that Luke has inserted into that order after the baptism. From the Marcan temptation account Luke retains only a few words, "for forty days in the desert" and "being tempted," as well as the mention of the Spirit (now recast in Lucan terminology). Luke, however, omits the details about the beasts and the angels—the motif of Paradise Regained—with which the Marcan account ends (1:13b); for him this episode has no idyllic aspect.

For the unspecified mode of the testing of Jesus in the Marcan account Luke substitutes "Q" material (4:2–13; cf. Matt 4:1–11). Whereas in Matthew Jesus is said to have been "led by the Spirit into the desert to be tested by the devil" (4:1) and the infinitive of purpose thus attributes the experience to both heavenly and diabolic influence, Luke's modification makes it clear that Jesus, "filled with the holy Spirit," departs on his own from the Jordan and is led about for forty days by the Spirit in the desert, where he is "tempted by the devil" (4:2). In other words, Luke portrays the testing of Jesus as undertaken at the devil's initiative, and not as an experience purposefully guided by the Spirit.[7] He thus keeps the devil and the holy Spirit apart.

Moreover, the order of the temptation scenes is significant. Whereas in Matthew the order is desert—pinnacle—high mountain, it is in Luke desert—view of world kingdoms—Jerusalem pinnacle. The difference of order raises a question about the original sequence in "Q" and who may have changed it. A. Plummer seems to speak of the Lucan sequence as the "chronological order,"[8] yet nothing in that sequence hints at a temporal nuance. It is rather a literary or theological sequence. K. H. Rengstorf suggests that Luke has rearranged the original sequence so that it would be the reverse of the first three petitions in the Lucan form of the Our Father (11:2): "May your name be sanctified; may your kingdom come; give us each day our bread for subsistence."[9] This suggestion, however, is ingenious and subtle; who would ever think of it spontaneously? Similarly, H. Swanston has seen a connection between the Lucan sequence and that of the Exodus events referred to in Psalm 106.[10] Again, such a suggestion seems far-fetched. A more plausible interpretation of the episode seeks to explain the difference in terms of its climax: Matthew has made the mountain scene the climax because of the emphasis in his Gospel on the mountain-motif (the sermon on the mount, the new-Moses, etc.), whereas Luke has made the pinnacle of the Temple in the holy city the climax because of the importance of Jerusalem in the geographical perspective of his writings, the city of destiny toward which Jesus makes his way resolutely and where salvation is actually accomplished.[11]

Other considerations, however, reveal that the Matthean sequence is more original, viz., that of "Q" itself. There is not only the progress in the Matthean account from the desert-floor to the pinnacle of the Temple to a high mountain, but also the progress from the word of God as the real bread of life to the protection of life itself by using the word of God, and from the word of God to God himself, whose place and worship the devil in the end would arrogate to himself. Again, the quotations used by Jesus to rebuff the devil appear in Matthew in a simple reverse order of their Old Testament occurrence: Deut 8:3 in Matt 4:4; Deut 6:16 in Matt 4:7; and Deut 6:13 in Matt 4:10, whereas the last two are inverted in the Lucan form of the story and disturb the simplicity. Moreover, in the first two Matthean scenes the devil's challenge begins, "If you are the Son of God," an order that seems more original than the Lucan in which this condition appears in the first and last scenes. Lastly, the Lucan order seems secondary in that it brings Deut 6:16, "You shall not put the Lord your God to the test," into close relation with the distinctively Lucan ending of the episode, "So the devil, having exhausted every sort of temptation, departed from him for a while" (4:13). Thus, coupled with Luke's geographical perspective and interest in Jerusalem, his order suggests that he has changed the sequence of the scenes from the original in "Q."

All efforts to comprehend the function and purpose of these scenes in this preparatory stage of the Lucan Gospel encounter the question about the origin of this material. The fact that the specific details of the testing are unknown to Mark and yet appear in both Matthew and Luke argues for their existence in a preevangelical, non-Marcan source (usually called "Q"). But where did that tradition get the material? The test neither in Matthew nor in Luke gives any indication of anyone witnessing the temptations; the devil confronts Jesus alone. Apart from "Begone, Satan" (Matt 4:10), which not only stands out in contrast to the use of *diabolos* in the rest of the episode, but which almost certainly has been added by the First Evangelist to the "Q" tradition,[12] the only words spoken by Jesus are Old Testament quotations. Because quotations from the Old Testament in so much of the gospel tradition stem from Stage II of that tradition and from the early community's reflection, as it sought to relate the Jesus-story to God's salvific plan, the creation of the temptation scenes has often been attributed to "the work of Christian scribes."[13] Though it is impossible to establish the historicity of these scenes as an external, objective happening—and one is probably looking for the wrong thing in trying to do so—the real question is whether early Christian scribes, having come to venerate Jesus as the Son of God, would have concocted such fantasies about him, fabricating them out of whole cloth. Moreover, the threefold temptation scarcely resembles temptations that Christians themselves would have been experiencing and would have retrojected into the story of the ministry of Jesus itself for moralistic reasons.

It is, of course, possible to read such an episode as an apologetic explanation that arose in the early church to explain why Jesus never performed miracles on his own behalf or why he failed to respond to the sign-seeking challenges of his contemporaries who so confronted him in his ministry. Even if one were to admit a grain of truth in such an apologetic explanation, it is unsatisfactory in the long run. The text, neither in Matthew nor in Luke, ever presents these scenes as an *appearance* of Satan to Jesus, in a sort of ecstatic vision. We are merely told that he was tempted by the devil. In this regard these scenes differ from the vision that Jesus has of Satan's fall in 10:18.

Yet many modern commentators try to root the temptations of Jesus in his real-life experience. J. Dupont and others have sought to root them in the requests made of Jesus during his ministry for signs of his authority. Dupont has tried to steer a middle course between a naive literalist interpretation of the scenes and a parabolic explanation of them, often proposed by others, which he regards as "entièrement fictive." He concludes, "Jesus speaks of an experience which he lived through, but translates it into figurative language, suited to strike the minds of his listeners."[14] For Dupont it would be a "purely spiritual dialogue" that Jesus would have had with the devil.[15] I too would root these experiences of Jesus in his own public life and ministry, but I am not sure that a parabolic explanation of the origin of the scenes is necessarily "entirely fictitious" or that they have to be explained only in terms of a purely spiritual dialogue that would have been somehow translated.

Not only do the three Synoptic evangelists portray Jesus as tempted by the devil, but certain verses in the Johannine Gospel also reflect a tradition about trials that Jesus faced: 6:15 (they come to take him and make him a king), 6:26–34 (the people ask him to give them "this bread always"), 7:1–4 (the reaction of certain Judeans and of his own "brothers" to him). R. E. Brown has studied this aspect of the Fourth Gospel.[16] Moreover, the Epistle to the Hebrews makes much of the fact that Jesus was subject to temptation and weakness (4:15; 5:2; cf. 2:17a). Such references in the New Testament clearly speak of the reality of temptation in Jesus' life, even though they are, unfortunately, unspecified. Brown has noted this and suggests, that "Mt and Lk (or their common source) would be doing no injustice to historic fact if they dramatized such temptations within one scene, and unmasked the real tempter by placing these enticements directly in his mouth."[17] Whether one prefers Dupont's "figurative language" or Brown's "dramatization," or earlier commentators' "parabolic interpretation," one is closer to the correct explanation of the temptation scenes than that of a naive literalism.

These scenes depict temptations coming to Jesus from an external source; they do not suggest that he is dealing with an inner psychological crisis or personal conflict. They symbolize rather in their own way the effect that was made on him by the "trials" of his ministry, the hostility, opposition, and rejection that he encountered continually throughout it. Such trials were real enough in his life and constituted the basis of his personal reaction to them. Should he use his power to react to them? Would he thus prove unfaithful to his Father's call?

Without regarding these stories as *ipsissima verba Iesu,* I should suggest that they may nevertheless be a way that Jesus himself summed up in figurative, dramatic, or parabolic language and expressed his experience to his disciples. These "trials" had been for him a form of diabolic seduction, tempting him to use his power to change stones to bread and to manifest himself with éclat. He would have recounted his experience to his disciples in such a threefold parabolic manner, and thus they would not have had only a fictitious origin.

The basis for such as interpretation of the temptation scenes is found in the Lucan Gospel itself. The Lucan temptation episode ends significantly with the clause, *kai syntelesas panta peirasmon,* "having exhausted every (sort of) temptation," the devil departed (4:13). Thus, the three scenes stand symbolically for all the "temptations" that he had experienced. Jesus as Son has stood the test; he has been tested in his fidelity to his Father and been found faithful.

But there is more: the testing of Jesus by the devil thus invests his trials with a cosmic dimension, as the baptism scene had done for his ministry as a whole. For the temptation of Jesus is not recounted in and for itself; it announces rather the beginning of mighty cosmic struggle that the forces of evil will launch against the realization of God's plan of salvation, which Jesus has come to proclaim and to inaugurate. His experience in this seduction is unique, therefore, as is the ministry for which he has been sent. The cosmic dimension of his confrontation with the devil is further evident in that the scenes allude to three events of the Exodus in which Israel of old was put to the test in the desert. But where Israel of old failed, there Jesus succeeds. The use of the texts from Deuteronomy play upon that contrast and implicitly compare Jesus with Israel of old.[18] Thus Jesus displays his fidelity to his Father, and the temptations portray him confronted by Evil personified and triumphing as heaven's emissary and God's Son (3:22; 3:38).

The scenes have often been said, further, to have a "messianic character."[19] By this is normally meant that the scenes are not recorded in either Matthew or Luke for a hortatory purpose, i.e., to give Christians a model for withstanding diabolic temptation in their moral conduct or lives. This observation has some truth to it, but the character of these scenes should be more accurately expressed, since the title *Christos* or "Messiah" nowhere appears in them, and it is far from evident that the title "Son of God" is meant only in a messianic sense.

The distinctive ending of the Lucan account, "So the devil, having exhausted every sort of temptation, departed from him for a while" (4:13), gives the episode a forward-looking orientation, but it also contains a key to the proper understanding of these scenes. The prepositional phrase *achri kairou,* whether understood simply as "for a while" (as in Acts 13:11), or as some commentators would have it, "until an opportune (or critical) time," is almost universally understood as a reference to 22:3, where Satan is said to enter Judas Iscariot at the beginning of the passion. But the Lucan ending also contains the word *peirasmos,* which has to be related to Jesus' own *peirasmoi,* "trials," in 22:28. Before we discuss further the relation between these verses, however, we must look at the second topic.

II. The Alleged Satan-free Period of Jesus That Follows the Temptation

In an earlier chapter I discussed Hans Conzelmann's view of Lucan salvation history and his threefold division of it.[20] I follow his basic division, though I make some adjustments in detail. Luke does indeed reckon with a divine salvific plan embracing the Period of Israel (from creation to John the Baptist), the Period of Jesus (from John the Baptist to the ascension), and the Period of the Church under Stress (from the ascension to the parousia), the period in which Luke himself writes. One of the adjustments of Conzelmann's view of salvation history that seems called for is his contention that the Period of Jesus is "Satan-free." He bases this view on the devil's departure from Jesus *achri kairou,* "for a while" (4:13) and its relation to 22:3, where Satan enters into Judas at the beginning of the passion. I let Conzelmann speak for himself:

> The Temptation is finished decisively (*panta*), and the devil departs. A question of principle is involved here, for it means that where Jesus is from now on, there Satan is no more—*achri kairou* . . . a period free from Satan is now beginning, an epoch of a special kind in the centre of the whole course of redemptive history.[21]

> When Jesus was alive, was the time of salvation; Satan was far away, it was a time without temptation. . . . Since the Passion, however, Satan is present again and the disciples of Jesus are again subject to temptation (xxii, 36).[22]

> Between the 'Temptation' and the Passion he [Satan] is absent, then he reappears (Luke xxii, 3) and the 'temptations' are back again; but it is not explicitly stated that he is responsible for the Passion. In the preaching about Christ's suffering he is not mentioned either.[23]

> . . . the Church of Luke's time . . . knows that since the Passion of Jesus it is again subject to the attacks of Satan.[24]

Thus Conzelmann regards Luke 4:13 as the end of Jesus'
peirasmos, "temptation, trial," and Luke 22:3 as the reap-
pearance of Satan in the story, not necessarily for Jesus
himself (though the passion is about to begin), but for the
Church under Stress.

The question is, How valid is this view of the Period of
Jesus in Lucan theology? Three difficulties have been sensed
in Conzelmann's presentation of this Satan-free Period of
Jesus: (1) Where is the caesura that divides it from the third
period? (2) Is the Period of Jesus really Satan-free in the
Lucan story? and (3) Has Conzelmann rightly understood
the Lucan use of *peirasmos?*

(1) As for the caesura that divides the Period of Jesus
from the Period of the Church under Stress, Conzelmann
fluctuates. In his discussion of Luke 22:3 and the renewal of
peirasmos, he seems to make the beginning of the passion
the caesura between the periods. Yet elsewhere in his book
he speaks of the Last Supper or the ascension as the caesura.[25] But to make the beginning of the passion the caesura
runs counter to the Lucan view of the salvation achieved by
Jesus. Conzelmann rightly insists that the Period of Jesus is
the center of time (*Die Mitte der Zeit*), the time when salvation is wrought, but then the passion, death, and resurrection of Jesus must all belong to it. This not only corresponds
to Luke's view of Jesus' *exodos,* about which he speaks with
Moses and Elijah and which he must accomplish in Jerusalem (9:31). It also has to be understood of his transit to the
Father through death, burial, resurrection, and exaltation.
Moreover, the caesura has to be set at the ascension, since
this is undoubtedly behind the double reference to it in the
Lucan writings. In Luke 24:50–51 the ascension occurs on
the night of the day of the resurrection, but in Acts 1 it
occurs after an interval of "forty days" (1:3). Say what one

will about this Lucan inconsistency, the double reference to the ascension shows its importance for Luke and makes it the caesura for the second and third periods of salvation history. For, as we have already noted, it provides the background for the question that the disciples pose to the risen Christ in Acts 1:6b, "Lord, is it *at this time* that you are restoring the kingdom to Israel?" The "time" is expressly related to the ascension and reflects a conscious awareness of it as different from what preceded in the Period of Jesus.

(2) Is the Period of Jesus really Satan-free in the Lucan story? No one will contest the relationship between Luke 4:13 and 22:3: the departure of the devil from Jesus "for a while" and the eventual entrance of Satan into Judas at the beginning of the passion. But does that necessarily mean that the interval is Satan-free? The biggest objection to this interpretation comes from the fact that most of the references to Satan, Beelzebul, demons, and evil spirits occur precisely in this section of the Gospel (see pp. 147–51 above). Three of the five passages that mention "Satan" are found between 4:13 and 22:3.

No little part of the problem is the way one views the relation of the demons and evil spirits to Satan or Beelzebul. The latter are the names of the arch-adversary, as we have seen, but how are the demons and evil spirits related to them? In some instances it is not easy to say, since the demons and spirits are mentioned independently, and that may be no more than a protological way of explaining sickness or diseases, as I have already mentioned. In two or three Lucan passages the demons and spirits are clearly related to Satan or Beelzebul. In 13:10–17 (exclusive to Luke) a crippled woman is said at first to "have a spirit of infirmity" but later on to have been bound "by Satan" for eighteen years. Apropos of this passage, Conzelmann recognizes "the connection between Satan and the evil spirits,"[26] but he passes over the problem that this connection causes for his thesis. Again, in 10:17–18 at the return of the Seventy(-two), they tell of the demons that have submitted to them "at the use of your name," and Jesus proceeds to recount having watched Satan fall. Similarly, in Luke 11:15 we read of "Beelzebul, the prince of demons." Here, the least one can say is that the demons are thought of as under Beelzebul's domination.[27] Again, in the explanation of the parable of the seed sowed, "the devil" appears to snatch the word of God from listeners—in effect, to attack them and do them evil.[28] If, then, demons and spirits related to Satan or Beelzebul are afflicting human beings, to what extent is the Period of Jesus really Satan-free?

(3) Has Conzelmann rightly understood what is meant by *peirasmos* in the Lucan story? *Peirasmos* occurs in Luke 4:13; 8:13 (in the explanation of the parable: the seed sowed on rocky soil represents those who hear the word, but they being without root fall away in time of "trial"); 11:4 (at the end of the Our Father: "bring us not into temptation"); 22:28 (at the Last Supper Jesus refers to the apostles as "you who have stood by me in my trials"); 22:40 (at the agony on the Mount of Olives: "Pray that you enter not into temptation"); repeated in 22:46. It also occurs in Acts 20:19, where Paul in his speech to the elders at Miletus tells of the "temptations" that he has suffered because of plots of the Jews. Conzelmann would understand all these references after 4:13 as that which confronts ordinary Christians in the course of life (as *peirasmos* is indeed used in 1 Cor 10:13; Heb 2:18; cf. Jas 1:12). If one withstands it, one gains the crown of life, since one has been tested, purged, and not found wanting. But is this really the sense of *peirasmos* after 4:13 in the Lucan writings?[29] Rather, in every case in which it is used of Christian

disciples it has the pejorative sense of "apostasy." Thus in 8:13, in the explanation of the parable, Luke has deliberately substituted *peirasmos* for the Marcan *thlipsis ē diōgmos*, "tribulation or persecution" (4:17). The Marcan phrase may, indeed, mean ordinary temptation in Christian life, but Luke sharpens it by using *peirasmos* in the sense of apostasy. This is the meaning of the word at the end of the Our Father (11:4) and in the advice given to the disciples on the Mount of Olives (22:40,46); they are to pray against falling away. (This may also be the connotation for Paul in Acts 20:19.)

But the meaning of *peirasmos* in Luke 22:28 is another matter. There Jesus uses it in addressing the apostles at the Last Supper, as he speaks of them as "you who have stood by me in my trials" (*hoi diamemenēkotes met' emou en tois peirasmois mou*). Conzelmann would have us believe that these *peirasmoi* refer to the passion that is now beginning (and indirectly to the share that his followers will still have in the attacks of Satan during the Period of the Church). But *peirasmos* (in the plural!) is here used of Jesus himself, as in 4:13 ("every [sort of] temptation"). Moreover, the participle used of the apostles, *diamemenēkotes*, "having stood by," is in the perfect tense, i.e., denoting an action begun in the past with effects continuing into the present. This would mean that the "trials" to which Jesus alludes in this verse have already been in progress during the period of his ministry. Thus *peirasmoi* reflects the *panta peirasmon* of 4:13, and it is the basis for the parabolic, figurative, or dramatic interpretation of the temptation scenes themselves (see pp. 156–57 above). They are the "trials" that confronted Jesus in his ministry, the hostility, opposition, and rejection that he experienced. They became for him a diabolic seduction to use his power on his own behalf.

At his baptism Jesus is presented as a heaven-sent

agent, indeed God's Son (reiterated in the genealogy), but the temptation scenes stress a secondary, but equally programmatic aspect of the mission that he is about to undertake. They reveal the adversarial aspect of that mission and its cosmic dimensions. When Satan enters Judas (22:3), that is the time when "the hour and the power of darkness" (22:53) descend upon him in a new sense.

Moreover, in the prayer of Jesus on the Mount of Olives, "Please, Father, take this cup away from me," he continues, "Yet not my will, but yours be done!" (22:42). That prayer is not for strength against diabolic temptation, but for courage to face the destiny that is his. Jesus' experience is presented by Luke as unique; it includes the opposition, hostility, and rejection during his ministry—part of the role that he was to play in the realization of the Father's plan of salvation. But its climax comes with his passion and death. Though there is no direct attack of the devil on Jesus between 4:13 and 22:3, when he enters Judas, the latter verse reveals how Satan's attack is now to be renewed. It will be aimed at him through one of his own; Satan-inspired Judas will betray him and turn him over to his enemies. This becomes in reality not a renewed temptation, but a confrontation now summed up as "the hour and the power of darkness" (22:53).

But how is all this related to the fall of Satan in 10:18? To that question we may now turn.

III.   Jesus' Comment about Satan's Fall in Luke 10:17–20

As enigmatic as the temptation scenes in Luke 4 are, the comment of Jesus about Satan's fall in Luke 10 is not less so. It reads:

¹⁷The seventy(-two) returned full of joy and reported, "Lord, with the use of your name even the demons submit to us!" ¹⁸Jesus said to them, "I was watching Satan fall, like lightning, from heaven. ¹⁹See, I have given you authority to tread upon serpents and scorpions, and over all the power of the Enemy; and nothing shall harm you at all. ²⁰So do not rejoice at this that spirits submit to you; rather, rejoice that your names stand written in heaven!"

Jesus' threefold comment is recorded as his reaction to what the seventy(-two) disciples report about the success of their mission.

In this exclusively Lucan passage,³⁰ v. 17 is transitional and of Lucan composition, but it is a matter of debate whether v. 18, Jesus' comment on Satan's fall, was originally uttered in conjunction with vv. 19–20.³¹ Even if one admits with R. Bultmann that the original sense of v. 18 has been irretrievably lost to us,³² the strangeness of the saying may be one of the best reasons for ascribing it to Jesus himself. W. G. Kümmel has attributed it to "the oldest tradition,"³³ and J. Jeremias argues from the retention of *satanas* to its primitive formulation.³⁴ In any case, it is now found on the lips of Jesus at a crucial place in the Lucan Gospel. Being part of the episodes about Jesus sending out his followers to preach and heal during his ministry, it raises an important question as to how it functions in the Lucan story, and indeed in Luke's treatment of Satan.

What is the sense of Jesus' comment in general?³⁵ I have translated the verse, "I was watching Satan fall, like lightning, from heaven," intending that as a version of the generally accepted word-order or of that of P⁷⁵. Others, however, have rendered the verse thus: "I was watching Satan fall like lightning-from-heaven." Such a translation is supposed to describe Satan, the adversarial functionary of the heavenly court, deposed from his task there, and come to wreak havoc on earth. In such an interpretation Jesus' remark would express a warning about Satan's influence on human beings on earth.[36] He would be correcting the premature joy of the disciples who have returned, and his further remarks in vv. 19–20 would reassure them that he is now giving them authority over "all the power of the Enemy."

This interpretation, however, is not likely, because it does not explain the use of the participle *pesonta*, "falling," or its punctiliar aorist tense. Why should Satan be said to have "fallen" from heaven to attack human beings or to make mischief on earth? A. Plummer once remarked, "The point is not that the devil has come down to work mischief on earth, but that his power to work mischief is broken."[37] For this reason, many commentators prefer to see in Jesus' comment a cry of victory over the definitive defeat of Satan and the evil that he represents. It thus sums up in figurative language the outcome of the cosmic struggle that the programmatic scenes of temptation foreshadowed but did not express in terms of its resolution. The definitive outcome of the cosmic struggle will take place only with Jesus' passion, death, and resurrection, when "the hour and the power of darkness" (22:53) will have closed in upon him. But he already sees proleptically in the success of the disciples' mission the "fall" of Satan and all that he stands for.

To what kind of a vision does the verse refer? Two problems confront us in trying to answer that question. First, the meaning of the imperfect *etheōroun*. Does it mean "I was watching" or simply "I saw"? Normally, the imperfect would express continuous past action, "I was watching." However, the verb *theōrein* is used only in the present and the imperfect tenses, with *theasthai* serving as a substitute for its other tenses.[38] Hence some interpreters query the continuous past meaning and prefer to translate the imperfect simply as "I saw." In either case, the meaning of Jesus' comment is little affected.

Second, various labels have been put on the vision. Does it refer to a vision of the preexistent Jesus? To an ecstatic vision enjoyed by Jesus during his ministry? Or does it express a symbolic vision? As a vision of the preexistent Jesus, it would refer to a scene like that of Gen 6:1–4 (about the sons of God and the Nephilim) or that of Isa 14:12 (with its reference to Lucifer in the Latin Vulgate, "fallen from heaven"). Cf. Jude 6. Such an interpretation of the vision implied in Jesus' comment, however, is not probable since Luke never reckons with the preexistence of Jesus (unlike the Fourth Evangelist). Does the comment refer to an ecstatic vision enjoyed by Jesus during his ministry? *Per se* this is not impossible. W. G. Kümmel once espoused this interpretation: "The wording of the saying . . . suggests a visionary experience more strongly than a figure of speech."[39] More recently, U. B. Müller has argued in favor of it: a vision experienced by Jesus even while he was yet associated with John the Baptist; it would have been the cause of his own independent ministry of proclaiming the kingdom of God, a visionary call similar to that of the prophets of old (Isaiah, Jeremiah, Ezekiel, or Amos). As a result, Jesus' proclamation of the eschatological kingship of God would bring about the overthrow of Satan.[40] Even more recently, H. Merklein has argued that Jesus' comment in Luke 10:18 refers not only to a visionary experience, but to a revelation, maintaining that the most logical *Sitz im Leben* for it was the time that Jesus spent in the desert after his baptism and before he began his public ministry.[41] Indeed, the temptation scenes in 4:2–13 would only be a parallel description of the vision mentioned in 10:18. Merklein tends to relate to the same desert experience a revelation about Jesus' relation to God as *abba* as well as the revelation about the eschatological defeat of Satan.

Though the interpretation of Luke 10:18 as an ecstatic vision is not impossible, it tends to put too much stress on the verb *etheōroun*. Even though I have admitted the reality of temptation in the life of Jesus, I hesitate to see so specific a connection between the temptation scenes and this vision in 10:18. This vision is recounted only by Luke, and to relate it to the temptations (understood as in the "Q" tradition) and then to make them the expression of the *basic* visionary call in the ministry of Jesus, which neither Mark nor John knows, seems to be a case of overinterpretation. One has to reckon with the exclusive occurrence of this comment of Jesus in the Lucan Gospel, where it functions well in Luke's presentation of the double sending-out of apostles and disciples. Hence the interpretative solution ought to be sought in the thrust of the Lucan Gospel rather than in the life of Jesus itself.

For this reason I prefer the symbolic interpretation of the vision in 10:18. In the Lucan story it serves as a comment on the mission of the Twelve and especially of the Seventy(-two), summing up the effects of that mission: his watching reveals how their activity expressed victory over Satan's influence. That vision may be called "proleptic," in that it would refer to the eschatological defeat of evil; it may also be called "apocalyptic," in that the description uses apocalyptic stage-props to express that definitive defeat brought about by the power and authority given by Jesus to these followers. It may be called "symbolic," in that it understands the verb *etheōroun* in the sense of "I saw it coming" or "I knew all along."

Luke 10:18, then, proleptically depicts the definitive defeat of Satan, which was only programmatically implied in the temptation scenes of Luke 4. There, though the devil may have exhausted "every (sort of) temptation" in his testing of Jesus, who would prove himself loyal to his Father in the ministry about to be inaugurated, the definitive overthrow of the devil is not recounted. Yet that *peirasmos* of 4:13 is rooted in the "trials" (*peirasmoi,* 22:28) experienced in the course of Jesus' ministry. During them his followers loyally stood by him (22:28), and the vision of 10:18 intimates that the power and authority that he has passed on to them has been proleptically accomplishing its purpose. The cosmic arch-adversary is to be brought to defeat in his own ministry and in that of his followers.

Finally, the primary role of the Lucan Jesus is not expressed in such a defeat of Satan. There is a tendency on the part of some commentators to think that Jesus' ministry is mainly aimed at the defeat of Satan's "kingdom" (11:18). This is to misplace the emphasis, for it passes too quickly over what the Lucan Jesus expressly affirms as the goal of his mission: after a summary statement about his cures in Capernaum, the people try to prevent him from moving on, and he announces to them, "I must proclaim the kingdom of God in other towns as well, for that is what I was sent for" (4:43). In other words, the Lucan Jesus was above all conscious of his obligation to proclaim the kingdom of God and to set people free from all sorts of evil. In a secondary way, that may imply the freeing of them from their bondage to protological thinking about Satan and his kingdom. Satan and demons play a role in the Lucan story of Jesus, but in interpreting it one must not let a secondary theme dominate a primary emphasis: Jesus' role in proclaiming the kingdom of God.

Notes

1 See J. Jeremias, *Die Sprache,* 187–88. Jeremias notes that, whereas Luke normally substitutes common Greek terms for Semitic expressions in his Marcan source, he retains Semitic terms like *satanas* "in a consciously archaizing mode of speech and in dependence on tradition," when such a term is found in his private source. Thus, *satanas* (Mark 4:15) becomes *ho diabolos* (Luke 8:12), even though Luke writes *satanas* in Acts 5:3; 28:16, where the question of sources is debatable. Moreover, Luke retains *ho satanas* in 11:18, which is probably derived from "Q"; cf. Matt 12:26. But Mark 3:26 complicates the matter; see n. 3 below.

2 That *satanas* is ultimately derived from a pre-Christian Palestinian Jewish tradition can be seen from 11QPs^a 19:15 (*'l tšlṭ by śṭn,* "let not Satan rule over me"); 4Q504 1–2 iv 12. Cf. the use of *Maśṭēmāh,* a term developed from Hebrew *śāṭān,* in Qumran literature (1QS 3:23; 1QM 13:4,11; CD 16:5; 4Q511 152:3[?]); cf. *Jub.* 17:16; 23:12; 48:2–3.

3 Mark 3:22–27 also has a form of this episode about the Beelzebul controversy, but Luke chose to omit that episode, when he returned to the Marcan order of material after his Little Interpolation (6:20–8:3); his form of the controversy in chap. 11 is clearly the counterpart of the Matthean— hence from "Q."

4 For further details, see *Luke,* 920. The name appears in the Greek Old Testament only in Symmachus (4 Kgdms 1:2). Cf. G. Schwarz, *"Und Jesus sprach": Untersuchungen zur aramäischen Urgestalt der Worte Jesu* (2d ed.; BWANT 118; Stuttgart: Kohlhammer, 1987) 10.

5 It is so entitled in A. Huck and H. Lietzmann, *Synopsis of the First Three Gospels* (Oxford: Blackwell, 1959)

102. Cf. B. H. Throckmorton, *Gospel Parallels* (Camden, NJ/London: Nelson, 1967) 92.

⁶ See further B. Noack, *Satanás und Sotería: Untersuchungen zur neutestamentlichen Dämonologie* (Copenhagen: Gad, 1948). B. Gerhardsson, *The Testing of God's Son (Matt 4:1–11 & Par): An Analysis of an Early Christian Midrash* (ConB NT ser. 2; Lund: Gleerup, 1966). R. Schnackenburg, "Versuchung Jesu," *LTK* 10 (1965) 747–48. S. L. Johnson, "The Temptation of Christ," *BSac* 123 (1966) 342–52. J. Dupont, *Les tentations de Jésus au désert* (StudNeot, Studia 4; Bruges: Desclée de Brouwer, 1968). P. Pokorný, "The Temptation Stories and Their Intention," *NTS* 20 (1973–74) 115–27. W. Wilkens, "Die Versuchungsgeschichte Luk. 4,1–13 und die Komposition des Evangeliums," *TZ* 30 (1974) 262–72. H. Mahnke, *Die Versuchungsgeschichte im Rahmen der synoptischen Evangelien: Ein Beitrag zur frühen Christologie* (BBET 9; Frankfurt am M.: P. Lang, 1978). D. Zeller, "Die Versuchungen Jesu in der Logienquelle," *TTZ* 89 (1980) 61–73. A. Fuchs, "Versuchung Jesu," *SNTU* 9 (1984) 95–159.

⁷ See S. Brown, *Apostasy and Perseverance in the Theology of Luke* (AnBib 36; Rome: Biblical Institute, 1969) 17–18.

⁸ *Gospel according to S. Luke,* 110.

⁹ *Das Evangelium nach Lukas,* 63.

¹⁰ "The Lukan Temptation Narrative," *JTS* 17 (1966) 71. Verses 14–15 refer to the manna and quails; vv. 19–20, to the golden image; and vv. 32–33, to the story of Massah.

¹¹ See *Luke,* 164–71.

¹² *Pace* S. Brown (*Apostasy* [n. 7 above], 18 n. 58), who thinks that because the phrase is already in Mark 8:33, *hypage, satana* could also have been in "Q."

¹³ See R. Bultmann, *HST,* 254–56.

¹⁴ *Les tentations* (n. 6 above), 128.

[15] Ibid., 129; cf. 125 n. 22.

[16] See "Incidents that Are Units in the Synoptic Gospels but Dispersed in St. John," *CBQ* 23 (1961) 143–60, esp. 152–55. Cf. his *The Gospel According to John* (AB 29, 29a; Garden City, NY: Doubleday, 1966–70) 308.

[17] "Incidents" (n. 16 above), 155.

[18] For further details of this comparison, see *Luke,* 511–12.

[19] See, e.g., H. Riesenfeld, "Le caractère messianique de la tentation au désert," *La venue du Messie* (RechBib 6; Bruges: Desclée de Brouwer, 1962) 51–63. J. A. Kirk, "The Messianic Role of Jesus and the Temptation Narrative: A Contemporary Perspective," *EvQ* 58 (1972) 91–102.

[20] See pp. 61–63 above.

[21] *Theology,* 28.

[22] Ibid., 16.

[23] Ibid., 156.

[24] Ibid., 188 n. 4.

[25] Ibid., 13, 16, 203–4. Cf. W. C. Robinson, Jr., *Der Weg des Herrn: Studien zur Geschichte und Eschatologie im Lukas-Evangelium: Ein Gespräch mit Hans Conzelmann* (TF 36; Hamburg-Bergstedt: H. Reich, 1964) 23. S. Brown, *Apostasy* (n. 7 above) 12. G. Baumbach, *Das Verständnis des Bösen in den synoptischen Evangelien* (Theologische Arbeiten 19; Berlin: Evangelische Verlagsanstalt, 1963) 206.

[26] *Theology,* 157. He writes: "Therefore passages such as Luke xi, 17–23 do not mean that there is a constant conflict with Satan during Jesus' ministry; they have a symbolic meaning and are meant primarily to be a comfort to the Church of Luke's time, which knows that since the Passion of Jesus it is again subject to the attacks of Satan" (p. 188 n. 4). That this passage has reference solely to the "Church of Luke's time" is not immediately apparent, for one must ask

why Luke, who has composed a sequel about this church, relates this event to the ministry of Jesus.

[27] See G. Baumbach, *Das Verständnis* (n. 25 above) 182–83; cf. S. Brown, *Apostasy* (n. 7 above), 6.

[28] See E. E. Ellis, *Gospel of Luke*, 248 n. 3.

[29] See S. Brown, *Apostasy* (n. 7 above), 12–19.

[30] Some commentators think that there is an echo of this tradition in John 12:31.

[31] I. H. Marshall (*Gospel of Luke*, 427–28) regards vv. 17–20 as originally part of "Q," which Matthew has chosen to omit. But his suggestion encounters the difficulty of departing from the common understanding of "Q," which normally stands for material common to Matthew and Luke and absent from Mark.

Moreover, the *idou* of v. 19 may serve as a sign that vv. 19–20 were a unit, not originally joined to v. 18. See P. Grelot, "Etude critique de Luc 10,19," *RSR* 69 (1981) 87–100, esp. 88.

[32] *HST*, 158.

[33] *Promise and Fulfilment: The Eschatological Message of Jesus* (SBT 23; Naperville, Il: Allenson; London: SCM, 1957) 114.

[34] *Die Sprache*, 187–89.

[35] A prior question may concern the textual transmission of the verse. The preferred reading in the critical text of the New Testament is: *etheōroun ton satanan hōs astrapēn ek tou ouranou pesonta,* lit., "I was watching Satan like lightning from heaven falling." But in ms. B "from heaven" precedes "like lightning," whereas in P[75] "from heaven" follows the participle *pesonta.*

[36] See F. Spitta, "Der Satan als Blitz," *ZNW* 9 (1908) 160–63. S. W. Lewis, " 'I Beheld Satan Fall as Lightning from Heaven' (Luke x. 18)," *ExpTim* 25 (1913–14) 232–33.

[37] *Gospel according to S. Luke,* 278.

[38] BDF § 101; BDR § 101.32.

[39] *Promise and Fulfilment* (n. 33 above), 114.

[40] "Vision und Botschaft: Erwägungen zur prophetischen Struktur der Verkündigung Jesu," *ZTK* 74 (1977) 416–48, esp. 426–29.

[41] *Jesu Botschaft von der Gottesherrschaft* (SBS 111; Stuttgart: Katholisches Bibelwerk, 1983) 59–62.

7

The Jewish People and the Mosaic Law in Luke-Acts

If Luke has composed his Gospel and Acts with a specific view of salvation history divided into three periods,[1] what does he consider the role of the Mosaic law and the people of Israel to be in that plan of salvation? In particular, how are the Mosaic law and Israel related to the part of the plan inaugurated by the ministry, death, and resurrection of Jesus Christ?

This problem is not peculiarly Lucan, since other New Testament writers have also wrestled with it: What is the place of Israel in God's salvific plan, if he has intervened in a new way in human history through the Christ-event? Paul the Apostle, the evangelists Matthew and John, and the author of the Epistle to the Hebrews are other writers who have also wrestled with this problem, in one way or another.

Recent discussions of the law and the Jewish people in Luke-Acts, however, have brought to light various aspects of this problem in the Lucan view of salvation history.[2] Indeed, the problem is complex, and some ideas about it move in almost opposite directions. From this it is clear that the answer to the problem in the Lucan writings is not simple. It merits, then, some further attention. I shall deal with it under two headings: (1) Luke's view of the Mosaic Law; and (2) Luke's view of Israel or the Jewish people.

I.   Luke's View of the Mosaic Law

The Period of Israel, though it stretches from creation to the ministry of John the Baptist, is simply described in Luke 16:16 as "up until John it was the law and the prophets." After that description, the Lucan Jesus continues, "From that time on the kingdom of God is being preached." The implication in such a description of the two periods is that what was to be accomplished by Jesus' kingdom-preaching, new though it was, was somehow being attained through the law and the prophets before the kingdom-preaching began. If we may label what was being accomplished by Jesus as "salvation" and admit that it was somehow available to those who were guided by the law and the prophets, what happened to it, once the kingdom-preaching was begun?

In a sense, the Mosaic law continues for Luke to be a valid norm of human conduct in all three periods of salvation history and also a means of identifying God's people. This is seen in three ways.

(1) There is the *normative* sense of the law. In the infancy narrative the Lucan Gospel offers glimpses of human conduct in the Period of Israel when the law of Moses functions as its norm. The principal characters, Zechariah and Elizabeth, Mary and Joseph, Simeon and Anna are "upright in God's sight and living blamelessly according to all the commandments and requirements of the Lord" (1:6; cf. 1:28c,64c; 2:4,25,36,41). "All that was required by the law" is either predicated of them explicitly (2:39) or implied in the text. Indeed, Jesus himself from his childhood is portrayed living according to it, and not merely as an expression of supererogatory piety. These persons conduct themselves "according to the law of Moses" (2:22) or "according to what is prescribed in the law of the Lord" (2:24; cf. 2:23,27,39). Whether Luke uses *nomos,* "law," or *entolē,* command-

ment," or even the broader term *ethos,* "custom,"[3] the normative character of what is attributed either to Moses or to the Lord is thus clear in the lives of such Palestinian Jews. So Luke reckons with the validity of the Mosaic law in human conduct in the Period of Israel.

In the Period of Jesus the normative character of this law is at times affirmed by Jesus himself. When he is confronted by a lawyer who queries, "Teacher, what am I to do to inherit eternal life?" he answers, "What is written in the law? How do you read it?" And the lawyer answers, "You must love the Lord your God with all you heart, with all your soul, with all your might, and with all your mind; and you must love your neighbor as yourself." Then Jesus says to him, "You have answered correctly; do this and you shall live" (10:25–28).[4] Thus a classic summary of the whole law in two verses, using both Deut 6:5 and Lev 19:18, is acknowledged by the Lucan Jesus as a guide for human conduct in order that one may "inherit eternal life."

The validity of the same law is further couched in a hyperbolic statement found in an isolated verse of Luke 16. Its context is problematic. Chapter 16 of the Lucan Gospel is a peculiar construction in that it has two parables separated by a string of sayings. Verses 1–13 contain the parable of the dishonest manager and three applications that allegorize details of the parable; at the end of the chapter is found the other parable, of the rich man and Lazarus (vv. 19–31). The bloc of sayings between these parables follows on the third allegorization of the parable of the dishonest manager that reads, "You cannot serve both God and mammon" (16:13).[5] After that, the sayings run as follows:

> [14]Listening to all this were avaricious Pharisees who sneered at him. [15]So he said to them, "You are the ones who are always justifying your position in the sight of

> human beings; but God knows what is in your hearts.
> For what is of highest human value is an abomination in
> God's sight. [16]Up until John it was the law and the
> prophets; from that time on the kingdom of God is being
> preached, and everyone is pressed to enter it. [17]But it is
> easier for the sky and the earth to pass away than for one
> stroke of a letter of the law to drop out. [18]Anyone who
> divorces his wife and marries another woman commits
> adultery; and anyone who marries a woman divorced
> from her husband commits adultery."

Then follows the parable of the rich man and Lazarus. In this
bloc of sayings I am above all interested in v. 17, "It is easier
for the sky and the earth to pass away than for one stroke of
a letter of the law to drop out." With such a hyperbolic
comparison the Lucan Jesus affirms the validity of the Mosaic law; then his teaching on divorce and remarriage follows
in v. 18. The only aspect of his utterance on the latter subject
that concerns us now is whether there is really a connection
between v. 17 and v. 18, between the statement about the
validity of the law and the prohibition of divorce.

The similarity of wording in Jesus' utterance on divorce
here with Matt 5:32 makes it certain that Luke is using the
form of it that comes from the source "Q."[6] The lengthy
doublet in the Matthean Gospel (19:1–12) is a redactional
form of Mark 10:1–12, no counterpart of which is found in
the Lucan Gospel. Matthew has made the "Q" form of the
utterance part of his six antitheses in the sermon on the
mount (5:32). There he deliberately compares older legal
regulations with his own teaching: "You have heard it said to
the people of old . . . , but I say to you . . ." In that
Matthean setting the "Q" form of the utterance on divorce is
used as a corrective of the Old Testament tolerance of divorce. Because of that setting in the Matthean Gospel, some

interpreters would see Luke's use of the same utterance as an example of Mosaic legislation being corrected, i.e., a correction of the law just referred to in v. 17.[7]

But the question is whether that utterance of Jesus is intended by Luke as one challenging the law. There are those who argue that the three sayings of Jesus in vv. 16–18 represent a pre-Lucan unit.[8] Verses 16 and 17 clearly have to do with the Mosaic law: "Up until John it was the law and the prophets . . . it is easier for the sky and the earth to pass away than for one stroke of a letter of the law to drop out." But is it clear that the utterance on divorce (v. 18) is intended as related to that law, or even as a correction of it? The absolute form of the prohibition found here on Jesus' lips is hardly an example of Mosaic legislation, since the latter otherwise tolerated divorce. The absolute prohibition used here may go contrary to that law, but is it clearly intended as a correction of the law itself—as it is, indeed, in the Matthean sermon on the mount?

When all is said and done, there is no certainty that the sayings separating the two parables (vv. 1–13 and 19–31) were ever a pre-Lucan unit. Moreover, when one considers these sayings along with the immediately preceding bloc of three allegorizations of the first parable—allegorizations that were scarcely a unit in the pre-Lucan tradition[9]—one realizes how disparate and isolated the intervening sayings in this chapter really are. Again, whereas two of the allegorizations (vv. 8b–9 and 10–12) and the sayings about the avaricious Pharisees (vv. 14–15) have no counterparts in the other Synoptics (being exclusively Lucan), the two sayings about the law (vv. 16–17) and that about divorce (v. 18) have parallels in Matthew (being "Q" material), but they are found in completely different contexts in the Matthean Gospel (11:12–13; 5:18; 5:32). To me this means that Luke has made use of isolated utterances of Jesus, fashioning them into a loose unit that does not hang well together. The upshot is that there is no clear connection between Jesus' utterance on divorce in v. 18 and the two preceding sayings about the law and its validity in vv. 16–17. Hence it is far from clear that Luke is citing Jesus on the topic of divorce as an example of his "challenging" the Mosaic law, as S. G. Wilson has tried to put it. Unlike the Matthean setting, where the utterance forms part of six antitheses and is deliberately meant to be a corrective of the regulation of old, there is not a hint of such "a challenge to the authority" of the Mosaic ruling in the Lucan form.[10] Such a challenge would be ill-suited to the Lucan context, which has just made a hyperbolic statement about the validity of the Mosaic law. Yet the force of the sayings is not to be missed: the law of Moses is valid, but divorce is prohibited.[11]

At the end of the same chapter the Lucan Jesus recounts the parable of the rich man and Lazarus (vv. 19–31). Toward its conclusion the rich man begs Father Abraham to send Lazarus to warn his five brothers about their fate after death, unless they repent. Abraham replies, "They have Moses and the prophets; let them listen to them" (16:29; cf. v. 31). Here, not only the Mosaic law, but even the teaching of Old Testament prophets is cited as normative for Palestinian Jewish conduct.

Again, when the Lucan Jesus cures the lepers (one leper in 5:12–16 and ten in 17:11–19), he instructs them to go and "show yourselves to the priest(s) and make an offering for your purification, as Moses prescribed" (5:14; cfr. 17:14). Jesus thus enjoins on Jews and a Samaritan the execution of a specific command set forth in Lev 13:49, clearly regarding it as normative of conduct.

All these instances drawn from the Lucan Gospel reveal

the normative character of the Mosaic Law precisely in the Period of Jesus.

(2) The Lucan Jesus refers at times to "the law and the prophets" in a *predictive* sense.[12] For Luke makes use of an argument that has been called "proof from prophecy."[13] Sometimes he cites the Old Testament in the genuine sense of Old Testament prophecy, i.e., as an utterance of a spokesman of God. But at times he understands Old Testament passages, whether from the law, the prophets, or even the psalms, as predictive—as foretelling something to come in the divine order of things. This sense of the law and the prophets occurs especially in Luke's christological use of the Old Testament. Thus in the Emmaus incident, when the risen Christ converses with Cleopas and his companion on the road, he begins "with Moses and all the prophets and interprets for them what pertains to himself in every part of Scripture" (24:27). Again, later on when Christ appears to the Eleven and others in Jerusalem, he says, "All that was written about me in the law of Moses, in the Prophets, and in the Psalms must see fulfillment" (24:44). The same idea is implied in the conversation of Jesus with Moses and Elijah at his transfiguration: "they appeared in glory and were speaking of his departure, the one that he was to complete in Jerusalem" (9:31). Though one may be hard pressed to figure out what passages Luke has in mind in such christological use of the Old Testament, one can hardly deny the predictive nuance that he gives to "the law and the prophets" in the passages cited. Thus the Lucan Jesus is made to appeal to the Mosaic law not only in a normative sense, but also in a predictive sense.

(3) Another aspect of Jesus' attitude toward the Mosaic law may be termed *supplemental,*[14] i.e., that the law is being somehow supplemented. This is seen in the caesura-verse of

Luke 16:16, where Jesus affirms, "Up until John it was the law and the prophets; from that time on the kingdom of God is being preached, and everyone is pressed to enter it." Here Jesus' kingdom-preaching is at least seen as following on the law and the prophets. The exegetical problem in the verse is to decide whether that preaching is meant as a replacement of the law and the prophets or as a supplement to them. The verse has often been understood as though the kingdom-preaching were a replacement of the law.[15] It has been compared with the Pauline statement, "Christ is the end of the law" (Rom 10:4; cf. 1 Cor 10:11c). However, that would be to use a Pauline notion—and a highly contested one at that[16]—to interpret a Lucan problem. As we shall see, the sense of Luke 16:16b has to be that Jesus' kingdom-preaching is a supplement to the law and the prophets of the Period of Israel. Now in the Period of Jesus, when he appears in the Lucan Gospel as the kingdom-preacher par excellence, he views the law and the prophets as normative, and his preaching of the kingdom is supplemental to it. What is so viewed here will be even more evident in the Period of the Church under Stress. But before we come to that, another episode in the ministry of Jesus brings out the supplemental sense of the law.

In the episode of the rich young magistrate who comes to Jesus with a question, the Lucan form of the story runs as follows (18:18–25):

> [18]Once a magistrate put this question to him, "Good Teacher, what must I do to inherit eternal life?" [19]Jesus said to him, "Why do you address me as good? No one is good except God alone. [20]You know the commandments, 'You shall not commit adultery; you shall not murder; you shall not steal; you shall not bear false witness; honor your father and mother.' " [21]And he re-

plied, "I have observed all these since I was a youth."22
When Jesus heard this, he said to him, "For you then
one thing is missing: Sell all that you have, distribute it
to the poor, and you shall have treasure in heaven. Then
come, follow me!" 23When he heard this, he became
very sad; for he was extremely rich. 24When Jesus saw
him becoming sad, he said, "How hard it is for those
who have money to enter the kingdom of God! 25It is
easier for a camel to pass through the eye of a needle
than for a rich man to enter the kingdom of God."

The contrast between the commandments of the Decalogue
and Jesus' kingdom-preaching stands out. Something more
than allegiance to Moses and all the prophets is being demanded of this Palestinian Jewish magistrate; the supplement is seen in a demand of the kingdom-preacher himself.17

Does the Lucan Jesus, however, display a critical attitude toward the Mosaic law? This question is asked, not only
in light of the famous antitheses of the Matthean sermon on
the mount (Matt 5:21–48), but also because of several incidents in the Lucan Gospel where Jesus seems to teach something different or enters into dispute with Palestinian leaders
(e.g., about sabbath observance). S. G. Wilson in his treatment of the law in Luke's Gospel has a whole section in
which he depicts the Lucan Jesus "challenging the law." He
believes that there are sayings which "abrogate or alter the
demands of the law either directly or by implication."18 Wilson begins his discussion by citing the sabbath controversies
in chap. 6 (vv. 1–5 and 6–11). In the first, the disciples have
been plucking ears of grain, and some of the Pharisees object to their conduct, "Why do you do what is prohibited on
the sabbath?" Jesus defends his followers by citing the Old
Testament incident of what David did when he and his men

were hungry: how he took the presentation loaves and they ate them, even though no one but the priests were permitted to eat such bread (1 Sam 21:1–6; cf. Lev 24:8–9). Jesus ends by saying, "The Son of Man is lord of the sabbath." Now Wilson argues, "If the sabbath is subordinate to Jesus so is the law."[19]

One has, however, to take the Lucan story as it is. The plucking of ears of grain from a neighbor's field was permitted by Deut 23:26, provided that one did not put a sickle to the standing grain. Hence plucking itself was not a violation of the Mosaic law. What the Pharisees criticize is such activity on the sabbath. Though Exod 34:21 explicitly enjoins sabbath-rest at ploughing time and harvest time, it was the later fence built around the law by Pharisaic oral tradition that explained "plucking" as a form of "reaping" (*m. Sabb.* 7:2; cf. *y. Sabb.* 7.9b; Str-B 1. 617). So, in defending his followers and in declaring himself lord of the sabbath, Jesus is not expressly contravening the Mosaic law, but only a certain interpretation of it. Even if he cites an Old Testament example as a precedent, his justification of his followers' activity does not imply a contravention of the Torah as such.

Similarly in the second episode in chap. 6, when Jesus in a synagogue cures the stunted right hand of a man on the sabbath (vv. 6–11), his activity is not depicted as a refusal to recognize the normative value of the third commandment, "Remember the sabbath, to keep it holy" (Exod 20:8). In redacting the text of the episode, Luke introduces Jesus asking a question, "Let me ask you." The question itself enshrines Jesus' own pronouncement: "Is it allowed on the sabbath to do good to people or to do harm, to save a life or do away with it?" (6:9). Then, as lord of the sabbath, he bids the man stretch forth his hand. That command, however, does not mean that the Lucan Jesus has abrogated the remembrance of the sabbath or that he regards the obligation to keep it holy as no longer normative for human conduct. He reacts rather against a certain understanding of the sabbath.

In each of these episodes Luke has scarcely portrayed Jesus as critical of the Mosaic law, even if he clearly presents him as differing with a current interpretation of it. The same has to be said for his cure of the crippled woman (13:10–17) and of the man with dropsy (14:1–6).[20] Thus, for the Period of Jesus one must say that Luke regards the Mosaic Law as definitely normative, even though the kingdom is now being preached as a supplement to it.

As for the Period of the Church the normative character of the law of Moses is further recognized. In Acts Luke uses the word *nomos,* "law," seventeen times, mostly in the story about Stephen or in the account of Paul's ministry.

The early Christian community of Jerusalem is portrayed in Acts as living, in effect, in accordance with the law. Though Peter and others preach Jesus as the Messiah and announce his message, they continue to attend the Temple (2:46) and take part in its hours of prayer (3:1). Even Peter's initial reaction to the vision accorded him in the Cornelius incident is that of a Jew guided by levitical regulations: "Lord, I have never eaten anything common or unclean" (10:14; cf. Lev 11:4–8,10–20,23–43). Further, Stephen may be *charged* with having spoken against the law (6:13), but he it is who accuses his opponents of not keeping the law (7:35). Likewise, Paul, often charged with teaching "all the Jews who are among the Gentiles to forsake Moses, telling them not to circumcise their children or observe the customs" (21:21), is nonetheless portrayed as a Jew faithful to the law:[21] he has Timothy circumcised (16:3); he carries out a (Nazirite) vow (18:18) and sees to his own purification and pays the expenses of four men under a similar vow (21:23–24).[22] Paul is further depicted claiming that he was educated at the feet of Gamaliel (22:3–4) and attended at the time of his conversion by Ananias, "a devout man according to the law" (22:12).[23]

In all these references to the "law" in Acts, *nomos* clearly means "the law given to Israel on Sinai . . . the law of Israel."[24] It is not only that by which Israel was to find salvation, but it is also "the mark of distinction between Jews and non-Jews."[25] It is not a law of human origin, but was "promulgated by angels" (7:53) and filled with "living oracles" (7:38). Indeed, for Christians who have come to faith in Jesus Christ from Judaism, that law is still regarded as normative and as a mark of their identity as God's people—of their solidarity with the Israel of old. But to admit that brings me close to the topic of part II of this chapter. Before I turn to it, however, there is one last aspect of the law in the Lucan writings that calls for comment.

In the episode of Paul's preaching to the Jews in the synagogue of Antioch in Pisidia there is a statement about justification and the law that calls for clarification. After having mentioned how the "holy and sure blessings of David" have come through Jesus Christ whom God has raised from the dead, Paul continues:

> Therefore, let it be known to you, brethren, that through this man [Jesus] forgiveness of sins is proclaimed to you, and by him everyone who believes is acquitted (*dikaioutai*) of everything, of which you could not be acquitted by the law of Moses (13:38–39).

As we have already seen, this is the only place in Acts where Luke portrays Paul preaching justification by faith. He has, however, recast the Pauline teaching and subordinates "justification" to "forgiveness of sins," a mode that is absent from Paul's undisputed letters.[26] The Lucan formulation not only dulls the Pauline precision of justification in the forensic sense, but it seems to declare that there is a form of forgiveness of sins that the Mosaic law could not produce, but which faith in Christ Jesus does now provide. The relative pronoun *hōn* is best referred to the pronominal *pantōn* as its antecedent, "all things which. . . ." The Lucan sense would then be: Through Jesus Christ "forgiveness is offered for *everything*—which the Law never offered."[27] Indeed, if this be the sense of the verse for Luke, then the gospel that Paul is preaching is understood once again as a *supplement* to the law, now expressed in terms of the Christian view of forgiveness. "It does not follow that the law has been done away with or that it no longer has a role to play in Jewish or Jewish-Christian piety."[28]

With this we may now turn to the second part of our discussion.

II. Luke's View of Israel or the Jewish People

The Jewish people are first mentioned in the Lucan writings as "the children of Israel," in Gabriel's words to Zechariah about the future role of his son John: "He will turn many of the children of Israel to the Lord, their God. He will go before him with the spirit and power of Elijah, to turn the hearts of parents to children (Mal 3:24), to turn the disobedient to the understanding of the upright, and to make ready a people fit for the Lord" (1:16–17). Luke further refers to them as "the children of Israel" in Acts 5:21; 7:23,37; 9:15; 10:36; they are for him "the house of Israel"

(Acts 2:36; 7:43 [= Amos 5:25]) or "the people of Israel" (Acts 4:10,17; 13:24). In all such designations Luke is referring to those for whom the law and the prophets are normative and taken as a mark of their identity.

"Israel" alone is also often used as a name in the nongeographical, ethnic sense (Luke 1:54,68,80; 2:25,32,34; 4:25,27; 22:30; 24:21; Acts 1:6; 5:3; 13:17,23; 28:20). On occasion, "Israel" is specified as Yahweh's "servant" (Luke 1:54) or "his people" (Luke 1:68; cf. 2:32), and the Lord himself is called "the God of Israel" (Luke 1:68; cf. Acts 13:17).

The term *hoi Ioudaioi*, "the Jews," occurs only rarely in the Lucan Gospel: in a neutral sense in 7:3; 23:51; again, twice in the passion narrative, when Pilate interrogates Jesus, "Are you the king of the Jews?" (23:3) and in the inscription on the cross (23:38). But it occurs almost seventy times in Acts: in a neutral sense, often meaning the Jews as a nation distinct from others, sometimes even with the connotation of God's chosen people (2:5,10,14; 10:22,28,39; 11:19; 13:5,43; 14:1bis; 16:1,3,20; 17:1,10,17; 18:2bis,4–5,19,24; 19:10,17; 20:21; 21:21,39; 22:3,12; 24:5,24; 26:4; 28:17); more frequently, however, it is used in an adversarial sense, where the context deals with the persecution of Christians or with opposition to Paul (9:22–23; 12:3,11; 13:6,45,50; 14:2,4–5,19; 17:5,13; 18:12,14bis,28; 19:13–14,33–34; 20:3,19; 21:11,27; 22:30; 23:12,20,27; 24:9,18,27; 25:2,7–10,15,24; 26:2–3,7,21; 28:19,[29]); and once of believing Jews (21:20).[29]

Many of these designations are, as a matter of fact, traditional, and they clearly denote for Luke the people who worship "the Lord, God of Israel" (Luke 1:68; cf. Acts 13:17), the "God of Abraham, Isaac, and Jacob, the God of our fathers" (Acts 3:13; 5:30; 7:32,46; 22:14; 24:14), the God who has sworn an oath to "our father Abraham" (Luke

1:73).[30] This people is "the children of the family of Abraham" (Acts 13:26), those to whom he gave "the covenant of circumcision" (Acts 7:7–8).

It is, however, highly important for Luke that to this people belong the *promise(s)* made to it through the "fathers," i.e., the patriarchs (Luke 1:72; cf. Acts 7:17; 13:23). Luke expressly admits that "the promise belongs to you and to your children" (Acts 2:39); this he makes Peter say to the Jews assembled in Jerusalem on Pentecost. Thus, this "Israel" remains the Israel of old, the people identified by allegiance to the law and the prophets, by circumcision, and by this "promise made to the fathers" (Acts 13:32). Because of such promises "the message of salvation has been sent" to this people (13:36).[31] By contrast, Christians are never called "the Israel of God" by Luke, in contrast to the way that Paul names them in Gal 6:16.

Five characteristics of this people Israel may be singled out in Luke's treatment of them.

(1) Luke echoes Old Testament and intertestamental writers in describing this people; it is not perfect, for it is disobedient—not yet "fit for the Lord" (Luke 1:17).[32] Precisely because of this situation, the role of John the Baptist is so described: he is being sent "to turn many of the children of Israel to the Lord, their God . . . and the disobedient to the understanding of the upright" (1:16–17). Later on, Peter exhorts the Jews assembled in Jerusalem to "save yourselves from this crooked generation" (Acts 2:40); and Stephen accuses his opponents of not keeping the law itself (7:53).[33] For the repentance that Peter demands of such Jews John's own reform preaching was to be a preparation: a preparation of this people for God's visitation of it (which took place in the ministry and preaching of Jesus himself).[34]

(2) The "promise made to the fathers" and the hope of

Israel associated with it (Acts 26:6–7; 28:20)[35] now come to this people in a form that it does not expect. When Paul preaches in the synagogue of Antioch in Pisidia, he announces, "Of this man's [i.e., David's] posterity God has brought to Israel a Savior, Jesus, according to (his) promise" and "we now proclaim to you that what was promised to the patriarchs God has fulfilled for us, their children, in raising Jesus" from the dead (Acts 13:32–33). Likewise, Peter makes the same proclamation in his Pentecost sermon: "God has raised up this Jesus, and of this we are all witnesses. Exalted at God's right hand, then, and having received from the Father the promise of the holy Spirit, he has poured this out, which you see and hear" (Acts 2:32–33). Thus the promise(s) of old have taken on a new form in the ministry of Jesus and in the Spirit that he has poured out. When the Jerusalem Jews hear Peter's words, they ask him what they are to do. Peter replies, "Repent, and be baptized every one of you in the name of Jesus Christ for the forgiveness of your sins, and you shall receive the gift of the holy Spirit. For the promise is (made) to you and to your children . . ." (Acts 2:38–39). Then Luke records that about three thousand of these Jews welcomed the word and were baptized (2:41); they were added to the original hundred and twenty (1:15). The number grows to five thousand (4:4) and eventually to "many myriads" (21:20). So Jews, gathered in Jerusalem for the feast of the Assembly,[36] joined the reconstituted Twelve that have addressed their message about the crucified and resurrected Jesus the Messiah to Israel. They have thus become the first Jewish Christians, and in this way Israel becomes in the Lucan story "the divided people of God," to use the term of J. Jervell.[37] In this one sees the fulfillment of the oracle of Simeon, who spoke of "the fall and the rise of many in Israel" (Luke 2:34), foreshadowing the distinction of Jews marked off from Jewish Christians (cf. Acts 5:13). Though the latter still have a solidarity with Israel for whom the law and the prophets are a mark of identity, they have accepted the supplementary preaching of the kingdom.

Peter's words in the Jerusalem Temple are ominous; he refers to Moses and the promise that God has made to him: "The Lord God will raise up a prophet for you from your brethren, as he did me. You shall listen to him in everything that he tells you. And every person that does not listen to that prophet shall be rooted out of the people" (Acts 3:22–23; cf. Deut 18:19). It is important to recognize that Luke never uses of Jewish Christians the expression "the new Israel,"[38] for they remain in his eyes those for whom the law and the prophets, the circumcision, and the promises of old are normative and valid and a mark of their identification. For them "law" has to be understood, however, in the supplemental sense; it continues to be normative, but they have also acknowledged that "the kingdom of God is being preached" (Luke 16:16b) and they have been among those "pressed to enter it" (16:16c).[39] For Luke such Jewish Christians would no longer be part of disobedient Israel. The upshot of all this is "that the missionary proclamation has divided Israel into two groups: the repentant and the unrepentant," as Jervell has phrased it.[40] "The portion of Jews who believe in the Messiah and are willing to repent appears as the purified, restored, and true Israel . . . they are Jews who have accepted the gospel, to whom and for whom the promises have been fulfilled."[41] Such a distinction accounts for the neutral and the adversarial use of "the Jews" in many passages of Acts.

(3) Peter's words uttered on Pentecost give us a still further insight into Luke's understanding of this reconstituted Israel. At first Peter says to the assembled Jews, "Let all the house of Israel know for sure that this Jesus, whom

you crucified, God has made Lord and Messiah" (2:32,36).
Moreover, through this Jesus "the promise" made to the
fathers has been realized "for you and for your children, and
for all that are far off, everyone whom the Lord our God
calls to himself" (2:39). Just who are all those "that are far
off" is not explained at this point in Acts, but Lucan foreshadowing is at work: the gospel to be preached to the
Gentiles is being hinted at.

Peter's words imply that the promise made to Israel of
old is to be shared with others "whom the Lord our God calls
to himself." Later, when Peter preaches in the Temple, after
the cure of the cripple at its Beautiful Gate, he ends his
words to the assembled Jews: "You are the children of the
prophets and of the covenant that God made with your
fathers, when he said to Abraham, 'Through your posterity
shall all the families of the earth be blessed' (quoting Gen
22:18). Now God has raised up his servant and sent him to
you first, blessing you as each one turns from your wicked-
ness" (3:25–26). Thus, through the descendants of Abraham
are "all the families of the earth" to share in God's blessings
now made available through the resurrected Christ. In this
way Peter hints at the share that the Gentiles are to have in
the blessings of Israel. But how is this share in the promises
of old or in the blessings of Israel to be realized?

(4) Among the Jewish Christians of Jerusalem certain
converts from Pharisaism tried to insist that it was "necessary to circumcise" Gentile converts and "charge them to
keep the law of Moses" (Acts 15:5). Luke, however, depicts
more moderate Jewish Christians of Jerusalem not adopting
this decision.[42] At the so-called Council of Jerusalem Peter
becomes the spokesman for a different solution to this
problem—a solution eventually adopted by other Jewish
Christians. In his address to the apostles and elders assem-

bled in Jerusalem Peter asserts, "Through my mouth Gentiles have heard the gospel and have come to believe" (15:7). He then refuses to impose on Gentile converts the yoke of circumcision and observance of the Mosaic law, insisting rather, "through the grace of our Lord Jesus we believe that we are saved in the same way as they are" (15:11), i.e., Jewish Christians have come to salvation "through the grace of our Lord Jesus" just as much as Gentile Christians.[43] In this speech at the "Council," Peter alludes to his missionary experience at the conversion of Cornelius and his household. In that episode, when Peter had the vision about the food that he was told to eat, he protested, "Lord, I have never eaten anything common or unclean" (10:14–15). The implication of that vision was not lost on Peter, who eventually went not only to Caesarea but even into the house of Cornelius, a God-fearer indeed, but nonetheless a Gentile. There he made known the meaning of the vision: "God has shown me that I should not call *anyone* common or unclean" (10:28), and so the transition is made from food to people. Thus in the Lucan story Peter is made to declare that it is God himself who has ordained that Gentiles, who are uncircumcised and who do not live according to the law and the prophets, are not common or unclean—not unprivileged to share in that salvation and forgiveness promised to Israel of old and in its blessings that have now come to it "through a Savior, Jesus, according to (his) promise" (13:23).

Once again one notes that the Lucan sense of the supplement to the Mosaic law is at work. Through the preaching of the kingdom of God (begun in the Period of Jesus) "the grace of our Lord Jesus" (Acts 15:11) has now become available not only to the Jewish convert still under the law and the prophets, but also to the Gentile convert. The Gentiles, however, are given a share in that same salvation and grace *as Gentiles,* because through repentance and baptism they have been associated with reconstituted Israel. Indeed, they have thus become part of reconstituted Israel.

(5) Gentile Christians form part of reconstituted Israel because the very law and the prophets have made provision for them. This is seen in the role that James of Jerusalem plays at the "Council." James acknowledges the validity of what Peter has declared on the basis of his missionary experience: "God has deigned to take from the Gentiles a people for his name" (15:14). Moreover, James justifies this position by citing prophetic passages from the Old Testament itself to ratify the admission of the Gentiles to a share in the heritage of Israel. What James cites is actually a conflated quotation of Jer 12:15; Amos 9:11–12; Isa 45:21, which runs as follows:

> After this I will return and rebuild the dwelling of David that has fallen down; I will rebuild its ruins and set it up, so that the rest of mankind may seek the Lord—all the nations that are called by my name. (So) says the Lord who makes these things known from of old (15:16–18).

James seeks scriptural proof for the recognition of the share that the Gentiles have in the heritage of Israel.[44] Nevertheless, he demands of such Gentile Christians that they live among Jewish Christians as the law itself demands of pagan sojourners dwelling among the Israelites. He lists four prescriptions drawn from Leviticus 17–18 that such Gentile Christians must observe: they must "abstain from meats sacrificed to idols, from blood, from what has been strangled, and from illicit marital unions" (15:29).[45] In other words, Gentile Christians are associated with Jewish Christians and find with them the same salvation "through the grace of our Lord Jesus" (15:11), but they find it not because "the law and the prophets" have been abrogated and are no longer normative, but because the law and the prophets themselves have provided for their share in the very promises made to the fathers of old. That is why "God has deigned to take from the Gentiles a people for his name" (15:14). Thus reconstituted, Israel is composed of, first and foremost, repentant Jews who have accepted the apostolic proclamation of the gospel and welcomed that "savior that God has brought to Israel, Jesus, according to (his) promise" (13:23), but also the people taken from among the Gentiles for his name, associated with this Israel. Thus, the very law and the prophets that remain normative for the repentant Israel provides for the association of Gentile converts to it as the one reconstituted people of God.[46]

Luke writes for a Christian community that is predominantly Gentile. He is trying to explain to Theophilus and other Gentile Christians like him how they have come to share in the divine promises made to the Israel of old. Gentiles have come to share in that heritage as *Gentile Christians,* without the norm of the law and the prophets, save for those prescriptions that the law demanded of those who lived in close association with those for whom the law and the prophets were still normative. As Gentile Christians they have come to share in what the law and the prophets in the predictive sense promised of old—the hope of Israel. Thus Simeon's oracle has in the long run come to fulfillment, ". . . my eyes have seen your salvation, made ready by you in the sight of all peoples, a light to give revelation to the Gentiles and glory to your people Israel . . ." (2:29–32). As D. L. Tiede has put it, "The oracles of Simeon demonstrate that the question of the status of the Gentiles is fundamental to Luke's view of God's relationship to Israel."[47] Thus "all human beings" have seen "the salvation of God" (Luke 3:6; cf. Isa 40:5).

Notes

1 See pp. 61–63 above.

2 See J. van Goudoever, "The Place of Israel in Luke's Gospel," *NovT* 8 (1966) 111–23. A. George, "Israel dans l'oeuvre de Luc," *RB* 75 (1968) 481–525. K. Berger, *Die Gesetzesauslegung Jesu: Ihr historischer Hintergrund* (WMANT 40; Neukirchen-Vluyn: Neukirchener-V., 1972). J. Jervell, "The Law in Luke-Acts," *HTR* 64 (1971) 21–36; *Luke and the People of God: A New Look at Luke-Acts* (Minneapolis: Augsburg, 1962) 41–74. H. Hübner, *Das Gesetz in der synoptischen Tradition: Studien zur These einer progressiven Qumranisierung und Judaisierung innerhalb der synoptischen Tradition* (Witten: Luther-V., 1973). R. Banks, *Jesus and the Law in the Synoptic Tradition* (SNTSMS 28; Cambridge: University Press, 1975). S. G. Wilson, *Luke and the Law* (SNTSMS 50; Cambridge: University Press, 1983). J. B. Tyson, "The Jewish Public in Luke-Acts," *NTS* 30 (1984) 574–83. R. C. Tannehill, "Israel in Luke-Acts: A Tragic Story," *JBL* 104 (1985) 69–85. F. G. Downing, "Freedom from the Law in Luke-Acts," *JSNT* 26 (1986) 49–52. C. L. Blomberg, "The Law in Luke-Acts," *JSNT* 22 (1984) 53–80. R. C. Tannehill, "Rejection by Jews and Turning to Gentiles: The Pattern of Paul's Mission in Acts," *Society of Biblical Literature Seminar Papers Series* (§ 25; ed. K. H. Richards; Atlanta, GA: Scholars, 1986) 130–41. D. L. Tiede, " 'Glory to Thy People Israel!': Luke-Acts and the Jews," ibid., 142–51. J. T. Sanders, "The Jewish People in Luke-Acts," ibid., 110–29; *The Jews in Luke-Acts* (London: SCM, 1987).

3 *Ethos* may be used by Luke in a broad (Hellenistic?) sense to designate a way of life governed by generic traditions traced back to Moses (perhaps in Luke 1:9; 22:39; Acts 16:21; 25:16). But he may also use it in a more specific sense,

referring to distinct regulations (cf. Deut 16:1–6; Exod 23:15–17); thus in Acts 6:14 ("the customs that Moses delivered to us"); 15:1; 21:21; 26:3; 28:17. Note too the expression in Luke 2:27, *kata to eithismenon tou nomou*, "what has become customary under the law." See further S. G. Wilson, *Luke and the Law*, 4–11.

⁴ This episode seems at first sight to resemble Mark 12:28–31 (= Matt 22:34–40), but it develops so differently in the Lucan text that it is preferably ascribed to a different source, probably "L," which Luke has chosen to substitute for the Marcan form. See further *Luke*, 877–78; cf. S. G. Wilson, *Luke and the Law*, 14–17.

⁵ See J. Dupont, "Dieu ou Mammon (Mt 6,24; Lc 16,13)," *Cristianesimo nella storia* 5 (1984) 441–61.

⁶ See my article, "The Matthean Divorce Texts and Some New Palestinian Evidence," *TS* 37 (1976) 197–226, esp. 200–203; reprinted, *TAG*, 79–111, esp. 83–84.

⁷ So S. G. Wilson, *Luke and the Law*, 43–51.

⁸ See E. Rodenbusch, "Die Komposition von Lukas 16," *ZNW* 4 (1903) 243–54. V. Taylor, *Behind the Third Gospel: A Study of the Proto-Luke Hypothesis* (Oxford: Clarendon, 1926) 156–58. B. S. Easton, *The Gospel according to St. Luke: A Critical and Exegetical Commentary* (Edinburgh: Clark; New York: Scribner, 1926) 247–48. D. Daube, *The New Testament and Rabbinic Judaism* (London: Athlone, 1956) 292–93. H. Schürmann, *Traditionsgeschichtliche Untersuchungen zu den synoptischen Evangelien* (Düsseldorf: Patmos, 1968) 127–28.

⁹ See *Luke*, 1105–6.

¹⁰ See *Luke and the Law*, 47.

¹¹ See J. M. Creed, *The Gospel*, 206. He correctly notes that "the topic of divorce is introduced abruptly and leads no further." But is it really "introduced as a striking

instance of conflict between the teaching of Jesus and the Jewish law?" The "conflict," if there, is not even hinted at. The Old Testament at most tolerated divorce (see Mal 2:14–16). Hence Jesus' prohibition of it is not directly contrary to it. Moreover, the Essene community of Qumran also prohibited it (see 11QTemple 57:17–19; cf. *TAG*, 91–97).

[12] The phrase "the law and the prophets" is not always predictive, as Luke 16:16a makes clear, *pace* S. G. Wilson (*Luke and the Law*, 44). See further 16:29; Acts 13:15; 24:14.

[13] See P. Schubert, "The Structure and Significance of Luke 24," *Neutestamentliche Studien für Rudolf Bultmann zu seinem siebzigsten Geburtstag am 20. August* (BZNW 21; ed. W. Eltester; Berlin: Töpelmann, 1954) 165–86, esp. 173–74.

[14] I fashion this term in dependence on S. G. Wilson (*Luke and the Law*, 27), but I do not consider this supplement a "challenge" of the law.

[15] The question of the "replacement" of the law is tied up with that of Luke's attitude toward the Jewish people (see part II). For the replacement idea, see E. Haenchen, *The Acts of the Apostles* (Philaldelphia: Westminster, 1971) 98–103, esp. 100. Cf. his essay, "The Book of Acts as Source Material for the History of Early Christianity," *SLA*, 278. See also J. C. O'Neill, *The Theology of Acts in Its Historical Setting* (2d ed.; London: SPCK, 1970) 77–99. J. T. Sanders, "The Jewish People" (n. 2 above), 111. Just where H. Conzelmann stands in this matter is not clear. At times he speaks of "liberation from the Law" (*Theology*, 146–47), but he is not always consistent (see J. T. Sanders, "The Jewish People," 113).

[16] See C. E. B. Cranfield, "St. Paul and the Law," *SJT* 17 (1964) 43–68; "Romans 9:30–10:4," *Int* 34 (1980) 70–74.

H. Hübner, *Paul and the Law* (Edinburgh: Clark, 1986). H. Räisänen, *Paul and the Law* (WUNT 29; Tübingen [Mohr],1983; Philadelphia: Fortress, 1986). R. Badenas, *Christ the End of the Law: Romans 10.4 in Pauline Perspective* (JSNTSup 10; Sheffield: JSOT, 1985).

[17] See further C. Coulot, "La structuration de la péricope de l'homme riche et ses différentes lectures (Mc 10,17–31; Mt 19,16–30; Lc 18,18–30)," *RevScRel* 56 (1982) 240–52.

[18] *Luke and the Law,* 27–51, esp. 31–39. He discusses the four disputes about "the sabbath Law": Luke 6:1–5; 6:6–11; 13:10–17; 14:1–6 (the last two being exclusive to Luke). In fairness, I should add that Wilson's title for the section "Challenging the Law" ends with a question-mark, but the discussion itself comes out strongly on the side of showing Jesus critical of the law.

[19] Ibid., 35.

[20] Wilson's comment on 13:10–17 is correct: "The sabbath is thus declared to be the day for healing *par excellence,* a claim which operates on a different level from, and ultimately contradicts, rabbinic thinking. Jesus does not argue, as sages frequently do, about the legitimacy of certain exceptions to the sabbath command but views the sabbath in a totally different light as the most appropriate day on which to do good and save life (6:9)." It may, indeed, correct or contradict "rabbinic thinking," but it does not mean *eo ipso* that Jesus is critical of the Mosaic law itself.

[21] See further P. Vielhauer, "On the 'Paulinism' of Acts," *SLA,* 35–50.

[22] It is disputed by interpreters whether vv. 23–24 mean that Paul merely underwent some purification rite for seven days on his return to the holy land after being abroad or that he too joined in the Nazirite vow ritual with the four men for whom he was paying. For details, see E. Haenchen, *Acts* (n.

15 above), 611–12; I. H. Marshall, *The Acts of the Apostles: An Introduction and Commentary* (Leicester: Inter-Varsity, 1980) 345 n. 1.

[23] See further Acts 23:1–5; 26:4–5.

[24] J. Jervell, *Luke and the People of God,* 137.

[25] Ibid.

[26] See p. 6 above.

[27] See K. Lake and H. J. Cadbury, *Beginnings,* 4. 157.

[28] So S. G. Wilson, *Luke and the Law,* 59. Cf. P. Haudebert, "Abrogation ou accomplissement de la loi mosaïque? (Luc 16,16–18)," *Impacts* (Angers) (4/1984) 15–26.

[29] H. Conzelmann (*Theology,* 145) sees in the first two uses of *Ioudaioi* a "certain hardening," i.e., "a simple designation" takes on "a sharply polemical sense." Similarly, R. F. Zehnle (*Peter's Pentecost Discourse* [SBLMS 15; Nashville, TN: Abingdon, 1971] 65) thinks that after 13:43–45 *hoi Ioudaioi* becomes a technical term for Paul's opponents. Both of these views, however, seem to be a bit overdrawn. See further D. L. Tiede, " 'Glory' " (n. 2 above), 148 n. 18.

[30] Luke never depicts Christians as the children of Abraham, as does Paul in Rom 4:12. See N. A. Dahl, "The Story of Abraham in Luke–Acts," *SLA,* 139–58, esp. 140–41 and n. 7.

[31] See further R. C. Tannehill, "Rejection" (n. 2 above), 131.

[32] Recall such Old Testament declarations about Israel's disobedience as Deut 32:5,20,28; Ps 78:8; Isa 65:2; Jer 7:13,24–26; Ezek 3:7; Hos 9:17. Cf. *Jub.* 1:9,14,16–17; *4 Ezra* 2:33. Often this disobedience of Israel is cited as the reason why God's word goes to the nations; cf. D. L. Tiede, " 'Glory' " (n. 2 above) 148–50.

[33] See H. Conzelmann, *Theology,* 146.

34 See Luke 19:44.

35 See R. C. Tannehill, "Rejection" (n. 2 above), 136–37.

36 For this designation of the feast which draws Jews of the diaspora to Jerusalem (the Feast of Weeks), see my article, "The Ascension of Christ and Pentecost," *TS* 45 (1984) 409–40, esp. 430–31 n. 54.

37 *Luke and the People of God*, 41–74.

38 Though I once wrote that "Acts vaguely suggests that the Christian group looked on itself as the New Israel" ("Jewish Christianity in Acts in Light of the Qumran Scrolls," *SLA*, 236; *ESBNT*, 275), I should rephrase that today and speak more properly of them as part of a reconstituted Israel.

39 For this sense of *kai pas eis autēn biazetai*, lit., "and everyone is pressed into it," see *Luke*, 1114–18.

40 *Luke and the People of God*, 42.

41 Ibid.

42 See R. E. Brown, "Not Jewish Christianity and Gentile Christianity but Types of Jewish/Gentile Christianity," *CBQ* 45 (1983) 74–79.

43 In other words, "Jews and Gentiles alike are saved solely by the grace of God (verse 11)." So S. G. Wilson in dependence on J. L. Nolland, "A Fresh Look at Acts 15:10," *NTS* 27 (1980–81) 105–15, esp. 112–13. Nolland says that the infinitive *sōthēnai* might also be taken as "an infinitive of result": "But through the grace of our Lord Jesus, we *believe* (in order) to be saved, and so do they." F. F. Bruce (*The Acts of the Apostles* [2d ed.; London: Tyndale, 1952] 295) calls it rather an "epexegetic infin.," whereas K. Lake and H. J. Cadbury (*Beginnings*, 4. 174) hesitate between "the loose 'epexegetical construction of result' (or purpose)." But it can only be either an infinitive in indirect discourse or an infinitive of purpose (BDF § 390.1–2).

[44] See further N. A. Dahl, " 'A People for His Name' (Acts xv. 14)," *NTS* 4 (1957–58) 319–27. Dahl has shown that *laos* means Israel, or some group of it, in the Lucan writings, save for Acts 15:10 and 18:10. The exception made for 15:14 is clear, but I hesitate about that in 18:10.

[45] I continue to think that the allusion to Leviticus 17–18 is the best explanation of the four prescriptions in this difficult text. See my commentary on it, *JBC* art. 45 § 75–76. S. G. Wilson (*Luke and the Law,* 78–101) has devoted a lengthy discussion to this interpretation, which he rejects, and also to two others (that the prescriptions refer to pagan cultic practices or ethical rules). It is not possible to comment here on the details of his, often tortuous, argumentation. For the meaning of *porneia* as "illicit marital union," see my article, "The Matthean Divorce Texts" (n. 6 above), 213–21; reprinted, *TAG,* 87–89.

[46] See further J. Jervell, *Luke and the People of God,* 43.

[47] " 'Glory' " (n. 2 above), 150–51. Cf. K. Berger, "Das Canticum Simeonis (Lk 2:29–32)," *NovT* 27 (1985) 27–39.

8

"Today You Shall Be with Me in Paradise" (Luke 23:43)

The verse that serves as the title of this chapter calls attention to an important episode in the Lucan passion narrative. Its importance lies in the contribution that the episode makes to the Lucan understanding of Jesus' death and of the sequel to that death. It merits, then, further attention, but we must first make some introductory remarks about the context in which the episode appears.

In all four Gospels Jesus is crucified on Golgotha or the Place of the Skull (Mark 15:22; Matt 27:33; Luke 23:33; John 19:17).[1] Whereas in the Synoptic Gospels Simon of Cyrene is pressed into service by those that lead Jesus off to carry the cross to Golgotha (Mark 15:21; Matt 27:32; Luke 23:26), John's Gospel knows nothing of this detail. Rather, the chief priests "took Jesus; and he went out, bearing his own cross" (John 19:17). Each of the four evangelists, however, notes that with Jesus two others were crucified, one on either side of him (Mark 15:27; Matt 27:38; Luke 23:32–33; John 19:18) and that an inscription or *titlos* (= Latin "titulus") was used to announce the charge against Jesus (Mark 15:26; Matt 27:37; Luke 23:38; John 19:19), whereas nothing of the sort is mentioned about the other two.

Concerning the inscription on the cross, three things

should be noted. (1) The inscription is the only thing known to have been written about Jesus during his earthly lifetime. Yet it is preserved in four different wordings in the canonical Gospels. Whereas Mark has simply recorded it as "The King of the Jews" (15:26), Matthew has, "This is Jesus, the King of the Jews" (27:37), and Luke, "This (*or* This One) is the King of the Jews" (23:38).[2] John alone records, "Jesus of Nazareth (*or* the Nazorean), the King of the Jews" (19:19).[3] The substance of the inscription agrees in each case, but one might have expected that the evangelists would have reproduced at least this text exactly.[4] The diversity of the records says something about the historical character of the gospel tradition; one has to reckon with the obvious literary composition that has been at work.[5] (2) Perhaps because of such diversity, the inscription has been regarded as "secondary" in the gospel tradition, i.e., not part of the original tradition and (by implication) not historical.[6] Yet, as P. Winter has argued, the substance of the wording of the inscription speaks against its fabrication by Christians, who would scarcely have written that Jesus was "the King of the Jews."[7] (3) Though there is no evidence that the affixing of such an inscription to the cross stating the charge against the crucified person was the usual Roman practice in the execution of criminals,[8] that this was used in the case of Jesus speaks for the authenticity of the record, as A. E. Harvey has argued.[9] For whereas Mark (15:25) states simply, "And the inscription of the charge against him was written," Matthew (27:37) records that "they put over his head the charge against him." Luke (23:38) writes, "There was an inscription over him." Only John's Gospel (19:19–22) ascribes the writing of the *titlos*, "title," to Pontius Pilate: "and he put it on the cross." Moreover, only John further states that it was written "in Hebrew, in Latin, and in Greek." This last difference about

who put the inscription on the cross and in what languages
raises a question about the official or unofficial nature of the
inscription, despite the common attestation of its use in the
Synoptic and Johannine traditions.[10] In the Johannine Gospel nothing is recorded about the "two others" who were
crucified with Jesus. The Marcan Gospel merely records that
the two robbers (*lēstai*) "who had been crucified with him
kept taunting him" (15:32b), and the Matthean Gospel mentions the same (27:44); but neither of them supplies the
details of the taunts. The brief Marcan notice, however, is
expanded by Luke from his private source "L." J. Jeremias
in his study of the language of the Third Gospel finds Lucan
redaction at a minimum in this episode,[11] which supports the
Lucan use of an independent tradition. In any case, the
expansion that gives the details of the taunting is exclusive to
the Lucan Gospel. My discussion of this episode in vv. 39–43
will have three parts: (1) the meaning of the episode; (2) the
significance of the episode for the Lucan understanding of
Jesus' death; and (3) the significance of the episode for the
Lucan understanding of the sequel to Jesus' death and
burial.

I.   The Meaning of the Episode

The text of the passage reads:

One of the criminals who hung there kept taunting him,
"Are you really the Messiah? Then save yourself, and us
too!" But the other answered him with a rebuke, "Don't
you even fear God? After all, you are under the same
sentence yourself. For us it represents justice; we are
only getting what our deeds deserve. But this man has

done nothing improper." Then he said, "Jesus, remember me when you come into your kingdom!" Jesus replied to him, "Believe me, today you shall be with me in paradise."

Form-critically considered, the episode is one of the pronouncement stories of the gospel tradition, a narrative preserved for the sake of the punchline or pronouncement of Jesus enshrined in it, "Today, you shall be with me in paradise." The penitent criminal, who acknowledges Jesus' innocence and implicitly requests a share in the regal destiny that awaits Jesus, plays upon the nuance of the inscription itself, "This (*or* This One) is the King of the Jews." R. Bultmann has cited the episode as an example of the growth that took place in the narrative tradition, as it differentiates and individualizes: the story about men vaguely described in the Marcan Gospel as "those crucified with him" and taunting him now becomes an account in which one criminal sides with Jesus against the other.[12] Bultmann may be right, but who can say that the growth in the tradition is owing solely to such an inner dialectic; a later recollection of detail, derived from a different source, may just as easily explain the so-called growth in the tradition.

Luke calls the two others *kakourgoi,* as he had in vv. 32–33. These "evildoers" or "criminals" were being executed for misdeeds and crimes, but it is impossible to say whether they were Jews, not pagans, or in any way identified with a "Zealot" movement, as is often alleged.[13] Such an identification is not only guesswork, but presupposes that the "Zealot movement" was in existence at this early period in Palestinian history, which is quite debatable.[14]

At any rate, the unrepentant criminal taunts Jesus, "Are you really the Messiah? Then save yourself, and us

too!" (v. 39bc). He thus echoes the taunt of the "leader" of
the people, "He saved others; let him save himself, if he is
really God's Messiah" (v. 35). The unrepentant criminal
thus makes use of the important Lucan verb *sōzein,* "save."
The leaders have employed it in v. 35, and the soliders in v.
36. The implications of this triple use of the verb will be seen
in part II. What is to be noted now is that "saving" is related
to one acknowledged by the unrepentant criminal as "Messiah," even if only in a taunting way. Salvation is thus expected through an anointed agent of God.

The second criminal, however, implicitly expresses his
metanoia, "repentance," as he recognizes his guilt and that
he rightly hangs crucified: "For us it represents justice," or
lit., "at least we suffer justly." He is also made to declare
Jesus' innocence: "This man has done nothing improper,"
nothing *atopon,* "out of place," not to mention anything
criminal. In other words, through this dialogue between the
two criminals Luke dramatically achieves another declaration of Jesus' innocence in the passion narrative, this time
from an unofficial source, from one suffering the same fate
(condemnation to death). This declaration follows upon Pilate's triple declaration of Jesus' innocence (23:4b,14c,16)
and Pilate's recognition that not even Herod of Galilee, to
whom he had sent Jesus, found any charge against him
(23:15). Thus Luke uses one of the dregs of humanity, a
common criminal, to echo the official declarations of Palestinian political authorities, Pilate and Herod, about Jesus'
innocence.

The second criminal further requests that Jesus remember him when he comes into his "kingdom."[15] The request
stems from an implicit comparison of himself with Jesus,
who he judges will face a fate different from his own in the
after-life.[16] His mention of Jesus' "kingdom" plays on the

title hanging over Jesus' head, "This is the King of the Jews," and his reference to it implies that somehow through death this "king" is about to enter upon his regal status or destiny. His request is a plea for a gracious remembrance, for he can do nothing at this point to merit it. Implicitly, his request is an expression of faith in Jesus.

The climax in the episode is reached in Jesus' pronouncement, "Today you shall be with me in paradise."[17] Jesus turns the criminal's vague time-reference, "when you come into your kingdom," into a very specific "today." Moreover, he admits to the repentant criminal that he will share in his own destiny. Significantly, the Lucan Jesus uses the expression "to be with me," a formula similar to that which occurs elsewhere in the New Testament for the destiny of Christians. In 1 Thessalonians 4 Paul formulates that destiny in an analogous way, as he tries to console early Thessalonian Christians about the fate of their confreres who have fallen asleep before the parousia. Making use of apocalyptic stage-props, Paul attempts a description of that event. But when one prescinds from the apocalyptic paraphernalia such as God's trumpet, the archangel's cry, the clouds, etc., one sees that Paul's essential affirmation is "we shall be with the Lord forever" (4:17). Again, when Paul, faced with the prospect of death, debates with himself, he ponders, "For me to live is Christ, to die is gain. . . . I am hard pressed between the two; my desire is to depart and be with Christ, for that is far better" (Phil 1:22–23).[18] In this episode, however, the Lucan Jesus, already crucified, promises the repentant criminal a similar destiny, "Today, you shall be with me. . . ."

Jesus' promise ends with the phrase "in paradise," as the place where he will enter upon his kingdom and where the repentant criminal will share in his regal destiny. The noun *paradeisos,* "paradise," occurs twice elsewhere in the New Testament itself: in 2 Cor 12:4, where Paul boasts of his rapture to "the third heaven" or to "paradise" (because of this Pauline usage paradise has often been understood as a biblical term for "heaven"); and in Rev 2:7, where reference is made to "the tree of life which is in God's paradise" (an allusion to Gen 2:9 and especially Ezek 31:8). But neither of these meanings helps much to understand the word on the lips of the Lucan Jesus.

"Paradise" is originally of Old Persian provenience, *pairidaēza,* an "enclosed space, precinct." It came into the Greek language as *paradeisos* and normally denoted an "enclosed park, garden."[19] It occurs often enough in the Septuagint in this sense and is used of the "garden of Eden" (Gen 2:8–16; 3:1–24) or of "God's garden" (Ezek 31:8). In time, it acquired an eschatological nuance, as in Isa 51:3, where *paradeison Kyriou,* "garden of the Lord," is promised as part of the consolation and comfort for Zion. From such usage it came to denote in the intertestamental literature of the Jews the abode of assumed persons such as Enoch or the righteous in the after-life (*T. Levi* 18:10; *Life of Adam and Eve* 25:3). In the Aramaic fragments of the Books of Enoch from Qumran Cave 4 one reads of *pardēs qušṭ[āʾ],* "the paradise of righteousness."[20] Though it is difficult at first to ascertain what precise nuance Luke might have intended in using *paradeisos* in this episode, it is clear that his idea is related to this intertestamental Jewish usage. He puts it on the lips of the already crucified Jesus who is about to die and pass to the glory that the Messiah was bound to enter, as we shall see in part III. The important element now is that this crucified Jesus promises the repentant criminal a share in the same paradise with him. So much for the meaning of the episode itself.

II. The Significance of the Episode for the Lucan Understanding of Jesus' Death

In a sense this episode becomes the peak of the Lucan depiction of the crucifixion of Jesus, because it not only presents the third taunt against him, uttered by the first criminal after those of the leaders and the soldiers, but it also manifests for the last time Jesus' salvific mercy manifested toward one of the dregs of humanity. Taunted about his regal, messianic status by the first criminal, he is defended in the rebuke uttered by the second, who not only declares Jesus' innocence, but begs a share in his coming destiny.

To bring out the bearing that this episode has on the Lucan understanding of Jesus' death, I must explain briefly the outlook that a number of modern commentators have about this aspect of Luke's teaching. It has been expressed in various ways, but it comes down to this, that Luke seems to present the death of Jesus neither as sacrificial nor as an act of vicarious offering. This point is often made by asserting that "there is indeed no *theologia crucis* beyond the affirmation that the Christ must suffer, since so the prophetic scriptures had foretold."[21] Apropos of the speeches in Acts, E. Käsemann writes that "fabrication is interwoven with proclamation. A *theologia gloriae* is now in process of replacing the *theologia crucis.*" Because apocalyptic has been replaced by a theology of history, "the Cross of Jesus is no longer a scandal but only a misunderstanding on the part of the Jews which the intervention of God at Easter palpably and manifestly corrects."[22]

Such a thesis is often supported by noting Luke's glaring omission of anything like Mark 10:45, where Jesus sternly instructs the Twelve about the one who would be "great" or "the first" among them. He ends by saying, "For the Son of Man did not come to be served but to serve and to give his life as a ransom for many." Luke may derive from this Marcan episode a part of it, which he transposes to the Last Supper (Luke 22:24–27). There Jesus' words end thus: "For who is the greater, the one reclining at table or the one waiting on him? Surely it is the one who reclines. Yet I am here among you as the one who serves." But the concluding remark about the Son of Man giving his life as a ransom for many is strangely omitted by Luke—or, according to some interpreters, suppressed. This is allegedly because Luke has no real understanding of the salvific value of Jesus' death.[23] He has dulled the sharp, cutting edge of the Marcan proclamation about the vicarious character of Jesus' death because of his concern to historicize the story of the Christ-event. So runs the allegation.

No little part of such a view about Luke's understanding of Jesus' death stems from an implicit, or sometimes explicit, comparison of Lucan theology with Pauline theology. In the words of Käsemann quoted above, "the Cross of Jesus" is said to be in the Lucan writings "no longer a scandal." This is clearly an implicit reference to 1 Cor 1:23, "We preach Christ crucified, a stumbling block to Jews and folly to Gentiles." Again, J. M. Creed explicitly calls attention to "the entire absence of a Pauline interpretation of the Cross."[24] When such comparisons are made, one has to agree that Luke has no equivalent of the Pauline clauses, "who was handed over for our trespasses" (Rom 4:25) or "who died for our sins" (1 Cor 15:5); nor does he treat Jesus' death explicitly as an expiation for sin (Rom 3:25).[25]

Now Paul is admittedly a theologian superior to Luke. Paul's writings also reflect an earlier stage of understanding of the Christ-event. Being a missionary and "apostle to the Gentiles" (Rom 11:13), Paul is less bookish than Luke. Yet so much of this comparison is a question of degree. Luke also offers an interpretation of the Christ-event, but it seems unfair to compare Luke and Paul and to expect, as is often done, that Luke should put things the way Paul does. He has not proposed his interpretation of the ministry, passion, death, and resurrection of Jesus in essay-like letters written to cope with *ad-hoc* problems that give the author the opportunity to proclaim things in a radical and at times corrective fashion. Luke has rather chosen the narrative form for his proclamation of the Christ-event, punctuated indeed with sayings of Jesus and speeches of apostles. In the long run, is the Lucan appeal for faith, repentance and conversion, or baptism proposed in a narrative form any less demanding than Paul's appeal for faith that elicits God's grace of justification, reconciliation etc.? The real question about the Lucan story is whether God is portrayed in it bringing to realization his salvific plan *despite* the suffering and death of Jesus or *through* that suffering and death. In my opinion, it is the latter.[26]

Luke the storyteller has his own way of presenting such momentous soteriological truths. The main way that he expresses the effect of the Christ-event is as "salvation."[27] In part I of this chapter I called attention to the use of *sōzein,* "save," in this episode. In the course of five verses Luke uses it four times with reference to the crucified Jesus: the taunt of the leaders, "He saved others; let him save himself" (v. 35b); the ridicule of the soldiers, "If you are really the King of the Jews, then save yourself" (v. 37); and finally the taunt of the first criminal, "Are you really the Messiah? Then save yourself, and us too!" (v. 39). So Luke dramatically presents the effect of the Christ-event par excellence—in this peak scene of the crucifixion. What he has so dramatized could, indeed, have been expressed in abstract terminology: As he hangs on the cross, let him exercise his regal and messianic power of salvation. But Luke has chosen to put it concretely.

There is, however, still more drama to such a scene, for Jesus the Savior, about to die on the gibbet of infamy, not only tolerates the taunt of the first criminal, but, as the crucified one, he recognizes the repentance of the second criminal and addresses him with the word of salvation itself: "Today you shall be with me in paradise." Centuries ago, Ambrose commented, "The Lord always grants more than the request made."[28] That is true, but who fails to note the way the storyteller Luke has expressed that favor. Whatever the final phrase "in paradise" might mean, the Lucan Jesus, who hangs crucified and is about to die, promises this repentant criminal a share in his own destiny. It is, in other words, an acquittal uttered by him who is "the one ordained by God to be the judge of the living and the dead" (Acts 10:42).

Thus, in a dramatic scene exclusive to the Lucan Gospel, the evangelist succinctly expresses what the death of Christ means for humanity. What the crucified Jesus promises even to this criminal who represents the lowest of humanity, he promises to all human beings. Passage through death will mean his attainment of regal status, once he has entered his "glory" (Luke 24:26), but the attainment of that status will not be without salvific effect on suffering human beings—even on a crucified criminal. This is Luke's narrative and dramatic way of proposing his understanding of the death of Jesus and his *theologia crucis!*

III. The Significance of the Episode for the Lucan Understanding of the Sequel to Jesus' Death and Burial

After Jesus dies, Luke describes the burial of him by Joseph of Arimathea in "a rock-cut tomb, where no one had yet been laid" (23:53). In this description Luke presents his own version of what each of the other evangelists tell in parallel episodes about the death and burial of Jesus (Mark 15:33–47; Matt 27:45–61; John 19:28–42).

In choosing to speak of "the sequel to Jesus' death and burial," I am at the outset trying to formulate the matter in a neutral way, because of the varying terminology used in the New Testament about the *postmortem* phase of Christ's existence and activity. Yet only the Lucan Jesus speaks of that *postmortem* condition in an episode prior to it—in his reply to the repentant criminal. His reply brings out an important aspect of it.

Once again, one may not fault Luke for not having expressed the soteriological aspect of that sequel as clearly as does Paul. Nowhere in the Lucan writings do we find the author proclaiming as does Paul, "He was handed over (to death) for our trespasses and *raised for our justification*" (Rom 4:25). Nor does Luke assert as does the Apostle, "If you acknowledge with your lips that Jesus is Lord and believe in your hearts that God raised him from the dead, you will be saved" (Rom 10:9). Luke has, however, his own way of expressing the soteriological value of the sequel of Christ's death and burial, but before we attempt to describe it, we may look briefly at the various ways in which he speaks of the *postmortem* phase.

Since Luke was not among the earliest New Testament writers, we should not expect him to use mainly the primitive terms for expressing the sequel to Jesus' death and burial, but, as we shall see, he has retained some of them and employed them along with other more common terminology.

The first formulation of the sequel of Jesus' death and burial to surface in his writings is resurrection. In the story of the empty tomb (23:56b–24:12), Luke depicts two men in gleaming robes saying to the women who have come to the tomb, "He is not here, but has been raised!" (24:6a).[29] the verb *egerthē* is a theological passive, i.e., it means, "has been raised" by God,[30] as it meant already in the Marcan source from which Luke has derived it (16:6). The basic idea in the use of the verb *egeirein* is that Christ has been awakened (i.e., from the sleep of death). Sometimes Luke also uses the active verb *anastēsai*, "raise (up)," i.e., to cause to stand on one's feet. But Luke uses either of these verbs in the active with God as the subject in speaking of the resurrection of Jesus (*egeirein:* Acts 3:15; 4:10; 5:30; 10:40; 13:30,37; *anastēsai:* Acts 2:24,32; [3:26?]; 13:33–34; 17:31) or *egeirein* in the theological passive (*egerthēnai:* Luke 9:22;[31] 24:34). But Luke also formulates references to the resurrection in the intransitive, using *anastēnai,* "rise" (Luke 18:33; 24:7,46; Acts 10:41; 17:3). It is often thought that this intransitive use of "rise" reflects a later theology, stemming from the time when Christians, having become aware of Jesus' divinity, began to express the resurrection as effected by his own power.[32] Luke reflects the two ways that Christians of his own day were speaking about Christ's resurrection, but it should be recalled that the intransitive use, "rise," is found in the earliest of the Pauline letters (1 Thess 4:14).[33]

At any rate, the abundant references in the Lucan writings to the "resurrection" of Jesus are clear. One aspect of Lucan formulation, however, has to be singled out. In Acts 1:22, when Peter is explaining the need to reconstitute the Twelve after the death of Judas, he declares, "Now one of the men who have gone about with us during all the time that the Lord Jesus moved in and out among us, beginning from John's baptism until the day he was taken up from us—one of these must become with us a witness to his resurrection." Luke is here formulating criteria for membership in the

Twelve[34] and expresses the reference to the resurrection in the abstract.[35] What he really means is that the one to be chosen must have been a witness to the risen Christ—one of those to whom the risen Christ has appeared. Yet in formulating it abstractly, as a "witness to the resurrection," Luke has—unwittingly—introduced a nuance that can be misunderstood, at least by modern readers. For neither Luke himself nor any other New Testament writer has ever depicted anyone "witnessing" the resurrection. Indeed, in all four Gospels the passion narrative ends with an account of the story of the discovery of the empty tomb by women who go there after the sabbath has ended. They find the tomb open, the body of Jesus gone, and (in the Synoptics) heavenly messengers, who proclaim to them the *praeconium paschale,* the Easter message, "He is not here, but has been raised!" (Luke 24:6; cf. Mark 16:6; Matt 28:6). In none of the four accounts is the resurrection of Jesus itself described,[36] and no one is portrayed "witnessing" it.

Moreover, Luke never presents the resurrection of Christ as if it were a resuscitation, a reanimation, or a return to natural, terrestrial life. He is never portrayed as is the resuscitated son of the widow of Nain (Luke 7:15) or the daughter of Jairus (8:54–55), not to mention Lazarus in the Johannine Gospel (11:44), who is eventually depicted as "one of those reclining at table with him" (12:1–2). Though the risen Christ is described by Luke as walking with Cleopas and his companion to Emmaus and conversing with them, at the crucial moment at table when they "recognize" him "in the breaking of the bread," he "vanishes from their sight" (24:31,35, *aphantos egeneto ap' autōn*). Vanishing from sight is scarcely a normal mode of departure or withdrawal for someone in natural, terrestrial existence. The real question is, Whither did he vanish? Before I try to answer that question, however, I should like to recall one or other way in which Luke refers to the *postmortem* status of Jesus.

In Acts 2:32–33 Peter on Pentecost announces to the assembled Jews in Jerusalem, "This Jesus God has raised up (*anestēsen*) . . . ; being exalted (*hypsōtheis*), then, to God's right hand, and having received from the Father the promise of the holy Spirit, he has poured it out. . . ." Again, in Acts 5:30–31 Peter declares before the high priest and the Jerusalem sanhedrin, "The God of our fathers has raised (*ēgeiren*) Jesus, whom you put to death by hanging him on a tree. God exalted (*hypsōsen*) him to his right hand as Leader and Savior." In these two passages Luke joins to his assertion about Christ's resurrection the mention of his "exaltation" (to God's right hand).

Now the idea that God has exalted Jesus after his death and burial is one of the earliest ways in which Jesus' *postmortem* status is conceived in the New Testament. This mode of expression is found, for instance in the pre-Pauline liturgical hymn that the Apostle has adopted and incorporated in chap. 2 of his letter to the Philippians.[37] That six-strophied hymn describes various phases and aspects of Christ's existence: his divine preexistence, his humiliation in becoming human, his further humiliation in death, his celestial exaltation, the adoration of him by all the universe, and the new name (*Kyrios*) that is given to him as the exalted one. But this pre-Pauline hymn passes from Jesus' death to his exaltation without any mention of the resurrection; after reference to his death on the cross, it says simply, "Wherefore God superexalted him" (*hyperypsōsen*, 2:9). That text makes it seem as though Jesus passed from death (and burial) to a heavenly status.[38] The difference between this hymnic text and the Lucan affirmations in Acts is that Luke has joined the primitive mode of expression, exaltation, to that of resurrection, the more common way in which that *postmortem* status was being spoken of in his day. The primitive mode of expression took on in time another formulation, to which I shall return.

"Being exalted to the right hand of God," however, was given a different connotation by Luke. When the risen Christ walks the road to Emmaus with Cleopas and his companion, he asks them in the course of the conversation in which he has been explaining "all that the prophets have said": "Was not the Messiah bound to suffer all this before entering his glory?" Or, to put it more literally, "Was it not necessary for the Messiah to suffer these things and (so) enter his glory?"[39] Here, on the evening of the day of the discovery of the empty tomb, Christ uses the past tense of the impersonal verb *dei* and refers to himself as having already entered his glory. In other words, the sequel to his death and burial is now described as an entrance into glory—and one that has already taken place. Thus has his *exodos* (Luke 9:31) from terrestrial life been completed; he has made the transit to glory through his passion, death, and burial. Exalted to God's right hand, he already enjoys his *postmortem* status of glory in his Father's presence.

From that glory Christ appears to his followers—and that too supplies an answer to the question posed earlier, Whither did he vanish? He vanished to the status of glory, and from there he appears as the risen Christ to his own: to Simon Peter (Luke 24:34, reported but not described); to Cleopas and his companion (described in 24:13–35); and to the Eleven and "those who were with them" (described in 24:33,36).

This aspect of Christ's *postmortem* status provides the background for another formulation of it that appears in the episode being discussed in this chapter. As Jesus hangs on the cross and is about to die, he replies to the repentant criminal, "Today you shall be with me in paradise" (23:43). We have already seen that "in paradise" could easily be understood as the after-life condition of the righteous, as it was in some intertestamental literature; but now we see that it is to be defined much more specifically in Lucan terminology. For this evangelist "in paradise" is merely a biblical way of phrasing what he otherwise refers to as the entrance of Christ "into his glory" (24:26) or as the exaltation to God's right hand (Acts 2:33; 5:31).

Much more important, however, is the adverb "today," with which Jesus begins his reply to the repentant criminal. Its significance is seen when one recalls that there is no description of the resurrection in the account of the discovery of the empty tomb. As eloquent as the Easter proclamation is in that episode, "He is not here, but has been raised!" no one knows when that tomb was emptied. The women come to it, "when the sabbath was over" or "early on the first day of the week" (Mark 16:1–2; cf. Matt 28:1; Luke 24:1; John 20:1), and find the tomb opened and empty. Moreover, it is not said that the discovery of it was made "on the third day." The three days enter the picture because of the day of the crucifixion (called the Paraseve in John 19:14), the intervening sabbath, and the first day of the week (when the tomb is discovered empty).

The message given to the women who visit the tomb includes the advice, "Remember what he told you while he was still in Galilee: 'The Son of Man must be handed over into the hands of sinful men and be crucified; and he must rise again on the third day' " (Luke 24:6–7). Here Luke's text itself supplies an answer to the question how "the third day" came to be associated with the resurrection itself. The advice given to the women explicitly recalls the predictions of the

passion found in the ministry narrative (Luke 9:22; 18:33).[40]
We have already mentioned the problem that these predictions create because of formulation by hindsight;[41] part of that
formulation is precisely the reference to "the third day."[42] But
that formulation is found already in the pre-Pauline kerygmatic fragment used in 1 Cor 15:4: "that he was raised on the
third day according to the scriptures."[43] Yet this fragment of
the kerygma reveals the source of the expression and how the
three days associated with the discovery of the empty tomb
became "the third day." It has always been a problem to
explain what is meant by "according to the Scriptures" in that
fragment. Most interpreters refer it to Hos 6:2, "After two
days he will revive us; on the third day he will raise us up." But
since there is in no account of the discovery of the empty tomb
a description of the resurrection, as we have noted, or a
witnessing of it, one may rightly ask when the tomb was
emptied, when Christ's entrance into glory took place, or
when he was exalted to the Father's right hand. In the light of
this question one sees the significance of the answer that Jesus
gives to the repentant criminal, "Today you shall be with me
in paradise." Have we taken seriously enough the implication
of that adverb "today"?

What complicates the discussion of "today" in Jesus'
reply to the repentant criminal is the so-called *descensus ad
inferos,* which emerges later in the Christian tradition and
becomes part of the creeds.[44] If one tries to account for that,
as did many of the Fathers and medieval theologians, who
wrestled with this Lucan text,[45] then the import of the *Lucan*
references to the sequel of Jesus' death is missed. For Luke,
despite all the periodizing that he introduces into this phase
of Christ's existence, seems to know nothing of a *descensus
ad inferos* if that is to be understood as something more than
death itself. Indeed, we can only speculate about how long

an interval Luke may have considered between Jesus' death and burial and his entrance into glory. In this context the implications of "today" in the episode under discussion are eloquent.

I said above that I would return to another formulation which the primitive expression "exaltation" took on in time, and that is "ascension." This is not *per se* a Lucan mode of expression, even though we often refer to the account in Acts 1:9–11 as the "ascension." Luke has, however, his own ways of formulating this matter. At the beginning of the travel account in his Gospel, he writes, "As the days were drawing near when he was to be taken up . . ." (*tas hēmeras tēs analēmpseōs,* lit. "the days of his assumption," 9:51). The abstract noun *analēmpsis* is used here, whereas in the account in Acts the cognate verb is used, *analambanein* (Acts 1:2,11,22): "he was taken up" (i.e., by God—again, the theological passive).[46] However, Peter in his pentecostal sermon to the Jews of Jerusalem contrasts the risen Christ with David, who "did not ascend the heavens" (2:34), implying that Christ did "ascend" (*anebē,* "went up").[47] From this use of the verb *anabainein,* "go up, ascend," we derive in modern parlance the abstract "ascension," the Greek equivalent for which would be *anabasis,* which never occurs in the New Testament.

At the end of his Gospel Luke depicts the so-called ascension of Christ as occurring on the evening of the day of the discovery of the empty tomb (24:50–51), whereas at the beginning of Acts it occurs some forty days later (1:3,9–11; but cf. 13:31).[48] What has to be stressed now is that in either case it denotes the final appearance of the risen Christ to his followers assembled as a group; he appears from glory to take his final departure from them in visible form. From this point on they will see him no more in such a form; henceforth his presence among them will be known to them "in the breaking of the bread" (24:35) and in "the promise of my Father" (24:49), the promise explained in Acts 1:4 as the holy Spirit, which he in his exalted state pours out on them (Acts 2:35). Thus the primitive idea of "exaltation" has been dramatized and periodized under the pen of the storyteller Luke; it has become his "assumption" after forty days.[49] Other New Testament writers may refer to the "ascension" of Christ, such as John 20:17 and Eph 4:8–10, but only Luke has given us a description of the event.

When one reflects, then, on the different ways that Luke has formulated the sequel to the death and burial of Jesus in his writings—exaltation (as in the primitive tradition), resurrection (as in the common current expression of his day), "being taken up" or "ascending" (as in other late traditions)—one can see that the two specifically Lucan expressions are "entering upon his glory" (24:26) and being "today . . . in paradise" (24:43). It is this last mode of expression that comes to the fore in the episode of the two criminals on the crosses with the crucified Christ. In this episode the mercy of the Lucan Jesus Christ is manifest once again,[50] and its significance is seen both for the proper understanding of Lucan *theologia crucis* and the death of Jesus as well as of the sequel to that death. That transfer to paradise also has its soteriological effect, in that the repentant criminal is made to share in it.

Notes

¹ That Jesus of Nazareth "was crucified under Pontius Pilate" is a statement about an historical fact that has entered the ancient Christian creeds alongside such "articles of faith" as his virginal "birth" and his resurrection. Its "historical" character is supported by the extrabiblical testimony of the Roman historian Tacitus: ". . . Christus Tiberio imperitante per procuratorem Pontium Pilatum supplicio adfectus erat" (*Annales* 15.44.4; LCL 4. 282), "While Tiberius was reigning, Christ was put to death by the procurator Pontius Pilate." This is "the earliest record of the event in any non-Christian writer" (H. Furneaux, *Cornelii Taciti annalium ab excessu divi Augusti libri: The Annals of Tacitus* [2 vols.; 2d ed.; Oxford: Clarendon, 1896–1907] 2. 374).

On crucifixion in ancient Palestine, see M. Hengel, *Crucifixion in the Ancient World and the Folly of the Message of the Cross* (Philadelphia: Fortress, 1977) esp. 84–85. H.-R. Weber, *The Cross: Tradition and Interpretation* (London: SPCK, 1979). J. A. Fitzmyer, "Crucifixion in Ancient Palestine, Qumran Literature, and the New Testament," *CBQ* 40 (1978) 493–513; repr., *TAG*, 125–46. J. M. Baumgarten, "Hanging and Treason in Qumran and Roman Law," *Harry M. Orlinsky Volume* (Eretz-Israel 16; ed. B. A. Levine and A. Malamat; Jerusalem: Israel Exploration Society, 1982) 7*–16*.

² In the best Greek mss. of the Lucan Gospel (P⁷⁵, ℵ¹, B, L, 0124, 1241) and in Coptic versions, v. 38 reads: *ēn de kai epigraphē ep' autō· ho basileus tōn Ioudaiōn houtos.* However, a variant is found in some Greek mss. (ℵ*, A, C³, D, R, W, Θ, Ψ) and in many minuscules of the Koine text-tradition: *(epi)gegrammenē ep' autō grammasin hellēnikois (kai) rhōmaikois (kai) hebraikois,* "inscribed above him in

Greek (and) Latin (and) Hebrew letters." This variant, however, is suspect because it is clearly inspired by the tradition in John 19:20. See B. M. Metzger, *TCGNT,* 181.

³ The apocryphal *Gos. Peter* records yet another form: "This is the King of Israel" (§ 11). This is undoubtedly the way a Christian would have phrased it.

⁴ Attempts have been made to explain the lack of agreement among the evangelists on the basis of the three languages mentioned in John 19:20. Thus, P.-F. Regard ("Le titre de la croix d'après les évangiles," *RArch* 5/28 [1928] 95–105) recognizes the four different canonical forms of the inscription and admits that no one of them reproduces exactly the inscription of history. For him, the Marcan form presents only the common substance ("la teneur générale," 97), and nothing specific. Though John 19:20 says that the title was composed in three languages, it does not say "identically." Rather, Matthew, Luke, and John has each formulated it independently according to "the character and content of each Gospel" (ibid.). What *hellēnisti* and *rhōmaïsti* mean is clear; one may hesitate about *hebraïsti,* whether it means "in Hebrew" or "in Aramaic" (cf. John 5:2; 19:13,17; Acts 21:40; 22:2; 26:14; Rev 9:11; 16:16). What was written *hebraïsti* should be looked for in Matthew's Greek wording (perhaps without the name "Jesus"). The pronounced Roman influence in John's Gospel (cf. 19:15), where even the Jews admit Caesar as king, suggests that John 19:19 gives "the Greek translation of the Latin inscription on the cross" (101). Luke would have preserved the original Greek text of the inscription. Many of Regard's suggestions may seem plausible, but he has written with little concern for the Synoptic relationships and the form-critical problems of the Gospel texts. Fantasy characterizes some of his speculation.

The same has to be said for the attempt made by G. M.

Lee, who apparently wrote without knowledge of Regard's work (see "The Inscription on the Cross," *PEQ* 100 [1968] 144). He maintains that each evangelist "would wish to give the inscription as accurately as possible" and thinks that its "full draft" ran as follows: "This is Jesus of Nazareth the King of the Jews." Only the vowelless Hebrew/Aramaic form could have included all this. The Greek form, however, is preserved by Mark, who got it from Simon of Cyrene, a diaspora Jew who could not read the Semitic form. Luke inherited the Latin form ("Hic est Rex Iudaeorum") from his stay in Rome, translated it into Greek, and put the demonstrative at the end. Matthew preserves in Greek the Hebrew form, but without *Nṣry'*, because his informant could not read the whole text, since the nail riveting the inscription to the cross had been driven through part of the space occupied by this word. John read the text correctly, but dispensed with the "unnecessary demonstrative."

5 The three stages of the gospel tradition have to be recalled; see p. 64 above.

6 See R. Bultmann, *Die Geschichte der synoptischen Tradition* (2d ed.; Göttingen: Vandenhoeck & Ruprecht, 1931) 293: "sekundär." Cf. *HST,* 272, where the sentence has been omitted.

7 Winter claims that the wording is not only Jews-despising but Roman (*On the Trial of Jesus* [Studia judaica 1; Berlin: de Gruyter, 1961] 108–9; 2d ed. [1974] 155). Many others consider the (substantial) wording of the inscription to be historical: C. G. Montefiore, *The Synoptic Gospels: Edited with an Introduction and a Commentary* (2 vols.; London: Macmillan, 1927) 1. 381. M. Dibelius, *Jesus* (Philadelphia: Westminster, 1949) 95. T. A. Burkill, "The Trial of Jesus," *VC* 12 (1958) 1–18, esp. 16. J. Blinzler, *Der Prozess Jesu* (4th ed.; Regensburg: Pustet, 1969) 362–63.

⁸ Appeal is often made to Suetonius, *Caligula* 32.2.4; *Domitian* 10.1.3; Dio Cassius, *Rom. hist.* 54.3.7; Eusebius, *HE* 5.1.44 (LCL 1.426). In such passages ancient charges (*aitiai*) are mentioned, which had been formulated on placards against criminals or martyrs who were to be executed, but these are not considered relevant since none of them is said to have been affixed to a cross. The later testimonies of Hesychios (*Lexicon,* s.v. *sanis*) or Socrates (*Hist. eccl.* 1.17; PG 67. 117), which mention the use of a *sanis,* "wooden tablet," in reference to crucifixion, are not clearly independent of the Gospel accounts. See further E. Dinkler, *Signum crucis: Aufsätze zum Neuen Testament und zur christlichen Archäologie* (Tübingen: Mohr [Siebeck], 1967) 306. Though Dinkler admits the historicity of a *titlos* in Jesus' crucifixion, he points out that the affixing of it to a cross is without parallel in contemporary sources (n. 72). Cf. H.-W. Kuhn, "Jesus als Gekreuzigter in der frühchristlichen Verkündigung bis zur Mitte des 2. Jahrhunderts," *ZTK* 72 (1975) 1–46, esp. 5 n. 13

⁹ *Jesus and the Constraints of History: The Bampton Lectures, 1980* (London: Duckworth, 1982) 11.

¹⁰ Whereas in Matt 27:37 the "they" can refer only to the governor's soldiers (see 27:27), in the *Gos. Peter* (§ 11), "and they wrote on it," the "they" would refer to "the people" (§ 5).

The importance of this inscription cannot be underestimated, even if one cannot be certain about its official character. This is especially true if the thesis of N. A. Dahl is taken as valid ("The Crucified Messiah," *The Crucified Messiah and Other Essays* [Minneapolis: Augsburg, 1974] 23–28). Dahl maintains that the inscription on the cross proved to be the catalyst in the development whereby the *crucified* Jesus eventually came to be recognized by early Christians as the Messiah (*or* Christ). The title, "the King of the Jews," used to identify the crucified Jesus, was associated with contemporary Palestinian Jewish messianic expectations and led such early Christians to associate with Jesus' name the title "Messiah" or "Christ." In the New Testament tradition *Christos* becomes not only a title commonly used of him, but for many writers it acts almost as a second name, Jesus Christ. Moreover, it was eventually used to designate Jesus' followers as "Christians" (Acts 11:26; 26:28; cf. Tacitus, *Annales* 15.44.4 [n. 1 above]). Again, P. Winter (*On the Trial* [n. 7 above], 107; 2d. ed., 154) thinks that the Johannine form of the inscription, written in three languages, becomes Pilate's prophetic confession of Jesus' kingship over the peoples of all the tongues that Pilate—unwittingly?—ordered to be put on the cross. Winter also thinks that the inscription led to the eventual reinterpretation of Ps 96:10, whereby *mlk yhwh* or *Kyrios ebasileusen* became *Kyrios ebasileusen apo xylou*, "The Lord has reigned from the wood (of the tree)"; cf. Justin, *Dial. with Trypho* 73.1. On contemporary Jewish messianic expectations, see *Luke* 197–200, 471–72, 774–75.

[11] *Die Sprache*, 306–7. Cf. V. Taylor, *The Passion Narrative of St Luke: A Critical and Historical Investigation* (SNTSMS 19; ed. O. E. Evans; Cambridge: University Press, 1972) 95. Also *Luke*, 1507.

[12] *HST*, 309–10.

[13] See I. H. Marshall, *The Gospel of Luke*, 871; K. H. Rengstorf, *Das Evangelium nach Lukas*, 262. Cf. the interpretation of J. A. Bengel: "Latronem hunc fuisse Judaeum; alterum, ex gentibus: ex utriusque sermone et aliis rebus colligi potest. Nam ille Judaeorum more, nomen *Christi* exagitat; hic nomen *Regis,* ut milites, sed meliore ratione animadvertit. Accedit, quod Dominus beatitutinem ei promittens, non ad verba promissionum erga *patres,* sed ad

primas origines de *paradiso* alludit" (*Gnomon Novi Testamenti* [3d ed.; Berlin: Schlawitz, 1860] 192 [originally published, 1742]).

[14] See M. Smith, "Zealots and Sicarii, Their Origins and Relation," *HTR* 64 (1971) 1–19.

[15] The preferred reading of Luke 23:42 is *Iēsou, mnēstheti mou hotan elthēs eis tēn basileian sou,* as in mss. P[75], B, L and in Coptic versions. But the mss. ℵ, A, C[2], R, W, *f*[1,13], and the Koine text-tradition read *elthēs en tē basileia sou,* "when you come in your kingdom," a reference to the parousia. Again, ms. D (supported by Ital[d]) reads, *strapheis pros ton kyrion eipen autō· mnēsthēs mou en tē hēmera tēs eleuseōs sou,* "turning toward the Lord, he said to him, 'Remember me in the day of your coming.' " This again refers to the parousia. But both of these readings are judged inferior because they attempt to eliminate the problem of the relation of "today" to "in Paradise." For a far-fetched attempt to defend the latter of these two readings on the basis of an Aramaic substratum, see F. Altheim and R. Stiehl, "Aramäische Herrenworte," *Die Araber in der alten Welt* (5 vols.; Berlin: de Gruyter) 5/2 (1969) 361–67, esp. 361–63. I also retain the usual punctuation, putting a comma after *legō* and before *sēmeron;* the attempt to read "today" with the preceding words is a subterfuge to eliminate the problem of "today . . . in paradise," about which more will be said in part III.

[16] For a discussion of contemporary Palestinian Jewish beliefs about the after-life, see P. Grelot, " 'Aujourd'hui tu seras avec moi dans le paradis' (*Luc,* xxiii, 43)," *RB* 74 (1967) 194–214. Cf. P. Volz, *Die Eschatologie der jüdischen Gemeinde im neutestamentlichen Zeitalter* (2d ed.; Tübingen: Mohr [Siebeck], 1934) 229–56.

[17] Ms. D reads rather, *apokritheis de ho Iēsous eipen*

autō tō epiplēssontī tharsei, sēmeron . . . , "Jesus replied and said to the one rebuking, 'Take courage, today. . . .' " See B. M. Metzer, *TCGNT,* 181.

[18] See further 1 Thess 5:10; 2 Cor 5:8; Rom 6:8. For a fuller discussion of such New Testament phrases as "to be with," "to have with," "to do with," see P. Grelot, " 'Aujourd'hui' " (n. 16 above), 205–10. Cf. R. J. Karris, "Luke's Soteriology of With-ness," *CurTM* 12 (1985) 346–52. Centuries ago Ambrose caught the sense of Jesus' promise: "Vita est enim esse cum Christo; quia ubi Christus, ibi regnum" (*Expos. ev. sec. Lucam* 10.121; CCLat 14. 379).

[19] See Xenophon, *Anab.* 1.2.7; 2.4.14; *Cyrop.* 1.3.14; Theophrastus, *Hist. plant.* 4.4.1.

[20] See 4QEn^e 1 xxvi 21; cf. 4QEn astr^b 23:9. See J. T. Milik, *The Books of Enoch: Aramaic Fragments of Qumran Cave 4* (Oxford: Clarendon, 1976) 232, 289; cf. his article, "Hénoch au pays des aromates (ch xxvii à xxxii): Fragments araméens de la grotte 4 de Qumran," *RB* 65 (1958) 71–77, esp. 75–76. See further J. Jeremias, "Paradeisos," *TDNT* 5. 7675–73; H. Balz, "Paradeisos," *EWNT* 3. 40–41; P. Grelot, " 'Aujourd'hui' " (n. 16 above), 197–205; Str-B 4/2. 118–65.

[21] See J. M. Creed, *The Gospel,* lxxvi.

[22] "Ministry and Community in the New Testament," *Essays on New Testament Themes* (SBT 41; London: SCM, 1964) 63–94, esp. 92. Cf. H. Conzelmann, *Theology,* 201; H. J. Cadbury, *The Making of Luke-Acts* (London: SPCK, 1927; repr., 1958) 280–82; C. H. Talbert, *Luke and the Gnostics: An Examination of the Lucan Purpose* (Nashville: Abingdon, 1966) 71–82.

[23] The omission is problematic, because it is not clear just how Luke has used the Marcan material. Has he omitted merely Mark 10:45? Or rather the whole of Mark 10:35–45?

He seems to have used part of the episode in 12:50, i.e., what corresponds to Mark 10:38–39, but the strife of the apostles he has transferred to the Last Supper (22:24–27), omitting Mark 10:45. Hence the problem.

²⁴ *The Gospel,* lxxii.

²⁵ See further F. Bovon, *Luc le théologien: Vingt-cinq ans de recherche (1950–1975)* (Neuchâtel/Paris: Delachaux et Niestlé, 1978) 176–77.

²⁶ For further discussion of the soteriological character of Jesus' death in Lucan theology, see R. Zehnle, "The Salvific Character of Jesus' Death in Lucan Soteriology," *TS* 30 (1969) 420–44. G. Baumbach, "Gott und Welt in der Theologie des Lukas," *BLit* 45 (1972) 241–55, esp. 242. A. George, "Le sens de la mort de Jésus pour Luc," *RB* 80 (1973) 186–217. V. Fusco, "La morte del Messia (Lc. 23,26–49)," *Gesù e la sua morte: Atti della XXVII settimana biblica* (Brescia: Paideia, 1984) 51–73. F. J. Matera, "The Death of Jesus according to Luke: A Question of Sources," *CBQ* 47 (1985) 469–85. R. J. Karris, "Luke 23:47 and the Lucan View of Jesus' Death," *JBL* 105 (1986) 65–74.

²⁷ For the Lucan use of *sōzein* and *sōtēria,* see *Luke,* 222–23. Cf. B. H. Throckmorton, "*Sōzein, sōtēria* in Luke-Acts," *SE VI* (TU 112) 515–26. W. Radl, "*Sōzō,*" *EWNT* 3. 765–70. K. Giles, "Salvation in Lukan Theology (1)," *Reformed Theological Review* 42 (1983) 10–16.

²⁸ *Expos. ev. sec. Lucam* 10.121; CCLat 14. 379.

²⁹ Verse 6a is omitted in ms. D and in several mss. of the Old Latin version, but it is found in the most important Greek mss. (P⁷⁵, ℵ, A, B, C, W). The ms. W, however, reads *anestē,* "has risen." Verse 6a belongs to the original text of Luke, and it can no longer be regarded as a "Western Non-Interpolation," *pace* Westcott and Hort. See further *Luke,* 130–31; cf. B. M. Metzger, *TCGNT,* 191–93.

30 See M. Zerwick, *Biblical Greek* (Rome: Biblical Institute, 1963) § 236.

31 Though the passive of *egeirein* occurs in Luke 9:33, the intransitive *anastēsetai* is found in the parallel pronouncement of 18:33. In these passages, the first and the third of the classic announcements of the passion inherited from the Marcan source, reference is made to the "resurrection" of Jesus. The formulation of such announcements in the course of the ministry narrative is a matter of no little debate. They seem to many interpreters to have been formulated with hindsight, especially the part of them that refers precisely to the resurrection. See further *Luke,* 777–81. Because of this problem, I have not introduced these passages into the main discussion of the sequel to the death and burial of Jesus.

32 Some interpreters have at times even tried to insist that the passive forms of *egeirein,* used of Jesus' resurrection, should be translated by the intransitive "rise" (see J. A. Lacy, "*ēgerthē*—He Has Risen," *TBT* 36 [1968] 2532–35). Since, however, Luke elsewhere clearly ascribes the resurrection of Jesus to "God" (using the active of *egeirein*—see the main text) rather than to Jesus' self-activity, it is better to understand *ēgerthē* as a real passive. It obviously reflects a more primitive mode of thinking about the resurrection. Cf. J. Kremer, "Auferstanden—auferweckt," *BZ* 23 (1979) 97–98.

33 In the same letter (1:10b) Paul uses the active *ēgeiren* of God, "whom he raised from the dead." Since this verse is part of what is often regarded as a pre-Pauline kerygmatic fragment, it may reflect the more primitive way of speaking about the resurrection.

34 The Lucan criteria are three: (1) one had to be a witness to the risen Christ—one to whom Christ has appeared; (2) a witness to Jesus' earthly ministry from John's

baptism on; and (3) a "man" (*anēr*). Contrast the Pauline criteria in 1 Cor 9:1–2.

[35] See also 4:33. Note that Luke further speaks abstractly of the *anastasis*, "resurrection," in Acts 2:31; 4:2; 17:18(?), 32(?); 24:21; 26:23.

[36] A description of the resurrection eventually surfaces in the gospel tradition in the apocryphal *Gos. Peter* § 35–42 (see *Luke*, 1538; cf. *HSNTA*, 1. 185–86). See further R. E. Brown, "The *Gospel of Peter* and Canonical Gospel Priority," *NTS* 33 (1987) 321–43.

[37] See further *JBC* art. 50, § 16–19.

[38] A similar transition is found in the primitive hymnic fragment embedded in 1 Tim 3:16: "Who was manifested in the flesh, vindicated through the Spirit, seen by angels, proclaimed among the nations, believed in throughout the world, taken up in glory." Again, the absence of mention of the resurrection is noteworthy.

[39] The Greek text reads: *ouchi tauta edei pathein ton Christon kai eiselthein eis tēn doxan autou.*

[40] Cf. Mark 8:31; 9:31; 10:34; Matt 16:21; 20:19.

[41] See n. 31 above.

[42] Note how it is used neutrally in 24:21 (in Luke's own dramatic composition of the Emmaus story—see *Luke*, 1554–55).

[43] It is repeated by Luke in Peter's speech in Acts 10:40.

[44] It is in part also dependent on an interpretation of 1 Pet 3:18–19. See W. J. Dalton, *Christ's Proclamation to the Spirits: A Study of 1 Peter 3:18–4:6* (AnBib 23; Rome: Biblical Institute, 1965). Dalton maintains that Christ's preaching to the spirits in 1 Pet 3:19 has nothing to do with a descent, but refers rather to Christ's ascension. Dalton sketches the history of the interpretation of this difficult passage.

[45] See G. W. MacRae, "With Me in Paradise," *Worship* 35 (1960–61) 235–40, esp. 238–39; cf. P. Grelot, " 'Aujourd'hui' " (n. 16 above), 211–14.

[46] The passive *anephereto*, "was carried up," is used in Luke 24:51; and *eperthē*, "was lifted up," in Acts 1:9. These are simply literary variants of *anelēmphthē* (Acts 1:2,11,22).

[47] Note the difference here, in that this is a mere statement of fact (implying that Christ ascended); no description of the event, however, is given. The same can be said for John 20:17; Eph 4:8–10; and by implication for Rom 10:6–7. Only Luke has described the "ascension" of Christ (Acts 1:10–11) and done for it what the *Gos. Peter* 35–42 has done for the resurrection.

[48] The reason for this we have already explained; see p. 62 above.

[49] For reasons why Luke has so separated the so-called ascension, see my article, "The Ascension of Christ and Pentecost," *TS* 45 (1984) 409–40. Cf. E. LaVerdiere, "Jesus' Resurrection and Ascension," *Emmanuel* 92 (1986) 250–57.

[50] "It is the last and most impressive use that the Son of Man made on earth of His power to forgive sins" (Eb. Nestle, "Luke xxiii.43," *ExpTim* 11 [1899–1900] 429). Cf. J. F. Maile, "The Ascension in Luke-Acts," *Tyndale Bulletin* 37 (1986) 29–59.

Indices

Scripture Index

Index of Subjects

Sophists, 121
Sosipater, 9
Sosthenes, 9
Stephen, 185
Stoics, 121, 149
Suetonius, 226
Synoptic gospels, 30, 43, 57–58, 87, 89, 95–96, 216
Synoptic problem, 33–34, 52
Syntyche, 14

Tabitha of Joppa, 119
Tacitus, 223, 227
Talmid, 120–22
Teacher of righteousness, 120–21, 142
Temple (of Jerusalem), 34, 37, 74, 92, 95–96, 113, 120, 136, 153, 185
Temptation of Jesus, 151–58
Tertullian, 2, 8, 11
Testimony, 135
Testament of Levi, 209
Theologia crucis, 210, 222

Theophrastus, 229
Tiberius Caesar, 107, 223
Timothy, 9–10, 185
Titus, 9–10
Troas, 4, 11, 15, 17–18
Twelve, the, 123, 125–26, 133, 135–36, 168, 210, 215–16
Tychicus, 10

Virgil, 20, 81
Virginal conception of Jesus, 40, 49, 53, 66, 80

Way, the, 134–35, 145
We-sections of Acts, 3–5, 7, 9, 11, 13, 15–22
Wen-Amun, Journey of, 19
Widow of Nain, 216

Xenophon, 121, 143, 229

Zealot movement, 206, 228
Zechariah, husband of Elizabeth, 34, 42, 46–47, 49, 65, 68, 92, 95, 136, 176, 187

Index of Modern Authors

Adam, A., 112
Albright, W. F., 25
Allison, D. C., Jr., 114
Altheim, F., 228

Badenas, R., 199
Baer, H. von, 61
Bailey, J. A., 54
Baldi, D., 113
Balz, H., 229
Banks, R., 196
Baumbach, G., 172–73, 230
Baumgarten, J. M., 223
Bea, A., 55
Beall, T. S., 112
Beare, F. W., 12
Beker, J. C., vi
Bellet, P., 56
Bengel, J. A., 227
Benoit, P., 14, 84, 112

Bergeaud, J., 111
Berger, K., 196, 202
Best, E., 113, 144
Betz, H. D., 80, 143
Betz, O., 113
Beumer, J., 24
Blinzler, J., 225
Blomberg, C. L., 196
Bovon, F., 25, 62, 82, 230
Brodie, L. T., 51
Brown, R. E., xii, 27, 49, 51–52, 54–55, 84, 113–15, 156, 171, 201, 232
Brown, S., 23, 171–73
Brownlee, W. H., 112, 142
Bruce, F. F., 8, 24, 201
Buchanan, C. O., 12
Bultmann, R., xii, 45, 55, 105, 165, 171, 206, 225
Burkill, T. A., 225
Burrows, E., 45
Butler, C., 53

Cadbury, H. J., 25, 200–1, 229
Caird, C. G., 12
Cerfaux, L., 12
Collins, R. F., 8, 116
Conrad, E. W., 49, 56
Conzelmann, H., xii, 62–63, 80, 82, 85, 106, 145, 158–63, 198, 200, 229
Coulot, C., 144, 199
Cranfield, C. E. B., 198
Creed, J. M., xii, 111, 197, 211, 229
Crossan, J. D., 32, 52
Cullmann, O., 81

Dahl, N. A., 200, 202, 226
Dalton, W. J., 232
Daube, D., 197
Davis, C. T., 53
Deissmann, A., 14
Dibelius, M., 13, 45, 55, 225
Dinkler, E., 226
Dodd, C. H., 12
Donahue, J. R., 144
Downing, F. G., 196
Drury, J., 52–53
Duncan, G. S., 14
Dunn, J. D. G., 113
Dupont, J., 17, 26, 145, 155, 171, 197

Easton, B. S., 197
Ellis, E. E., xii, 23
Eltester, W., 198
Enslin, M. S., 23
Evans, O. E., 227

Faierstein, M., 114
Farkasfalvy, D., 24
Farmer, W. R., 24, 52–53
Farrer, A., 53
Feine, P., 14
Ferguson, E., 8, 24
Fitzmyer, J. A., xii, 53, 83, 114, 197, 201–2, 223, 233
Flanagan, J. W., 81, 115
Foakes-Jackson, F. J., xiii
Frisque, J., 81
Fuchs, A., 171
Fujita, N. S., 112

Furneaux, H., 223
Fusco, V., 230

Gamble, H. Y., 8, 24
George, A., 26, 196, 230
Gerhardsson, B., 171
Geyser, A. S., 111
Giles, K., 230
Glover, R., 23
Gnilka, J., 81, 113
Goguel, M., 14
Goudoever, J. van, 196
Goulder, M. D., 23
Grelot, P., 173, 228–29, 233
Griesbach, J. J., 33–34
Gundry, R. H., 34
Guthrie, D., 12
Guthrie, W. K. C., 143

Hackenberg, W., 80
Haenchen, E., 198–99
Hamman, P. A., 113
Harrison, E. F., 12
Harvey, A. E., 204
Haudebert, P., 200
Heard, R. G., 25
Hengel, M., 223
Hennecke, E., xii
Higgins, A. J. B., 115
Horgan, M. P., 142
Hubbard, B. J., 55
Huck, A., 170
Hübner, H., 196, 199

Jeremias, J., xii, 112, 170, 205, 229
Jervell, J., xiii, 196, 200
Johnson, S. L., 171

Käsemann, E., 116, 210–11
Karris, R. J., 229–30
Kasser, R., 24
Keck, L. E., xiii, 116
Kilpatrick, G. D., 85
Kirk, J. A., 172
Kittel, G., 141
Klassen, W., xiii
Koester, H., 32, 52